Transformation

Advance Praise

"*Transformation: Toward a Peoples' Democracy* is one part history, two parts guidebook, three parts love letter. Suzanne Pharr's words – persistent, relevant, and fierce – come to us from across five decades of social justice work. Read this book, talk about it, use it in your organizing – whether it be from your bed or in the streets, in prisons or classrooms, over kitchen tables or social media, in non-profit meetings or anti-oppression workshops. Pharr's stories, strategic thinking, and analysis will teach us, move us, nourish us."

– Eli Clare, author of *Brilliant Imperfection: Grappling with Cure and Exile and Pride: Disability, Queerness, and Liberation*

"If you know about Suzanne Pharr, this is a book of infinite attachments to what she believes in. It's a compilation of her ongoing life's works – and it is a great read. Through it, you can understand her revolutionary journey and I have found it extremely helpful to my own journey and what I'm doing. I highly recommend it. It leaves you thinking of a life that's pure, and never stops resisting, rebelling, refusing, revolting, and reclaiming when it comes to the powers that be that are standing between us and a world where we're all treated with the fairness, dignity and respect that every human being deserves."

– With love, Miss Major,
House of GG

"What a gift Suzanne Pharr has given us! This book is precisely what movements for social justice need at this political moment; radical analyses, an optimistic vision, a commitment to intersectional and intergenerational work and – perhaps most importantly - the possibility of political joy that comes from a life-long commitment to freedom work. Pharr's brilliant mind, generous spirit and love for organizing is like a political balm. Readers will be refreshed, inspired and deeply moved. What a timely and important gift!"

– Beth E Richie, author of *Arrested Justice*
Founder, INCITE
Professor and Department Head,
Criminology, Law and Justice and Black Studies
University of Illinois at Chicago

"Suzanne brilliantly analyses the development of the U.S. anti-fascist movement to offer wisdom based on her lived experiences spanning six decades. She never uses a single-issue approach in her intersectional inspiring work because she connects the dots between all social justice and human rights movements. She's as vital to read as Audre Lorde, Cherrie Moraga, Gloria Anzaldúa, and Adrienne Rich. Anyone reading this book will recognize what a gift she's given us."

– Loretta J. Ross, Activist, Public Intellectual, Professor

"For half a century Suzanne Pharr has given U.S. justice movements and the people and organizations within them her deep intelligence, vision, strategic acumen and great good sense. She has grounded us, founded us, made our work more intelligible, towed us out of ditches, forged our alliances, insisted we behave, listened us through our convulsions and confusions, and helped us find our ways. From our front lines and our front porches, Pharr has given us such 'Suzanne moments' when we most needed them. We can only, then, be immensely grateful that *Transformation*... brings us this wonderfully curated collection of Pharr's work just (we hope) in the nick of time, and for the ages."

– Mab Segrest, author of *Memoir of a Race Traitor and Administrations of Lunacy: Racism and the Haunting of American Psychiatry at the Milledgeville Asylum*

Transformation
Toward a People's Democracy

Essays and Speeches

by Suzanne Pharr

Edited by Christian Matheis

Virginia Tech Women's and Gender Studies Program
in association with

VIRGINIA TECH.
PUBLISHING

B L A C K S B U R G ◉ V I R G I N I A

First published 2021 by the Virginia Tech Women's and Gender Studies Program in association with Virginia Tech Publishing

Virginia Tech Women's and Gender Studies Program
317 Major Williams Hall
220 Stanger Street
Blacksburg, VA 24061

Virginia Tech Publishing
University Libraries at Virginia Tech
560 Drillfield Drive
Blacksburg, VA 24061

Cataloging in Publication Data
Transformation: toward a people's democracy / by Suzanne Pharr, edited by Christian Matheis. Blacksburg, Virginia : Virginia Tech Women's and Gender Studies Program, in association with Virginia Tech Publishing, 2021 | Includes bibliographical references.

ISBN: 978-1-949373-67-7 (pbk) | ISBN: 978-1-949373-68-4 (PDF) | ISBN: 978-1-949373-69-1 (epub) | DOI: https://doi.org/10.21061/transformation

1. Social Movements—United States. 2. Sexual Minorities—United States. 3. Feminism— United States. I. Pharr, Suzanne, author. II. Matheis, Christian, editor.

Cover image by Renée DeLapp
Cover design by Suzanne Pharr with Christian Matheis

A Poem

My heart is moved by all I cannot save:
so much has been destroyed
I have to cast my lot with those
who age after age, perversely,
with no extraordinary power,
reconstitute the world.

– Adrienne Rich, 1977

Contents

Part III. Missed Connections

Part IV. Making Connections

Appreciation

For this book

My great appreciation, gratitude and love to Kelly Mitchell-Clark, Lynn Frost, Kerry Lobel, Damita Marks, and Janet Perkins for their work at the Women's Project that made this writing possible –

And to Renée DeLapp who has lovingly supported my work and life for almost three decades –

And to Christian Matheis who brought this book to life.

For my political growth

Movements are built from connections between people and the exchange of ideas. From 1980 to 2000, my political growth was fed by the hundreds who interacted with me in workshops, discussions after speeches, conferences, retreats, and on the ground activism. In particular, my awareness and understanding were expanded by people from the frontlines of social justice work who were always willing to hold conversations filled with friendship, sharp analysis, challenge, and laughter in pursuit of a different world. I cannot name them all, and I offer apologies to those I may have overlooked, but I want to appreciate here some of the many who built ideas and friendships with me:

Freeman McKindra, Tom McRae, Wayne Jarvis, Peggy Halsey, Mrs. Evangeline K Brown, Ann Gallmeyer, Ann Adams, Amy Edgington, Jean Hardisty, Chip Berlet, Jean Grossholtz, Beth Richie, P. Catlin Fullwood, Val Kanuha, Barbara Hart, Susan Schechter, Karen Artichoker, Sue Julian, Loretta Ross, Jane Sapp, Barbara Ellen Smith, Carmen Vasquez, Amber Hollibaugh, Eli Clare, Urvashi Vaid, Robert Bray, Gary Schwartz, Eric Rofes,

Sue Hyde, Helen Zia, Ellen Gurzinsky, Suzanne Goldberg, Katherine Acey, Barbara Smith, Kay Whitlock, Mandy Carter, Mab Segrest, Joan Garner, Pat Hussein, Pam McMichael, Carla Wallace, Graciela Sanchez, Thalia Zapatos, Jack Danger, Brigette Sarabe, Scot Nakagawa, Deb Ross, Eric Ward, Holly Pruett, Bob Ralphs, Jamie Dawson, Tarso Ramos, Lee Schore, Jerry Atkin, Eric Ward, Amara Perez, Marcy Westerling – and Harriet Barlow who offered Blue Mountain Center so many times for us to hold extended conversations about social change.

For loving encouragement and promotion of this book

Jade Brooks, Trishala Deb, Pooja Gehi, Jess George, Steph Guilloud, Paulina Hernandez, Abbie Illenberger, Soya Jung, Miss Major, Alyssa Pharr, Beth Richie, Lisa Weiner-Mahfuz.

**– Suzanne Pharr
July 2021**

Acknowledgments

Publication of this book was supported by

Sue Hyde, Executive Director, Wild Geese Foundation
Southerners on New Ground (SONG)
Community and Justice Studies at Guilford College
The Center for Principled Problem Solving and Excellence
in Teaching at Guilford College
University Libraries at Virginia Tech
Women's and Gender Studies at Virginia Tech
Kathleen Herbst
Isaac Magaña

I

Beginnings

Editor's Introduction

This is a Movement Book

How did I end up editing a book by a southern feminist queer octogenarian whose work spans over five decades? My connection to Suzanne Pharr grew from the time I invited her to the university where I was teaching in 2007 to give a talk on the rise of the Right. That was during the waning years of the second George W. Bush administration, a time when many of us cut our teeth organizing on the defensive against regressive attacks on LGBTQ+ communities. The Right gained much ground in those years by doing as the Right always has done – by eroding civil rights, passing destructive financial policies that benefit private corporations, and burying the country and the world further and further in profiteering wars abroad. Late in 2007 I returned from working in a campus LGBTQ center in Pennsylvania to Oregon to teach direct-action organizing and policy advocacy at Oregon State University. I felt rejuvenated by Pharr's talk earlier that year and I had a renewed focus thanks to her specific call for political education. In my teaching and scholarship I turned to Pharr's 1996 *In the Time of the Right: Reflections on Liberation* as a guiding text. Working through the text with students in courses on organizing and policy advocacy allowed me to reconsider my understanding of power, relationships, and solidarity.

A decade or so later in the fall of 2018, not long after I joined the faculty in Community and Justice Studies at Guilford College, I opened my email to find a message from Pharr. She had found some of my publications that reference her work and we reconnected by email. When we spoke she explained that she was in the process of finding a home for her lifelong collection of writings, notes, and records. Pharr wanted a way to share her writings – especially during this most recent period of white supremacist neo-fascism. I offered the idea of an open access e-

3

book since it seemed like an ideal model – one consistent with her vision and goals for sharing this work. A movement book was born.

What is a movement book?

There is ongoing debate among organizers and scholars about how social movements begin and end, and even more debate about what even constitutes a movement in the first place. Likewise, there are countless scholarly and historical resources to learn about social justice movements through various kinds of research and storytelling. Historians, archivists, theorists, and activists offer all manner of insight into the historical significance of movement work, primarily focused on key figures and their impact. One can readily find autobiographies of movement organizers, books of theory about movements, and archives full of records documenting movement work. But a movement book is a different kind of resource. This movement book is about movement work. As Pharr puts it in "Farming Our Politics,"

> Movement work, like small farming, is slow. It requires thoughtful, careful steps, autonomy and independent thought, diversity and inclusiveness. It requires resistance to adversity and a commitment to begin again after losses and defeats. Movement work is people putting their acts of resistance and creation and growth together, people who refuse to let the seeds disappear and who save them for the future, people who refuse to destroy a village in order to save it, people who believe that change is made one person at a time, until our numbers are legion.

This book is about the work itself – the analysis, organizing, lessons, dynamics, and strategy of a movement – and it speaks to those who feel lost and in need of guidance and inspiration.

Why do we need movement books like this one?

Suzanne Pharr's work takes us through her analysis of the ongoing threat to community life and democracy posed by rightwing politicians and pundits, corporations, and theocratic ideologues. The stories and examples told throughout these writings give a picture of coalitions, struggles, strategies, wins, and losses in the work to disrupt and dismantle intersectional oppression. Known as a multi-talented organizer, strategist, and writer, Pharr's extensive and vocal opposition to rightwing totalitarianism and hate-based violence seeks to bridge narrowly defined political agendas and "single-issue politics" that leave us open to further division and disempowerment. Her tactical wisdom over the past six decades helped to set the context for what we have witnessed in recent years as increasingly coordinated progressive movements against intersectional oppression. There is a great need at present for us to think in intergenerational terms. Organizing movements for the long-term, for more than episodic and reactionary one-off demonstrations and protests, is a deep need. To be clear, reactionary demonstrations are necessary in the face of system injustice. The long-range movement work brought to light in this collection places demonstrations in the context of a broad strategy made up from many different kinds of tactics, protests included. This movement book illustrates portions of the work Pharr and others carried out over a period of decades so that others can borrow from, replicate, and improve on the analysis and tactics. We need to organize not just for weeks, months, and years, but with a vision that spans decades and centuries.

The Right has long organized under a fascist view of sameness, demonizing differences and fomenting intergroup hostilities. There was a time when it would have been nearly unimaginable that Black Lives Matter, Me Too, Water Protectors, Occupy, Border Witnesses, and the plethora of other liberatory social justice movements would speak with and coordinate among one another. As these movements continue to foster coalitions and to build both diverse and common visions of a just and dignifying future it is important to understand the interventions Pharr and her contemporaries helped make possible. Systematic, intersectional oppression is centuries – if not millennia – in the making. These old oppressive systems will yield if we understand and commit to the lengthy work that imparts to future generations careful lessons and strategies, and relationships that resist disruption by fascist politics. This book is one part of the work to sustain intergenerational movements.

Suzanne Pharr's movement work

Pharr's movement organizing is grounded in her work to end violence against women and children, work that grew while organizing in Arkansas to monitor and end hate violence against women, people of color, LGBTQ people, and Jews. Along with that grounding she holds a foundational and unruly place in contemporary social justice movements. Foundational in a cohort of lesbian activists engaged in early and ongoing scrutiny of the neo-conservative infiltration of democratic institutions, unruly in her persistent and unflinching analysis of power through a liberatory lens. Pharr's particular contributions to that generational work shine through this remarkable collection.

This book complements Pharr's two previous book-length works, *Homophobia: A Weapon of Sexism* (1988) and *In the Time of the Right: Reflections on Liberation* (1996). Her writings are a staple in community organizing and in academic circles alike, marking her place among a group of generative figures who influence grassroots politics and scholarly discourses with far-reaching and long-lasting resolve. That is no small accomplishment, but its historical significance may not be entirely obvious to readers who are unfamiliar with the way U.S. social justice movements underwent vicious political, economic, and cultural backlash against civil rights and broad economic welfare. Pharr and her peers altered the activist and scholarly landscape by talking *openly and simultaneously* about oppression, economic exploitation, and the intersectional divisions among marginalized groups. It is not only the fact that she openly and thoroughly discusses these intersections that makes her writings pivotal, but also that Pharr speaks of oppression as something that can be resisted and replaced with justice. One tactic Pharr explains throughout the collection is to do work that makes justice so attractive that people cannot stomach living without it.

Throughout this book Pharr gives us a clear picture of the struggle. She shows how the parts are connected and exemplifies the kinds of outcomes to work toward as well as the need for ongoing organizing. Her careful attention to many different focal points has made a lasting impact on social struggles in the U.S. as well as in other countries. In 2018, for instance, Pharr's analysis of the intersections of sex, gender, and sexuality was cited in the opinion of a Justice of the Supreme Court of India ruling on gay rights (*Navtej Singh Johar & Ors. v. Union of India thr. Secretary Ministry of Law and Justice*).[1] The case functionally decriminalizes consensual sexual relations among adults, ending the criminalization of "homosexual sex" and opening a path for LGBTQ+ civil rights. The decision most immediately and positively impacts over 1 billion people in India, and has been praised globally as a widely significant ruling for civil rights overall. In some ways India changed overnight and millions breathe more freely and live more openly, and at the same time it will take many years of grassroots work to translate the legal ruling into a holistic sense of shared dignity free of sexism, homophobia, and transphobia. Imagine, a recent fundamental change for billions of people on the other side of the world is tied to decades-old work in Arkansas and ongoing efforts to stop violence against women.

Movement work and political education

This book is also a model of political education. That is, it is a book designed to help readers build their understanding of the relationships, patterns, themes, and different forms of power that impact our lives. Anyone can use the term "power" and in fact it is often used so interchangeably and unconscientiously that it becomes a cipher, meaning everything and nothing all at the same time. Few of us pause to ask, where and from whom did we first learn to think carefully about power? What are different kinds of power and how do they harm or heal? This book offers lessons about power in various forms (collective responsibility, mutuality, cooperation, strength, force, power-over, etc.). It shows how different forces and agendas are connected even when they have been carefully hidden and covered in propaganda. The writings contained in this collection map out Pharr's analysis of

1. https://indianexpress.com/article/india/section-377-verdict-live-updates-supreme-court-decriminalisation-of-homosexuality-5342203/?#liveblogstart

power, oppression, and economic exploitation. They bring to light the less apparent intersections of racism, sexism, heterosexism, transphobia, ableism, nationalism, and other forms of institutionalized cruelty so they can be challenged and replaced. The political education in this book is also visionary. Pharr reminds us along the way that to confront fascism and intersectional discrimination we must understand the past and present, and we must also continuously ask "who benefits?" from a particular course of action, and "what would it be like if we all had access to a fair share?"

The political education in this movement book calls us to reject the isolation and defeat we feel when we internalize the politics of domination used by the Right. Pharr provides a historical perspective on discrimination and fascism, speaks to our current moment, and reminds us of the pressing need for liberatory visions of social justice organized across a broad reach of identities. The essays also weave across generational differences to remind readers of a time when many people close to my age can recall a decisive shift in resistance oppression – a turning point Pharr helped to craft and continues to embolden. For over five decades Pharr and her peers have helped to bring about a far-reaching and thriving national network of politically educated organizers and strategists who continue to create spaces of visionary direct-action. The writings ahead are about recent history, our political struggle here and now, and they are about the kind of society and world we can yet create.

How is this book organized?

Throughout the first section, "The Right," Pharr chronicles attacks on U.S. democratic institutions carried out by a network of rightwing political, corporate, and theocratic groups, and gives voice to the harms these attacks cause. Beginning with a reflection on the election of Ronald Reagan, Pharr analyzes the deliberate and coordinated scapegoating of marginalized communities and the concurrent takeover of the U.S. economy through privatization and corporate welfare. The essays provide an accessible exposé, uncovering the ways the Right utilizes financial and economic control over public policy and media, narrowly defined cultural norms and stereotypes, makes political appointments to the judiciary, and enacts other means to consolidate dominance and control. The resulting erosion of public participation in democratic processes and the degradation of community life are evident all around us, and recently in ways that have become the new norm for more and more people. As Pharr shows us, the decades-long decline in infrastructure, civil rights, and social trust was not accidental, nor was it the result of any normal sociological evolution.

In "Part II: Missed Connections," Pharr methodically outlines the ways that pundits on The Right gaslight us by tapping into internalized oppression, horizontal hostility, scapegoating, and other common elements of oppression. Their goal is to disrupt the livelihood and dignity of marginalized groups, sowing mistrust and hostility among targeted groups so that broad intersectional movements become unlikely. The early essays in this section illustrate how different forms of structural oppression intersect and manifest within identity-based organizations causing intergroup animosity and, ultimately, leaving oppression entrenched within social justice movements. Racism within LGBTQ+ movements, homophobia and transphobia in movements for racial justice, sexism in anti-racist networks, and divisions along lines of socioeconomic status and labor conditions leave our movements vulnerable.

Unless we take notice of the need for organizing at the level of systems, she explains, we will focus too narrowly on individual change (i.e. philanthropy, individual civic service, counseling) and ignore the bigger-picture strategies that covertly undermine liberatory organizing. Pharr gives special attention to the challenges of finding funding for radical and progressive organizations, pointing to the Black Panthers, Zapatistas, and ACT-UP (AIDS Coalition to Unleash Power) as models of resource sharing, mutual aid, and collectivity. At the close of the section, Pharr warns us about the decades-long shift toward solely individualized solutions, such as personal therapy, and calls us to remember that the greatest advancements in civil rights and liberatory politics stem from collective storytelling and reflection (e.g. consciousness-raising groups) and collective action.

"Part III: Making Connections" opens with a head-on critique of the divisions among activists and oppressed groups, and a clarion call to notice the interconnected nature of systemic discrimination. Throughout this section, Pharr emphasizes the need for an integrated analysis of violence against women and minoritized groups, and she guides us to frame issues with an expanded and unapologetic vision. With a thriving vision of social justice that is organized on the basis of multi-issue coalition politics we can, she argues, make use of some of the divisions caused by toxic politics, turning those divisions into throughlines for resistance. Pharr explains in "The Struggle for Democracy" (1993), "the religious Right has put our issues on the lips of everyone in America. Everybody is talking about it. And why is this going to make us victorious? Because they have given us the greatest opportunity to do public education about who we are that we could have ever dreamed of" (Pg. 287). Turning mean-spirited divisions into opportunities requires strategy, the linking of critical analyses with long-term solutions – to understand how coalitions formed from differing visions of social justice bolster rather than weaken anti-oppression efforts. These connections are part of why multi-issue and multi-identity coalitions can, at present, resist further scapegoating and gaslighting. For instance, think of recent attempts by the Right to target Critical Race Theory rather than target a particular group. This attempt to scapegoat a body of activist-scholarship rather than singling out a vulnerable population is not new. The targets may differ but the tactics remain the same. But the attack signals an opportunity to exploit the fascistic thinking at play. Pharr's writings suggest that the relationships among marginalized groups prevent the Right from picking off targeted communities and in desperation they turn to attack theories and concepts. Ideological attacks on communism, multiculturalism, school curriculum, sexual health education, Critical Race Theory, and other scholarly resources reflect a vulnerability in the Right's domination politics. If we are wise,

Pharr shows us, our coalitions can turn the Right's desperate ideological attempts at culture war to our advantage.

In the closing set of essays, "Part IV: Crossing Divides, Finding Ways Forward" Pharr points to the kinds of liberatory social change we need to imagine and tell one another about if there is to be truly broad-based, shared collective action for a socially just democracy. Pharr gets to the roots of long-lasting social justice organizing, naming key opportunities for building coalitions in unlikely places and in unexpected moments. "Building a Gay and Lesbian Liberation Movement" makes a declaration of dignity and, as Pharr writes, "we come to our liberation work with the full power of our humanity demanding no more and no less than the full benefits of freedom" (Pg. 300). In essays such as "Lesbian Battering: Social Change Urged" and "Future Directions of the Battered Women's Movement – Or – Being a Dreamer of Dreams" Pharr illustrates the basis of programs by, for, and about those in need versus governmental and/or for-profit services that serve only to domesticate us and make us more resilient at living with oppression always at our heels. In "Rural Organizing: Building Communities Across Difference" Pharr points to the tactical necessity of rural organizing, and in "A Match Made in Heaven" she demonstrates the importance of insight into those who seem at once enemies of social justice but who turn out to be caught up themselves in the false and misleading messages perpetrated by religious and corporate pundits. Finally, "Reflections on Liberation" originally appeared as the final chapter in *In the Time of the Right...* and it is reproduced here in its entirety as a reminder that in the face of violence, hate, and division we need movements built around commitments to lift up humanity.

Ways to use this book

Share this book

As an open access publication distributed under the Creative Commons we hope this text will pass through activist and scholarly networks as broadly and freely as possible. Use it to organize. Use it to teach. Use it for research. Where possible, expand on the ideas, reuse the examples, and riff on the writings. This is a people's book, a book of political education, please share it widely.

Read the story, follow the themes, use the tools

The collection tells a coherent story across a decades-long arc of movement work. Reading the essays in order from beginning to end shows how Pharr's movement work began, grew, and changed. The overall story shows the intricacy of analysis, resistance, planning, and action that pose a challenge to domination politics – the manipulative schemes that pit different groups against one another while eroding communal, social, and global welfare. The essays can also be taken as free-standing pieces, each addressing a particular problem with a focused analysis and solution. Whether reading the collection as a whole or borrowing from different parts, it serves as a flexible guide to movement organizing, academic instruction, and scholarly research. At www.suzannepharr.com there are also various video recordings that complement and expand upon the different themes in this book.

Put these lessons in the hands of those who need it

For decades Pharr has helped to organize grassroots and civil rights resistance to oppression and economic exploitation by providing plain, accessible, and common sense descriptions of the destructive policies and conditions that turn people against one another. Pharr writes for everyday readers, and especially for those who have been left out of and excluded from a fair share of power. These essays use accessible language, free of alienating jargon that tends to further exclude those who are most in need of social justice.

Over and again Pharr shows throughout the essays in this anthology the ongoing direct attacks on people of color, women, LGBQ+ and Trans communities, immigrants, disabled persons, and those living in poverty were carefully conceived, planned, and carried out by rightwing operatives who seek to maintain corporate and theocratic dominance. But those systemic forces remain entrenched because they are so pervasive as to be obscured and normalized to the extent that they are simultaneously everywhere all the time and difficult to detect. These writings paint the historical picture so it can be understood more clearly by a wide audience whether or not they have organizing experience and/or academic preparation. Share the lessons in this book knowing they require no specialized training or experience to use.

Read it for inspiration and examples of strategy

It is one thing to have questions and ideas, to demonstrate a critical diagnosis. It is another thing to have solutions and plans of action. And yet another thing to bring people together to build, revise, and act on a plan. Pharr uses common sense concepts in the context of tactical, well-planned resistance – or *strategy*. Drawing primarily on the work of the Women's Project and the organization's revolutionary presence as a feminist, anti-racist, anti-poverty powerhouse of social change, Pharr highlights the need for strategy in response to systemic oppression in all of its intersecting forms. This book is not in itself a book of strategies and yet the examples and emphasis on strategy make this collection unique and timely.

Let it help you question divisions and build relationships

One of Pharr's most significant contributions is her emphasis on relationships and her rejection of within-movement elitism. She shows us why and how to resist the erosion of community that can plague organized movements. The Right has manufactured careful attacks on marginalized communities, and they do so because once stereotypes and human differences are weaponized they know that marginalized communities more readily turn on one another than on our oppressors. Our relationships in community and coalition help us to resist divide-and-conquer tactics. Pharr shows the priority of both respecting differences and finding commonality. That is, common ground and shared interests are key to movement work but finding what is common in our struggles is not helpful if we sacrifice certain marginalized identities and experiences in an ill-fated attempt to make "progress." Pharr shows the necessity of bringing our full selves to the work, and of declaring movements a place where a full range of differences can thrive.

In the spirit of a people's democracy

As a movement book we hope this will be helpful to activists, teachers, scholars, and anyone else in search of a beacon to help find a way through our present-day storm of fascism, capitalist exploitation, and globalized oppression to a just future. This book tells a story about organizing people, changing systems, and building power among the marginalized. The voice and writing invite readers to reject separation and embrace collective dignity. Growing and sustaining liberatory movements takes political education and it takes work, and this book is about that work. As you read and reflect on these snapshots from the life and work of Suzanne Pharr I hope you will feel a greater sense that a people's democracy is feasible and winnable, and within our power to create.

– Christian Matheis
Greensboro, NC
2021

Author's Introduction

In my eighth decade, I have a sense of wonderment when I look at this collection I share with you. From a distance, these writings represent analysis and reflection in a time when we were witnessing a slow but seismic shift in this country, one that landed us today in the major crises of 2020-2021. They bear witness to strategies and tactics used to divide this country and to grow authoritarianism built on wealth and race and gender. Though grounded in the present, they are predictive, beginning in 1980 with the election of Ronald Reagan. But, as we know, prediction is not prevention, and today we have a sharply divided country, with growing state, police, and civilian violence. However, the crises we face today are leading us to revisit the values we have known to be true in the past and are lifted up in these writings. There is a way forward.

Some of my wonder is how I came to write this analysis and commentary, what it was in my life that prepared and motivated me. Was it that I was a child of the recovery from the Great Depression and World War II that showed me how communities had to pull together to survive? Or because I grew up the youngest of eight children on a small farm in Georgia where you worked with community because your wellbeing depended upon it? Or because of my deep love of basketball where you have to work as a team to win and to overcome your losses? Or was it just something as simple as growing up a queer girl in a time when there was no place to breathe the air of freedom and it made me forever push for places where that air could flow unimpaired?

There are many gifts in life that are what the novelist Carson McCullers called "an accident of fate." I think of those moments as when life changes, for good or bad. My life was changed the day I read *The Combahee River Collective Statement* in the late 1970s.[1] It was the first time I had heard or seen a clear intersectional analysis and the bold vision and collective power of Black feminists. All of my social change work since that moment has been touched by that statement.

Another life-changer happened in the late 1970s after I surfaced from living on feminist land and took a job as Director of Head Start in Northwest Arkansas. Within a year I was under serious attack for being a lesbian, and after weathering public hearings and keeping my job long enough to create a shelter for sexually abused children, I fled. Freeman McKindra of Little Rock offered me a job as a VISTA worker interviewing elderly people about their need for services in rural areas. It was this job that taught me about the needs of rural Arkansans – needs that were so much like those I saw during my childhood in rural Georgia – and the Women's Project was born.

The majority of the articles in this book were written while working for the Women's Project and published in *Transformation*, its quarterly newsletter. The Women's Project was a scrappy little Arkansas organization that from 1981 to 1998 worked across rural and urban communities to bring about social change. Its political mission was aligned with *The Combahee River Collective Statement*: to eliminate sexism and racism, with a focus on violence and economic injustice. From our mission statement:

> We take risks in our work; we take unpopular stands. We work for all women and against all forms of discrimination and oppression. We believe that we cannot work for all women and against sexism unless we also work against racism, classism, ageism, anti-Semitism, heterosexism and homophobia. We see the connections among these oppressions as the context for violence against women in this society.

We believed that people could be transformed and we practiced relational organizing that was intersectional. We strived for political integrity, believing that we could not demand fairness and equality and justice from the world unless we practiced these

1. *The Combahee River Collective Statement.* United States, April 1977.

ourselves. A Black and white, straight and queer staff, we refused to talk about sexism without talking about racism and vice versa – they were always linked, and we linked all other oppressions to them. We were determined to fight systemic sexism and racism and economic injustice from within, and we thought the critical areas for change were shared power and shared resources. We paid all staff the same, believing that an hour of one woman's hard work was equal in worth to another woman's hard work, no matter what the job. Everyone participated in decision making about what the work would be and how the resources would be used. Our work was to create the structure to bring people from around the state into the work to change our communities and to build the political education and skills and resources to do it.

It was the work of these people – staff, interns, board and hundreds of people who became the Women's Project around the state – that made it possible for me to observe up close the times we were living in, the threats, dangers, and the possibilities. Though never thinking of myself as a writer before, I became an organizer who also wrote to name our experiences, examine them, and describe what was happening in the world around us. For example, when the rightwing Good News Methodists attacked the United Methodist Church (our fiscal sponsor for the first five years) because we had lesbians on staff, we began our study of the religious Right and our work against it. That work led us to the observation of and opposition to far Right groups such as the KKK and the Covenant Sword and Arm of the Lord. What followed was the creation of the Women's Watchcare Network, where we organized women around the state to document hate crimes against people of color, women, LGBTQ people, Jews and Catholics. In the end, we did massive, painful documentation of the murders of women. Then, after we gained this experience, in 1992 the Women's Project sent me to organize for the No on 9 campaign in Oregon, a campaign fighting an anti-gay ballot measure created by a local rightwing group and supported nationally by the well-organized religious and secular Right. In the end, we had a story of the growth and strategies of the Right.

This social history begins with the election of Ronald Reagan in 1980 and the simultaneous rise of neoliberalism and the religious Right. In these articles and speeches you will see the deliberate blaming of Black and brown people (particularly immigrants) for virtually all social problems: drug abuse and related violence, welfare fraud, crime, the failure of public education, high taxes, and deterioration of our neighborhoods. Built on this resentment and the creation of a myth of scarcity ("there isn't enough to go around" and "you are taking something from me"), there came a decades long plan to radically reduce taxation and gut our social programs and infrastructure.

In the two-plus decades these articles cover, you will see how the religious Right was central in the effort to create and mobilize resentment by creating wedge issues and fighting to maintain systems of domination – and how these wedges were purposed to organize people of color and low-income workers against the rising demand for the rights of people of color, women, and queer people. And then these wedges were used among white evangelicals and working-class white people as indicators of the loss of the moral and economic center of the country. These divisions still live today.

Readers will recognize the evolution of movement language, analysis, and identities from the late 20 Century documented here to the 21st century we experience today: a shift from focusing on multiculturalism to examining colonization, from defending the rights of LGBTQ+ people to expanding and demanding a broad understanding of gender, and from working for integration and equity to seeking abolition and reparations. Movements evolve or die. Our social justice movements have shown we can and will evolve—and we are growing.

This book is for those who long for and fight for social justice, for a world where every person counts and, as the old movement song says, where everyone has the right to the tree of life. Within these documents, there are examples of our great collective work for social justice as well as examples of how we failed or fell short of our dreams or missed opportunities to replace division with unity.

There are themes that run throughout: a focus on community and local work; a Gandhian belief that every step toward liberation must have liberation in it; the struggle between power/profit and community values/human needs; the affirmation that every person counts and we leave some people out at our peril; and the belief that the reconfiguration of the family and community is at the center of the battle for liberation or dominance. The overarching theme is the need to grow an inclusive and just people's democracy, and an argument that it is worth fighting to defend and build the fragile unfinished democracy we have.

In the spirit of this democracy, this collection is offered for any way you might use it on the path to ward off authoritarianism and to build a people's democracy, to resist division and to build unity, to reimagine and bring about a radical transformation of the world.

– Suzanne Pharr
Little Rock, AR
2021

Beginnings

Alarm – and an Early Call to Action (2021)

The 1980 Ronald Reagan election brought dramatic change to this country, and both the Right and the Left responded vigorously, the Right on offense building power and institutional control and the Left on defense trying to defend and build a multi-racial democracy. By then, the Right had created a strong network and infrastructure of political and religious institutions with an eager growing base. The election of Reagan gave them the charismatic leader who could make the economic and social changes to achieve dominance.

And now we are recovering from the last four years of another charismatic President, with a dangerously divided country and democracy under siege in a time of multiple life-threatening crises. We are facing world-changing threats and we are seeking ways to defend our people and to create a fair and just world.

It has been helpful to me to go back forty years in our history to revisit our threats, successes and failures. What is clear to me is that we on the Left have known what to do, even when we failed in it: connect with and fight for people across all our differences in race, gender, economic status, religion, and ability; make human rights the basis for equality and survival; practice the politics and behaviors we are fighting for, individually and within our organizations; keep culture and spirit vibrantly alive.

As evidence of what we knew and with hope for the future, I am beginning this book's conversation with two short speeches. The first was given in late November 1980, just as we were all recognizing that Reagan was the new President. The protest took place on a rainy highway in rural Arkansas at the entrance to the land where 18 Titan II missiles lay buried, ready for a directive from the new hawkish President. The second is an excerpt from a speech that was given in July 1981 six months into Reagan's presidency, addressing the horrors of the recent Family Protection Act that was a central piece of the Right's dream of the future.

Speech for Women's March Against Titan II Missiles (1980)

We are here today because we are women and men and children who live with faith and belief that positive change is possible, that we with our spirits and strength can bring that change about, that we can shape a new and better world out of the near disaster of this one.[1] We are here because we want to use our lives for the good, not for evil; because we want to create, not destroy; because we want to nurture, not diminish. We are here to say NO to the forces of war and destruction and to say YES to peace and creation. We are here seeking a better world.

We are here because we are a gentle, loving people, because we are strong and able and we want to be a voice for those who are not so strong, for those who are voiceless in their suffering. We are here because we are against violence, whether it is against women and children in the streets or in the home, or whether it's against all of us through war. We are here because we want good lives for all peoples, not just the white and rich and powerful. We are against the oppression that takes away the freedoms that create good lives: the freedom from economic want, the freedom to choose who we love, how and where we live, the freedom to do productive work, the freedoms of the 1st Amendment. We are here to speak for the many Americans who are losing those freedoms we call human rights. We call this loss of freedom *oppression.* And we say that the constant threat of nuclear war oppresses us all, every living thing on this small, green planet which is but a pinpoint of light in the cosmos.

Hence we have come to the place where 18 missiles surround us in their subterranean wait for the signal to be fired

1. November 1980. A speech given in Damascus, AR at a rally and march protesting the recent installation of nuclear missiles. https://encyclopediaofarkansas.net/entries/titan-ii-missile-explosion-2543/

for them to be sent to Russia to kill women, men and children much like ourselves, those who probably also feel themselves to have had little voice against nuclear warheads and heads of state.[2] We have come here to say YES to our belief in humankind all over the planet, women, men and children of all colors and beliefs, magnificent in our differences and beautiful in our similarities. We are here to say YES to our planet's survival, not just for a few paltry humans dragging themselves out of the nuclear debris and shaking off the radioactive dust, but for the survival of all of us on a planet that is green and growing and where life and freedom are not to be constantly jeopardized by the threat of nuclear or environmental or social destruction. We are here to say YES to a better way of life where we can live all around this planet with human rights and freedoms and love for one another and the natural world, knowing and respecting the deep connections among all living things.

And who are we? Well, there have been lots of new groups and political allies and parties springing up during the last few years. But we – I think we are yet a new one, born in the wake of a conservative tide in this country. We are the New Resistance gathering together, ready to grow in numbers and fight underground and aboveground and wherever it is necessary for the freedom and rights and preservation of life of all of us who share this small, green planet earth whose future hangs by a gossamer thread which we must dedicate our lives to protecting. Born of this day, we are the New resistance, already on the move. By tomorrow, our numbers will be swelling. We are indeed the hope for our future.

The Family Protection Act (1981)

Things fall apart, the center cannot hold.

Mere anarchy is loosed upon the world.

---

2. https://encyclopediaofarkansas.net/entries/titan-ii-icbm-launch-complex-sites-7760/

The blood-dimmed tide is loosed and everywhere

The ceremony of innocence is drowned.

The best lack all conviction while the worst

Are full of passionate intensity.

— "The Second Coming" by William Butler Yeats, 1919.

...I was asked to come here tonight to talk about the Family Protection Act (FPA).[3] This is a big one. We now have more evidence than we ever wished for to prove to us that the worst are full of passionate intensity, and that they are moving rapidly and effectively to eliminate basic rights and freedoms that have been hard won, and if we don't reinforce our deepest convictions with some courage and action, then we are in for some dark days in this nation and world.

Here is a summary of the most criticized aspects of the bill: It would prohibit federal intervention in child abuse, spouse abuse and juvenile delinquency; prohibit the use of federal funds for any group that "presents homosexuality as an acceptable lifestyle;" prohibit the use of federal funds in schools that use textbooks that do not show women in their "traditionally defined roles;" and it would provide tax breaks for church schools; prohibit abortion or contraceptive information to be given to teenagers without their parent's consent; reaffirm corporal punishment for children; give a tax exemption of $1000 to *married* parents who have a child; prohibit legal services from handling cases having to do with divorce, abortion or homosexual rights.

As you can see, the FPA goes against almost all of the advances we have made in the women's movement. What concerns me the most is that it creates a general climate of oppression, suggesting approval for the abuse of children, women, heterosexuals. It seems a step toward fascism in this country

3. Excerpt from a speech given at a meeting of the Fayetteville, AR chapter of the National Organization for Women (NOW) in June 1981.

with its return to state's rights and Christian male dominance. One of the FPA bills thrusts is into the schools, advocating a strict conformity to a single norm established by the new Right. We could then produce generations of students who are taught to accept what they are given, rather than to develop critical and analytical minds. And that is frightening, for as Erich Fromm says in his essay, "The Illusion of Individuality," "the human automaton is fertile ground for the seeds of fascism."[4]

Some people are saying that it appears we are returning to the days of the 50s and McCarthyism. If that were so, I wouldn't be so deeply worried as I am now. Instead, it seems to me that a more likely parallel is to the 1920s and 1930s in Germany.

...One of the things that plagues me as I work across the state is trying to decide if I am being an alarmist in my interpretation of the signs I see of those seeds Fromm mentions – or if I fail in this interpretation, whether I might be on the side of those millions in Germany who failed to read the signs and take action against them. I don't want to watch one person after another taken away while I say, "Oh, I can do without that one. It doesn't affect me so much," until finally all our backs are against the wall. Right now, the worst of what's happening is affecting people of color, low income women, and homosexuals. And it is here where we need to dig in and say *No*. It's now that we must act against racism, homophobia, sexism, classism – and in real ways that are more than just talk.

My greatest fear is that we will move toward a police state, all under the banner of keeping middleclass families safe. One bad step was the Supreme Court decision to uphold the legality of building a barricade that prohibited anyone Black from walking through a white neighborhood in Memphis *(City of Memphis vs. Greene, 1981)*. The court said that this was not a civil rights issue but instead simply a matter of ensuring the safety of the white neighborhood. With unemployment running at 25% in Black communities, and almost twice that for Black teenagers, it seems

4. Fromm, Erich. *The Fear of Freedom*. United Kingdom, Routledge & Kegan Paul, 1943. Pgs. 207-220

we might have an increase in crime and possibly riots similar to those in Britain. And what will our response be? My fear is that we will continue to fail to go to the source of the problem but instead will bring down all the force of our police and military establishment – all in the name of "protecting the citizens," that is, the white middleclass who will support this move in their fear and misunderstanding.

The ultimate question is what can we do and is there a glimmer of hope anywhere? As I travel the state working with women—work that leads mostly to Black communities—I gain great hope from the fact that I meet hundreds of strong women who are deeply concerned about women's issues and are willing to put large parts of their lives into the struggle for equality and human rights. These are not women who are heard from in the media, they are unsung, but they have gathered strength from surviving the hardness of their lives, they have found community with each other, and they are moving.

In May I went to the National Women's Studies Association conference in Connecticut and found many other reasons for hope. Drawing women from all over the country, the conference was called "Women Respond to Racism" and the women there explored racism with deep courage, some pain, and much growth. To me it was a sign of great hope and courage that the keynote speakers were the great poets, Audre Lorde and Adrienne Rich, one Black and one white, both lesbians. The major performance of the conference was by Sweet Honey in the Rock, powerful Black movement singers, and the book that riveted everyone's attention was the pioneering *This Bridge Called My Back: Writings by Radical Women of Color* (1983).[5]

...It is clear we have to engage ourselves wholeheartedly in the struggle for human rights. Here in Arkansas that means joining in the fight against racism: examining what is happening in our schools, prisons, the uses of welfare, housing and employment opportunities. And importantly, we have to examine what we do

---

5. Cherrie moraga, ed. *This Bridge Called My Back: Writings by Radical Women of Color.* United States, Kitchen Table, Women of Color Press, 1983.

in our lives that assumes race and class privilege, both consciously and unconsciously, and by so doing helps maintain race and class inequality.

In every aspect of our lives, we must follow Adrienne Rich's advice and become "disloyal to civilization." Our disloyalty will take the form of refusing to support patriarchy; refusing to accept white and male as the norm that all others are judged against; refusing to support the death seeking of militarism and nuclear proliferation; refusing to support a free enterprise system that exploits and dehumanizes its citizens while also slowly killing them through the abuse of the environment; refusing to support racism, sexism and homophobia with our willingness to shield ourselves behind white heterosexuality; and refusing to accept violence and aggression against women, people of color, homosexuals, the elderly and the poor.

This disloyalty is frightening because as Rich says, it makes outlaws of us all, stripping us of the safety granted us by being on the "chosen" secure side of middleclass America. It is frightening because it allows us no illusions, no excuses concerning our participation in the forces of dehumanization...

We must radicalize our lives by critical analysis and examination of what is happening in our society. Then we must act to make ourselves one with those we are carefully taught to think of as the *other* and dismiss as not being as human as ourselves. We must move toward a humanization of this culture through acting out the feminist principles that seek equality and a life of quality for all. And finally, we must accept the enormous responsibility of transforming this world and of creating with our every action the better world we choose to live in.

II

The Right

— Notes from the South and Oregon

1.

Divisions that Kill: The Enemy Without and Within

1992

When the verdict came down to acquit the cops who brutally beat Rodney King and people began burning their communities and attacking each other I thought to myself, the rightwing is achieving its goal to divide and conquer us as a people.[1]

Then, when the media immediately turned away from an analysis of the injustice of the verdict to focus solely upon the violent response to it and George Bush told the nation that what was happening in Los Angeles was not about civil rights or protest or equality but the "brutality of the mob" I thought, the Christian Right is victorious in its strategy to strip events from their political context and to frame them as morality, not as a matter of justice and injustice but of good and evil behavior of certain groups of people.

My outrage pounded in my temples as I sat riveted to the TV, and I saw my own face mirrored everywhere: in those who stole goods and torched buildings, in the white truck driver beaten nearly to death, in the Asian grocers armed to defend their shops, in the women who cried for the loss of their community. I felt torn apart. Horrified, I thought, these divisions are killing us, and they did not come to us by chance or through the natural order of things. These divisions have been encouraged and manipulated for decades by those who oppose our liberation.

---

1. Originally published in the July/August 1992 issue of *Transformation* (Vol. 7, No. 4), the Women's Project newsletter.

As I watched buildings burn and people die during the long May Day weekend, I thought of other miscarriages of justice such as the 1978 verdict to sentence Dan White to only six years of prison for killing gay San Francisco Supervisor Harvey Milk and Mayor George Moscone. And then there was the 1991 refusal of California Governor Pete Wilson to sign into law legislation providing civil rights to lesbians and gay men. As with the Rodney King verdict, these actions came to symbolize decades of injustice and our people took to the streets in outrage. As Martin Luther King, Jr. said, riot became the language of the unheard.

In the riots that followed these actions, we found ourselves without the leadership and vision for uniting our people to turn our rage against the source of our oppression. Instead, we turned much of it against each other. Our disunity had for too long been manipulated by the Right through pitting us against one another for the crumbs of access, resources and privileges: disrupting our work by FBI infiltration of our movements; destroying our leaders through police attacks such as those upon the American Indian Movement and the Black Panthers, and relentless shifting of blame from those who benefit from oppression to those who suffer from it. Angry, frustrated, and on the defensive, we have been led to adopt their values and tactics and to oblige them by doing part of their destructive work.

While we turn upon each other in our frustration, pain, and rage, the Christian Right's "foot soldiers of the Lord" who oppose our very existence march on to increasing successes on every front. Creating a climate of division and hatred, they shape public opinion to oppose our liberation and, in the end, to kill us. It was not by accident that the Harvey Milk murder occurred during the Anita Bryant campaign against lesbian and gay civil rights and just after the unsuccessful statewide effort by John Briggs for a ballot measure to prevent lesbians and gay men from teaching school in California. Similarly, the Rodney King verdict came after a year of highly publicized racist campaigning by Pat Buchanan and David Duke and Bush's sniping against the 1990 Civil Rights Restoration Act.

Since the early 1970s, the Christian Right has launched a political attack against lesbians and gay men, people of color, and feminists that has affected every adult and child in this country. It has made significant headway in dismantling the gains of the Civil Rights Movement and has become a major threat to the fundamental principles of democracy.

The Christian Right is united through homophobia, racism, and sexism in pursuit of their goal of merging church and state, institutionalizing a narrow view of morality, and maintaining social control by eliminating rights and freedoms. This broad coalition of highly organized Christian fundamentalists and evangelicals, politicians and businessmen has been a major force in creating the political climate we know today. It is backed by conservative think tanks like the Heritage Foundation and the Rutherford Institute that provide legal and legislative strategies, Pat Robertson's Christian Broadcasting Network that deliver its message, and Operation Rescue, Eagle Forum, and Concerned Women for America that provide hundreds of thousands of "foot soldiers. Working on a variety of fronts, this network has created strategies to infiltrate and control all our institutions, from school boards to the Supreme Court.

While our racism, sexism, and homophobia have often separated us from one another, these religious conservatives lump us together because they see people of color, feminists, lesbians and gay men as standing in the way of their goal to merge church and state: to give legislated dominance to white Christian males who receive their authority from Biblical scriptures. Indeed, they see us as being the cause of the breakdown of order in society. According to their logic, those rights and protections which give us voice in a democratic society are the cause of immorality and social chaos and must be thwarted or dismantled. The Civil Rights Movement's demand that power be shared by all is a block to their authoritarian vision.

Attacking the idea that some people are inferior by race and must be dominated, the Civil Rights Movement issued a call to conscience and to reason. It said that true democracy calls for justice, participation, and freedom. For most of us, indoctrinated to believe in a democracy that supported the interests of white males, this was a new and profoundly moving idea. Imagine: a demand for justice, participation, and freedom. The words rang in our ears.

Not only did African-Americans hear the call but also other people of color: Asians, Latinos, Native Americans. Other movements were birthed. It occurred to women that if racial discrimination prevented participation in democracy, so then must discrimination based on sex. It was a heady, movement-building idea. Lesbians and gay men looked at our lives, and everywhere we looked, we saw an absence of justice, open participation, and freedom to be who we are. Then Stonewall gave us the historic, symbolic moment to move toward liberation.

The civil rights movement not only marked the way for other great liberation movements, but its very successes led to a reaction to it and all who embarked upon the long and arduous path to equal rights. It was not by coincidence that it was in the late 1960s, during the presidential campaign of George Wallace of Alabama, that we began to feel the impact of the organized Christian Right.

Over the past two decades, the Christian Right claimed these victories:

- A campaign against homosexuality led by singer and orange juice promoter, Anita Bryant;

- The effort to defeat the Equal Rights Amendment led by Eagle Forum's Phyllis Schlafly;

- A highly organized Christian coalition led by Pat Robertson to elect Ronald Reagan;

- A widespread attack led by Operation Rescue to dismantle piece by piece abortion rights;

- An assault upon affirmative action laws led by Jesse Helms, among others.

These are only a few of their efforts. The Christian Right has created "armies of God" to infiltrate all of our institutions in pursuit of their goal of institutionalizing their narrow vision of morality. They have been at the center of the effort to restrict funding for AIDS prevention education and services; the attack on the battered women's movement as "anti-family;" the crusade for teaching creationism rather than evolution and the fundamentals of Christian thought instead of secular humanism: and the drive for censorship rather than freedom of speech. Their efforts to infiltrate and dominate institutions have touched the lives of every person in the U.S.

In the 1990s we have seen national testing of their racist agenda in their support of the gubernatorial campaign of David Duke in Louisiana and the presidential campaign of Pat Buchanan, their sexist agenda in the efforts of Operation Rescue to close abortion clinics in Wichita, KS, and Buffalo, NY, and their homophobic agenda in Colorado and Oregon. For six months I have been given an opportunity to do close observation of the Christian Right in Oregon where the Oregon Citizens Alliance (OCA) is attempting to pass a constitutional amendment to legally declare homosexuality, along with sadism, masochism, and pedophilia, to be "abnormal and perverse" behaviors and to prevent the state and local governments from spending any monies to "promote homosexuality." If passed, this ballot initiative would amend a state constitution for the first time in U.S. history to take away rights rather than to give them. Each national test of strategies is a prelude to their duplication throughout the country.

Many of these strategies could be summarized by the title of the popular film, "Sex, Lies, and Videotape" (1989). A stunning example is the use of mis/dis-information by the Oregon Citizen's Alliance (OCA) to divide people against one another and to bring bigotry to the ballot box. An analysis of the video, *No Special Rights*, they produced to distribute to 10,000 churches, schools, and individuals reveals themes common to the national Christian Right's work to destroy the rights of women, people of color, and lesbians and gay men.

The video is produced by the OCA's No Special Rights Committee which echoes a theme that the Right uses across the country: they argue that because all people are covered equally by the Constitution as framed by our "founding fathers" (excluding the Bill of Rights), that to ask for access, opportunity, or protection from discrimination is to ask tor a "special right." The slogan for David Duke's gubernatorial campaign was "Equal Rights for All; Special Rights for None." Under this banner, he attacked affirmative action and people of color and women who benefit from it. In framing the video, the OCA says lesbians and gay men are trying to get status as a "minority" which receives "special rights." Hence, they must keep lesbians and gay men from being part of affirmative action and quotas as well as prevent the state and local governments from promoting the "abnormal and perverse behavior" of homosexuality. They call for the state constitution to be amended to eliminate the category of sexual orientation along with any rights and protections.

Obsessed by sex, the Christian Right has had great success in coalescing people and developing a constituency when they concentrate on abortion and homosexuality. Both are highly charged emotional issues which go right to the heart of sexism. Male domination could not survive if all people were granted fully supported choice and self-determination over their bodies and lives. Because there is so much confusion and ignorance about both abortion and homosexuality, the Right can manipulate information and emotions to gain support tor its sexist agenda.

In Oregon, as well as the rest of the country, the lesbian and gay community makes a vulnerable target because as a people we have had visibility only since Stonewall in 1969: 23 years is a very short time for the general public to gain knowledge of a group. Consequently, false and distorted information can be fed to people who are generally ignorant of anything but the most gross stereotypes.

The OCA's video does just that. Filmed with a personal camcorder at the 1987 National Gay and Lesbian March on Washington and the 1991 San Francisco Pride March, the video strings together a series of images which they hope will convince people that we are sex fiends and perverts, we are anti-family and anti-religion, we are the uncaring carriers of disease, we sexually molest children, and, wealthy and powerful from federal and state tax dollars, we have a militant homosexual agenda that, using AIDS education, as an excuse, works through schools and the legislature to change laws that constrain our behavior and to present homosexuality as healthy and normal.

For 30 minutes the video bombards us with shots of naked men wagging their penises, barebreasted women, people in leather with paraphernalia, men and women with their children, groups such as lesbian/gay youth, strippers, parenting groups, fathers, teachers, Dykes on Bikes, Sisters of Perpetual Indulgence, Hookers from Hell, and individuals such as a man dressed as a faggot Christ carrying a cross, another licking the enormous rubber penis of his friend. There are interviews with proponents of sadomasochism giving graphic details, a man talking about how he was led innocently into sadomasochism, church people talking about redefining the Bible and church beliefs to justify the homosexual lifestyle, and as the centerpiece of the video, members of North American Man/Boy Love Association arguing on behalf of sex with children. Running as a sub-title under many of these images is the question, "Gay Pride?" or the statement, "This is what gay rights means."

What does the Christian Right hope to achieve with this video that has been distributed in Oregon and is now beginning to appear in other states? It advances the development of *coded language for rapid communication of bigoted information* that will lead people to join ranks with the Christian Right in their efforts to legislate discrimination and exclusion.

The Willie Horton video created by George Bush demonstrates the development of coded language. In this television ad, the viewing audience was exposed time and again to the message that Dukakis had paroled an African-American murderer and rapist who then raped and killed again. The successful goal was to create a shorthand that said rapists and murderers are African American, and liberals are soft on rapists and murderers. In his campaign, David Duke took this theme even further in developing these codes:

- Affirmative action is coded as the loss of "qualified" white people's jobs and women and people of color are held responsible;

- Drugs and crime are linked with community breakdown caused by people of color;

- Welfare is presented as the cause of the economic crisis brought about by people of color who abuse the system;

- Destruction of the family is associated with feminists who support reproductive rights and lesbians and gay men who do not produce families.

Relying on its audience not to know that 95% of those who sexually abuse children are heterosexual men, the OCA video leads viewers to associate all lesbians and gay men with the sexual molestation of children. It is the perpetuation of a *"big lie" – the lie told so often that it becomes the truth to uninformed people.* What is omitted is the information that heterosexual men sexually abuse both girls and boys most often within relationships of trust. Also omitted is that the majority of the lesbian and gay community believes that sex with children, whether consensual or not, is sexual abuse. The wrong of child sexual molestation cannot be rationalized by the intimacy of family relationships or so-called "man-boy" love. Because of the distortion of the truth, our children remain vulnerable to abuse because we warn them of only the least likely perpetrators and we do not warn them of trusted heterosexual men who exploit trust.

This "big lie" that lesbians and gay men recruit and sexually molest children is the linchpin of the emotional argument at the center of discrimination against us. Using this argument, the video goes on the offensive to frame the gay and lesbian movement in the context of morality rather than civil rights. Behavior is displayed which is perceived by most to be wrong, i.e., the sexual abuse of children, and then that behavior is extended to an entire group of people so that we then begin to think of all of them as immoral. Hence, as we see the images of small children in the Lesbian and Gay Pride March juxtaposed with naked men and comments about man/boy love, we are led to think that the central focus of lesbians and gay men is the sexual abuse of children. Thus, an entire group of people becomes named as immoral and devalued as human beings. It is then only a short step to the removal of rights and protections and the instigation of violence. No doubt for many people in this country watching the L.A. riots, the Willie Horton ad entered their minds carrying the Bush campaign suggestion that all Black men are criminals. As stated by President Bush, the issue in L.A. was morality, not civil rights, and one was justified in using "whatever force necessary" to stop the rioters.

This mis/dis-information is used to wedge us apart from our allies. The OCA has gone into African American churches in Portland and told their members that while they were clean, upstanding Christians in their Civil Rights Movement, these perverted and diseased homosexuals now want the same rights African Americans fought so hard for. They remind them that there are very few opportunities to go around, and that they must protect what little there is available for them. Abortion rights are also presented as genocide against the African-American community and women's participation in affirmative action as an attack on the position of Black males. Through presenting the idea of deserving and undeserving victims of hatred and oppression, the Right reinforces the idea of hierarchies of oppression, and divides us from another.

Pitted against one another with our rights assaulted at every turn, we often turn against each other in the desperate scramble to keep what little we have. While the OCA video influences the church audience it was created for, it also creates divisions among lesbians and gay men. The reaction to it is similar to the community response to the L.A. riots. Because it plays directly to *internalized oppression* – to the negative messages about ourselves that we have come to believe along with the rest of the population

– many lesbians and gay men who seek acceptance by the larger society condemn those in the video and distance themselves from them. People separate themselves off into "good queers/bad queers."

Another divisive result of the video is that it is so assaultive and the potential for our destruction so great, some lesbians and gay men begin feeling that we are the most victimized minority. People then talk about homophobia as the worst oppression and AIDS as the ultimate genocide. In doing so, we isolate ourselves from other oppressed groups and fail to connect with each other under the attack that is common to all of us. focusing on ourselves, we fail to recognize that this attack is not the worst thing that has ever happened to a people. Horrible as it is, it is no more terrible than the daily violence that kills thousands of women each year and damages millions more, than the decimation of communities of color by the police, than the deaths from lack of healthcare among the poor, than the loss of Native-American lands, than the genocide of the Jews. It is equally terrible and connected to all.

Perhaps the worst danger to our liberation is that our fear, anger, and defensiveness lead us to take on the tactics of the enemy:

- As the Right attacks our dignity and worth, we respond by attacking those within the movement who are different from us;

- As they invade our right to privacy, we respond by outing our own people;

- As they pit us against each other for the crumbs of benefits, we fight each other for recognition that our particular issue (AIDS funding, breast cancer research, civil rights legislation, hate crimes laws, domestic partnerships) is the most important;

- As they attack our leadership, we attack and refuse to support our leaders;

- As they distort and silence the voices of oppressed

people, we shout down and silence those we disagree with;

- As they block equality and participation for oppressed people, we subordinate the concerns of women, people of color, and people with disabilities in our movement.

In the end, we have to ask, who is served by our tactics? Who benefits most?

Our inability to agree on the answers to these questions makes us fractured in our vision and strategies, with each of us as activists participating in some way in what we would define as "the movement" but often fighting in disunity and *horizontal hostility* among ourselves. In particular, we have been divided by sexism and racism, with lines drawn between men and women, between white people and people of color. I fear that our disconnection will kill us.

We must begin a process of doing what we jokingly call "getting over ourselves" so that we can develop a vision and leadership that brings us together. This means we will have to stop shouting, "Me, me!" and learn to harmonize on "Us, us." Developing the *politics of inclusion* will not be easy because we have many barriers to overcome and because we have no model for it. But I am convinced that this is the only road to both survival and liberation. The Christian Right, on the other hand, has an easier time in creating its politics of exclusion. Recognizing that most people are disturbed by the social and political chaos in the U.S., they offer us a vision of the past. They ask us to look in the rearview mirror to the 1940s and 1950s when white soldiers returned from the war with the G.I. bill to go to school, finding jobs plentiful, housing available, and there was a sense of stability and order. What they call for, of course, is a racist, sexist, and homophobic vision, for this was a time of legalized segregation, when male authority was unchallenged by women, when abortion was illegal, and when lesbians and gay men were invisible. They speak of this as the time of "traditional family values." For many of us, it was the time of family horrors when rape, battering, incest and alcoholism were kept as secrets within the family. Nevertheless, the Christian Right is able to unite frightened and uninformed people in a nostalgia for the past when social order and benefits for the few were bought at the expense of women, people of color, lesbians and gay men.

Our vision of inclusion is built on the future, not the past; we are creating that which has not been before. If we can understand that the Right uses divisiveness to destroy our vision of inclusion, then we can learn that our most effective work of resistance and liberation is to make connections, both politically and personally. Making true connections may be the most cutting-edge work for the 1990s.

I have seen this work taking place in rural Oregon communities this spring where people are coming together to talk about claiming their communities. Lesbians and gay men, people of color, feminists, ministers, social workers, labor unionists, domestic violence workers, blue collar workers, etc., are gathering in common cause to say to each other that this attack by the OCA against the lesbian and gay community is actually a fundamental threat to democracy that affects everyone. They are sick of the Christian Right framing the issues and controlling the public debate for the past two decades. It is clear to them from looking at their school boards, for example, that the Right has infiltrated deeply into their communities, and they are scared. Instead of allowing the Right to create the rules of community life and to determine who gets to participate, these community people want to work together for a common vision that includes everyone. This means that people who usually have little to do with each other are now sitting side by side and learning about each other's lives. This process gives me great hope. I think people are hungry for true information and for a way to work together for justice.

While many progressive people agree that we must work against racism, sexism, homophobia, antisemitism, etc., I'm not sure that we always understand how intricately these oppressions are linked and how deeply they are connected to our very survival. For instance, do white lesbians and gay men truly understand that fighting against racism is key to our freedom? As we pursue liberation, we will have to build *politics of connection* from those glimpses we get of our shared destiny with other oppressed people. As do most people, I came to this recognition from personal experience which showed me both the connections and a vision for what could be.

When I was a senior in high school in 1957 in Lawrenceville, Georgia, I was wildly in love with playing basketball and wildly in love with a girl, and I was trying to figure out what was wrong with me. In my small farming community of white Christians who believed in a literal interpretation of the *Bible*, there was no context for figuring out who I was as a lesbian or how to live a whole and complete life.

In my confusion and isolation as a young lesbian, I joined my girlfriend in double dates with our steady boyfriends when they finished their football games. Afterwards, we two girls went home together in sanctioned "spend the nights" where we expressed the love and sexual feelings that were most true to our inner selves. We were deeply conflicted and secretive. We all watched "Rebel Without a Cause" (1955) and then night after night took our older brothers' '55 Chevys out on lonely roads to play "chicken." As we barreled down abandoned roads at 80 to 90 miles per hour head on toward our friends in another car, daring the other to be the first to avoid the impending collision, you can bet I was identifying with James Dean and Sal Mineo, not Natalie Wood. Confused and distressed, I had deep inside me a sense of abandon and a desire to risk my life because I couldn't make any sense of it. I thought there was something profoundly wrong with me, so much so that I could never expect a place of rest and acceptance among people I loved.

Little did I know in 1957 that 500 miles due west in Little Rock, Arkansas, Mrs. Daisy Bates as head of the NAACP was organizing a team of African-American teenagers to perform an act of courage that would give me my life. Each day, with awesome dignity, Mrs. Bates and the Little Rock Nine walked through crowds of jeering, hostile white people and national guardsmen to demand that quality education be an equal right, not a special right for white people.

Though Black people have been denied access and equality for almost four centuries, these young people found the courage to stand in the face of a history of subordination and hatred to demand that the door of education be opened to everyone. Their actions were one of the bold steps in the creation of the Civil Rights Movement that came to change the lives of all oppressed people, of all people in the U.S. Certainly it changed mine. It gave me my life. The Civil Rights Movement, along with the women's and lesbian and gay movements, gave me the understanding that I am a person of worth and dignity. Because of these great movements that called for justice, participation, and freedom for all of us – including this queer girl from a poor Southern family – I was able to put the pieces of my life together to make a whole.

And now, in 1992, I have lived for ten years in a house across the street from Central High School in Little Rock, Arkansas, and every day I can sit on my screened porch and look across the garden at a rainbow of kids entering a fully integrated high school that is one of the best in the U.S. My life has been privileged by the friendship and mentorship of Mrs. Daisy Bates who is now a member of the Women's Project.

While I was away working against the Christian Right in Oregon this spring, I called my office one day and heard this story of hope and vision. There had been a small gathering of friends at my house that overlooks Central High School where three of us live: white and middle-aged, African-American and young, white and living in a wheelchair. At this dinner of friends, there were five lesbians, three white and two Black, and Mrs. Daisy Bates in her wheelchair, all eating Chinese food together and watching a slide show about Mrs. Bates' life. Of these lesbians, one created the Women's Project's lending library of women's and African-American literature, another is an activist for disability rights, one is writing a book about Mrs. Bates life, another writes poetry and incisive political articles about lesbian battering, and one spends her days working against biased violence against people of color, women, Jews and Catholics, lesbians and gay men. All sat there together, eating and laughing and talking, sharing friendship and politics and common cause. Hearing about it, I thought, this is a glimpse of what the world can and should be.

I also thought, this is *a truly moral vision*. The Christian Right frames our political efforts in terms of immorality and offers in the place of politics a narrow moral prescription. Yielding this terrain to the Right, progressive people rarely talk about the morality of our own vision. Could there be anything more moral than the idea that all people are of equal worth and deserve justice and full participation in their society? Is there anything more moral than the idea that people are connected to and responsible for one another? I don't think so.

Sometimes I feel our work is like that of celestial navigation. Before directional instruments were invented, sailors navigated the seas by fixing their compass on the North star; however, if they fixed on the wrong star, then everything thereafter was off course. We are working against years of a society fixing on the wrong star. This nation has built all its institutions and policies from the starting point of *a fundamental lie: that certain groups of people are inferior to others and hence should be subordinated to them.* Every direction taken from this fundamental lie puts us off course, and group after group gets lost. If one begins with the lie that people of color are inferior to white people, then it makes equal sense that women are inferior to men. And so it goes. It is our work to fix upon *the truth: that all people are of equal worth and deserve justice.*

We must do this work as though our lives depended upon it. Because they do – all of them, no matter what sex or race or sexual identity or class. The message from Los Angeles rings true: there must be justice for all of us or there will be peace for none.

2.

The Christian Right: A Threat to Democracy

1992

In Oregon and throughout the U.S., there is a battle going on to determine the political, social, and economic principles that shape our lives and our freedom.[1] The conflict is in schools, in courts, in legislatures, in every institution of our society. It is the battle between the forces of repression and the forces of liberation between the politics of exclusion and the politics of inclusion. It is a battle between the authoritarian ideology of the Christian Right and the liberation ideology of the Civil Rights Movement.

In contrast to the majority of Christians who believe in the separation of church and state, the Christian Right consists of organized rightwing Christians who merge politics and theology to produce a system of social control. Positioned within a conservative movement made up of the secular, political Right and the neo-Nazi Far Right, the Christian Right provides the grassroots activists who create the groundwork for sweeping societal change. Ordinary citizens are most likely to have their most direct contact with the politics of the Right through encounters with these "foot soldiers" of the Christian Right who pound away at the fundamental principles of democracy.

A Brief Overview of the Christian Right

The Christian Right is regressive and its goal is the influence and infiltration of institutions to put in place Christian authority. It is fundamentalist in its literal interpretation of the *Bible* and its

1. Originally published in the September/October 1992 issue of *Transformation* (Vol. 7, No. 5), the Women's Project newsletter.

belief in absolutist "law and order" and morality dictated by God's elect. It is made up of Christian fundamentalists (church-based) and born-again Christians (from Televangelism conversion). Not all Christians belong to the Christian Right nor do all fundamentalists. There are approximately fifty million Christian fundamentalists in the U.S. Of that number, only fifteen to twenty million are organized into the political and social agenda of the Christian Right. The remainder range from conservative to progressive, and all are simply exercising their basic right to practice the religious and spiritual beliefs of their choice.

The Christian Right organized in response to the Civil Rights Movement, coming together under the racist agenda of the presidential campaign of George Wallace. They viewed the Civil Rights Movement and eventually the legacy of this movement – the Women's Movement and the Lesbian and Gay Movement – as the cause of the breakdown of authority, stability, and law and order.

While both the Christian Right and the Civil Rights Movements of the 60s were church-based, they were completely opposite in point of view. The Civil Rights Movement put forth the message that true democracy calls for justice, liberation, and participation, and that call was heard by oppressed groups throughout the country, creating a basis for other movements, and giving hope to disenfranchised people for the future. The white Christian Right Movement put forth the message that inclusion and participation by diverse groups will destroy the old order of the 40s and 50s when segregation was legally enforced, male authority was unchallenged by women as a class, and lesbians and gay men were invisible. It called for a return to the past.

During the 1970s and 1980s, the Christian Right had considerable success in their attack against the gains of the Civil Rights Movement. In particular, they gained strength through initiating a campaign against homosexuality led by Anita Bryant, the defeat of the Equal Rights Amendment (ERA) led by the Eagle Forum, and the attack against abortion rights led by Operation Rescue.

Their greatest success came from the coalition formed to elect Ronald Reagan who in return legitimized them and gave them open access to influencing and infiltrating institutions. This reinforcement allowed them to speed up their campaign to eliminate affirmative action, gut welfare programs, broaden the death penalty, and fill the federal courts with judges of their theological/political position. (Reagan appointed 425 judges to federal district courts and U.S. circuit courts of appeals.) A strong, highly organized movement for social control and Christian authoritarianism is fully entrenched.

Most remarkably, though, many people during these two decades dismissed the Christian Right as a temporary aberration on the U.S. political scene. Perhaps they were minimized and trivialized because their public faces were those of buffoons: Jerry Falwell, Jimmy Swaggart, and Jim and Tammy Faye Baker. Or perhaps it was because the movement originated out of the South and attracted some of the national anti-Southern sentiment. Many saw this growing "army of God" as working class and uneducated, and thereby incapable of designing a plan for dramatic, far-reaching social and political change. In retrospect, we must recognize that the New Right, with the Christian Right deployed as grassroots "foot soldiers," has controlled the public agenda for almost two decades and has affected virtually every U.S. institution.

One cautionary note: while there is crossover in belief and activities of the Far Right and the secular and Christian New Right, (i.e., Duke and Buchanan) it is important not to confuse the two by calling the Christian Right "Nazis" or their agenda the Holocaust. The Far Right is revolutionary and its goal is the takeover of institutions for white supremacist authority. Made up of neo-Nazis, racist skinheads, Christian Patriots, Christian Identity churches, the KKK and Aryan Nations, it is racist, anti-Semitic, and focuses on white racial "purity."

Some of the Major Players

In order to accomplish this widespread movement that has achieved everything from placing members of the Christian Right on local school boards to placing them on the Supreme Court, there has to be a complex array of institutions and organizations to support the work. Here are a few of the most important cornerstones of the New Right movement:

- **Heritage Foundation.** The most prestigious conservative think tank in the U.S., located in Washington, D.C. and funded by the Coors family. It produces policy and strategies for the Right and acts as a watchdog of U.S. government activity.

- **Rutherford Institute.** The legal arm that develops legislative initiatives and legal challenges.

- **Christian Broadcasting Network.** Led by Pat Robertson, CBN is one of the televangelism networks that control 1,000 fulltime radio stations and 200 television stations that function worldwide. These networks perform two important functions: they get out the message of Christian moral absolutism and authority, and they raise enormous sums of money through donations from their viewers.

- **Operation Rescue.** Grassroots anti-abortion activists who, ironically, employ tactics copied from the Civil Rights Movement to deny constitutionally-protected rights.

- **Eagle Forum and Concerned Women of America.** Grassroots anti-feminist networks that train women ("kitchen table activists") to generate thousands of letters and phone calls to public officials, to do street activism, and to apply pressure on institutions, particularly school boards. Eagle Form has 80,000 members, and CWA is the largest conservative U.S. women's organization, with a reported 565,000 members and a $5.4 million budget.

- **Oregon Citizen's Alliance.** Born out of the 1986 Joe Lutz campaign for the U.S. Senate, the OCA has worked as a "religious army" of supposedly 15,000 to shape the politics of Oregon to "divine authority" and to reinstate the "traditional family" among its citizens. Since 1987, the OCA has organized *against* gun control, euthanasia, separation of church and state, divestment from corporations doing business in South Africa, reproductive rights, homosexuality, state-aided pre-kindergarten programs, gay foster parents, parental leave, and *for* prayer in the schools.

A Tested Agenda

The ultimate goal of the Christian Right is to dismantle the gains of the Civil Rights Movement and to subject social and political life to Christian authoritarianism. To achieve this goal, they must attack not only African Americans and other people of color who gained from the Civil Rights Movement, but also the gains of the Women's Movement, the Lesbian and Gay Movement, and eventually, the Disability Rights Movement.

They have found fertile ground in economic hard times marked by social and political chaos. Generally, people feel assaulted, at risk, and in search of stability and meaning in their lives. Perhaps the greatest sense of loss is economic, providing an easy arena for scapegoating. The Christian Right offers an explanation of disorder by saying that it stems from social and economic disruption caused by people of color, women, lesbians, and gay men who have unfairly taken jobs from white men, destroyed the economy by welfare fraud, and demolished the traditional family by demanding autonomy and choice.

In response to this climate of fear, the New Right has built a national campaign centered on the idea of "No Special Rights." Their position is that the Constitution already covers everyone equally, and that, despite racism, sexism, and homophobia, to ask for anti-discrimination laws or laws providing equal protection and access is to ask for "special rights." During 1991 and 1992 we have been able to see their agenda at work through three national testing sites. In each of these, strategies are tested for replication throughout the country.

The racist agenda was tested in Louisiana with the campaign of David Duke, where Far Right and Christian Right politics were merged. Duke was defeated by the extraordinary effort of the African American community which turned out 80% of its registered voters; otherwise, the 55% white vote would have elected Duke. In this case, the messenger (Duke) was defeated, but the message won by getting widespread publicity.

The sexist agenda was tested in Wichita, Kansas, with the highly orchestrated attack on abortion clinics by Operation Rescue which bussed in thousands of people for street activism. Thanks to a principled federal judge, they were thwarted. However, immediately thereafter, Operation Rescue held a press conference to say that their next targets would be two sites in North Carolina, and one each in Massachusetts, Louisiana, and Arkansas. They had established a successful model.

The homophobic agenda is being tested in Oregon through city initiatives and a state initiative for a constitutional amendment to declare homosexuality, sadism, masochism, and pedophilia to be "abnormal and perverse" behavior. Though initiatives are on the ballot in five other states, the Oregon initiative is the centerpiece because of its breadth and because it calls for a constitutional amendment. This initiative calls for two primary restrictions: for all policies and laws offering protection and access for homosexuals to be eliminated, and for all state and local governments (including schools) to eliminate funding that would "promote homosexuality." An almost identical ballot measure is being tested in Colorado as well.

Strategies of Confusion and Division

In each of these sites major strategies or tactics of the Christian Right can be observed. The "wedge approach" is a central strategy. The point of the wedge, or the point of entry, is on an emotionally charged issue such as abortion, homosexuality, or the failing economy. The Right then uses this issue to gain widespread support and to build a broad constituency base that can then be expanded to include the other issues on its agenda. For example, they provide information about abortion, affirmative action, parental leave, welfare, etc., to the membership and voting base built around the issue of homosexuality and then organize them to vote on these issues.

The second way the wedge is used is to divide communities against themselves and to break up the progressive base for social change. For instance, in Portland, the OCA is entering African American churches and writing letters to the African American newspaper to say that homosexuals are trying to take a share of the small piece of pie that African Americans earned the hard way.

A second critical strategy is to frame the issue as one of morality rather than civil rights. To do this, the Christian Right names certain behavior as immoral, attaches that behavior to a category of people, and then identifies that entire group as immoral and to be restrained and controlled. For example, David Duke, following a long line of racist politicians such as George Wallace, Reagan, and Bush, furthered the development of coded language to get the public to think spontaneously that when crime or drugs or welfare or affirmative action are mentioned, African Americans are the problem. Hence, when he and others name drugs, crime, and illegitimacy as immoral, then connect them to a single group of people – African Americans – the next step is to think that these people are not only connected to immorality but are immoral themselves.

Similarly, the tactic is to say that abortion is immoral, feminists support the right to choice, and therefore feminists are immoral. Another is to say that lesbianism is immoral and the equation goes like this: *feminists = manhaters = lesbians. Therefore, feminists are immoral.*

For this attachment of morality/immorality to a class of people, the Right must produce not only generalized and stereotyped information but also false and twisted information. An example of such information is their basic premise that the

Constitution provides rights and protections for everyone equally. They present this distorted information to a population that is essentially uninformed. While being taught to think with pride about the framing of the Constitution, we have not been taught that women and African Americans were not accorded full human status by the men who created a document to protect the rights of property and slave owning males.

The Christian Right's campaign against homosexuality and for "traditional family values" illustrates clearly the use of mis/disinformation to support the idea of morality as the central issue instead of civil rights. Lesbians and gays are particularly vulnerable because even though in existence for centuries, there has been group visibility only since the beginning of the lesbian and gay movement with Stonewall in 1969. This brief period of visibility creates vulnerability for two primary reasons. Lack of visibility means that there is widespread ignorance on the part of the general public concerning this area of sexuality and culture. Thus, when the Right puts out the information that lesbians and gay men are child molesters, the public accepts it as truth, despite the data that demonstrates that 95% of those sexually abusing children are heterosexual men. Once again, immoral behavior gets attached to a group and the issue of gay and lesbian rights is presented in such a way that the voters think that they enter the polling booth to pull the lever on whether it is right or wrong to be homosexual (which is simply a sexual identity, like heterosexuality), not whether it is right or wrong to deny basic human rights.

The second way the lesbian and gay community is vulnerable is because the policies and laws providing rights and protection are so new and therefore more easily attacked. Through providing misinformation, the Christian Right can get voters to overturn these laws, thereby setting precedent in the attack against all the gains of the Civil Rights Movement and beginning the domino effect.

Naming the Real Issue

What is facing us in this "holy war" is not a battleground for morality but a direct assault on democracy. While the Right keeps public debate focused on the issue of right and wrong behavior, good and bad people, their political agenda goes unheeded and is on a course to limit participation in the democratic process by those they consider less capable of their narrow definition of morality: people of color, women, lesbians and gay men, and Jews.

This fundamental threat to democracy is a clear and present danger: a small number of people through the merger of church and state will soon determine and limit the freedom of those who differ from them in religion, politics, or culture. Democracy must always protect the minority voice, must always guarantee the participation of everyone. In the efforts of the Right we see the politics of exclusion, the politics of authoritarianism and domination.

The central question is one of self-determination and choice. Do we as a people get to have determination of our own lives and communities through a governing system that provides access, opportunity, and protections equally to all citizens, no matter who we are? Or do we have a governing system of rigid social control determined by a theologically-based political group? Do we all get to sit down at the decision-making table of this society? Or do only the few? And who decides?

Crisis and Opportunity

An insistence upon democracy as named by the Civil Rights Movement – requiring justice, liberation, and participation – is the greatest threat to the Christian authoritarian agenda. It is the work of those of us who believe in freedom to develop a local and national movement of liberation that claims our communities in the name of all the many diverse peoples who occupy them. It is incumbent upon us at this critical juncture of history to establish the values that are inclusive of everyone and to reject the values of exclusion and repression.

Nothing is more central to democracy than an informed populace able to make critical judgments. We must remember, as Eric Fromm said in the 1940s when reflecting upon the Second World War, "The human automaton is fertile ground for the seeds of fascism." For instance, one of the great battlegrounds is schools. The Christian Right has entered school boards throughout the country to oppose sex education, school-based clinics, dispensing condoms, secular humanism (critical thinking and values clarification), teaching evolution, and to promote prayer in the schools, to insist upon teaching creationism and banning "objectionable" books. This work is at the heart of the greatest threat to democracy, for this is the highly orchestrated effort to gain control of the minds of our children to limit their access to information and their ability to do critical thinking.

Finally, to create this great movement for liberation, we must figure out how to include everyone in full opportunity and participation. We have no model for this work for a true democracy. To live the politics of inclusion means that we must first get over ourselves, that is, put an end to our own barriers to inclusion. It is bigotry that *unites* the Right wing because they see people of color, women, lesbians and gay men as the enemy to their power and control. And it is our bigotry – the racism, sexism, and homophobia within our organizations – that *divides* us on the progressive left and prevents us from developing a fully inclusive movement.

Our most critical work is to eliminate these divisions and to recognize the connection we have as targeted groups and the common ground we share in our dream of justice and liberation for all of us. Our work is more difficult than that of the Christian Right. Their vision is modeled on the past, the time of the television Cleavers, when the power to exclude gave a few white people security. Our vision, on the other hand, has no model because we look to our present diversity and to the future which requires building a democratic society that includes everyone. We have to protect the democracy that we have in the present while building the new inclusive society.

We have the excitement and challenge of developing new ground. While the massive homophobic attack of the OCA against the people of Oregon and Colorado has created an alarming crisis, it has also created an opportunity. The Christian Right has chosen these two states as testing sites for exclusion; so may we make them testing sites for inclusion. In the face of this clear and present danger, we have the opportunity to bring people together to overcome old divisions and to build in our communities and our nation a true inclusive, participatory democracy. It is a test of the thoughtfulness, goodwill, courage, and dignity of our people.

3.

Wedge Issues and the Politics of Blame

1996

During the 1990s, the Right has found an effective way not only to build its constituency but to divide other constituencies and to lead us to vote against our own interests.[1] They create and exploit controversial issues to wedge people apart, working with the already existing presence of society's racism, sexism, classism, and homophobia. In a time of social and economic disorder, they urge people to blame and stand in opposition to each other by promoting the themes of the *myth of scarcity* ("there's not enough to go around") and the mood of mean-spiritedness ("you are taking something from me").

The Right diverts our attention from the economic realities in which there is plenty of money to go around but it unfortunately goes into the hands of owners and CEOs, not the hands of workers. Instead, their representatives such as Rush Limbaugh and Newt Gingrich lead us to think that it is poor people, people of color, lesbians and gay men, and low income women who have made us fall upon hard times. They set up a politic of blame, intolerance, and exclusion, and encourage people to turn upon one another.

They suggest that if welfare is provided for poor mothers and children, then there will not be the pittance of Social Security for the old. If women and people of color are brought into the workplace, then white men will lose jobs. If lesbians, gay men, bisexual and transgender people receive civil rights, then people of color will lose them. If undocumented immigrants are offered services, then citizens will lose money and services. If children

1. This previously unpublished commentary was written in May of 1996.

are offered bilingual or special education, then other children will receive inadequate education.

We are led to believe that people who should be our natural allies are actually our enemies and we must compete with them for the little that trickles down. We are led to believe that we will succeed when we have fought each other hard enough to take our share from the pie. The reality is that the pie was divided and distributed long before we ever reached the table, and we are fighting over the crumbs at the bottom.

We are pitted against each other, both as identity groups and as individuals, for a small (and often temporary) piece of what should be our birthright: shelter, food, clothing, employment, health, education, and safety, all dispensed with fairness and justice. Meanwhile, workers are robbed of jobs with livable wages and working conditions, women and children are violently abused, families deteriorate, people of color are marginalized in the social and economic life of the country, the environment becomes less life-sustaining every day, and great numbers experience the degradation of poverty.

Rather than blaming the powerful – institutions, corporations, and the rich – individuals and groups such as people of color or lesbians and gay men are blamed for the fears and losses that people experience. We are told that it is "bad" people who are causing our economic and social problems when the actual cause is loss of jobs and taxation for public services – and the concentration of wealth and power in the hands of the few.

Scapegoating

This shifting of the blame from the larger causes of problems to individuals or particular groups is called *scapegoating*. Scapegoating offers a simple explanation for complex issues and relieves the real culprits of their responsibility for problems.

Lesbians, gay men, bisexual and transgender persons are blamed for the breakdown of the "traditional" family and its values; Mexican and Asian immigrants are blamed for job loss as well as the high cost of public services; and recipients of affirmative action are blamed for the loss of white men's jobs; welfare recipients are blamed for the federal deficit. All are viewed as "bad people" who are taking advantage of the system and who are taking something from "the rest of us."

Widely accepted scapegoating leads to the creation of harmful public policy. We currently are witnessing a barrage of initiatives and legislative actions to prevent lesbians and gay men from gaining civil rights or civil marriage; efforts to deny services to undocumented workers and their children; initiatives to eliminate affirmative action and equal access to education and work; an amazing number of proposals to eliminate welfare and punish poor women and children; and initiatives and legislation designed to destroy any organized workers' unions that can fight back.

Rightwing talk show hosts and politicians have worked to create a social climate of intolerance, selfishness, and mean spirited competition. People are viewed as good guys/bad guys, normal/perverted, workers/freeloaders, people who belong and deserve rights and services/those who are outsiders who cause problems. We cannot allow this country to be owned and controlled by few: it must be a place of inclusion, not exclusion; of generosity and sharing, not selfishness and greed. Our work is to put an end to scapegoating and to create an environment where all of us, with all our differences, can flourish. To do this, we must join together with other targeted groups – our allies – to expose the use of scapegoating to mask the real causes of problems. We will form relationships of solidarity to defend ourselves while creating a society where we all have equality and justice. We refuse to be pitted against one another.

4.

The Wolf At The Door

1993

This story of the wolf is not a fairy tale, whatever they say.[1] What is the religious Right doing dressed up in those sweet "I'll take care of you, my dear" grandmother outfits? Or is it in sheep's clothing? Whatever works at the moment. Here's what I say: beware of the wolf in drag.

Since the first of the year, we have observed the Religious Right employing a new strategy in communities of color to persuade them to organize around single issues, such as homosexuality, that in the end will lead to their own loss of freedom.

Some examples:

- We have just witnessed the Christian Coalition moving into communities of color in New York to organize them against those who represent "multiculturalism issues" in school board elections. Focusing on the inclusion of lesbians and gay men in the "rainbow curriculum," the Right successfully linked supporting multiculturalism to supporting teaching about homosexuality. The second connection they made was that supporting multiculturalism advanced the idea that parents could be forced to accept their children being taught subjects and ideas that the parents do not approve of. And who loses if multiculturalism is seen as

---

1. Originally published in a 1993 issue of *Transformation* (Vol. 8, No. 5), the Women's Project newsletter.

a bad thing? The wolf eats up the idea of curriculum that includes the history and ideas of people who are not white, heterosexual, European males.

- Paul Weyrich and National Empowerment Television are gleeful about the recent opportunity to organize local NAACP chapters against the national office. The issue: that the national NAACP supported lifting the ban against homosexuals in the military. Who loses if the national organization is weakened or destroyed? Who benefits if African Americans are divided against one another? This attack comes at a time when the NAACP has perhaps the greatest opportunity it has ever had to become a powerful national player, led by Ben Chavis who apparently has the vision to bring all people of color together under its umbrella. The wolf eats up the idea of strength through unity.

- In California there is a November ballot initiative advanced by the Right promoting school vouchers of $2,600 in state funds to help pay tuition for private or parochial schools. Their 1978 tax cutting Proposition 13 has already drastically weakened public schools. Analysts expect the voucher system to complete the total collapse of public school funding. Who stands to lose the most if the public schools are destroyed? The newest and poorest students. It is not by chance that this initiative appears in the state that has the most immigrants of color and the nation's largest people of color population. The wolf, creating a private and mostly segregated school system, eats up the hope of free and accessible education for everyone, regardless of race or financial status.

- In August the Traditional Values Coalition (TVC) released a new video as part of its obsessive, ongoing attack against lesbians and gay men. Entitled "Gay Rights: Special Rights," this video pits the African

American community against the lesbian and gay community, using the myth of scarcity argument that there are not enough rights to go around. No longer covert in this approach, TVC states on the video's flier: "SPECIAL RIGHTS FOR GAYS = LESS RIGHTS FOR YOU!" Who loses if the religious Right manages to argue that civil rights should be granted only to the "deserving" and the general public should decide by vote who deserves them and who does not? This attempt to recruit people of color in their attack on the gay and lesbian community happens at the same time that the Right consistently links people of color with criminal activity – especially in the areas of drugs, welfare, theft and murder. The wolf, through court cases and ballot initiatives, will manage gradually to eat up protections for people of color because they too are not "deserving."

***

The wolf is at the door of all of our communities but none more frighteningly so than communities of color. For example, immigrants. Our news media is currently full of stories of anti-immigrant sentiment in the U.S., with most suggesting that much of the population sees immigrants as a drain on U.S. resources and a cause of the present economic problems. California Governor Pete Wilson, in an open letter to President Clinton, called for refusing citizenship to U.S.-born children of "illegal" immigrants, denying education to "illegal" immigrants, cutting off health and other public benefits, and requiring them to carry an identification card. Again, the Right is invoking the *myth of scarcity*, suggesting that there is not enough to go around. Roger Hernandez, writing in the Aug. 13, 1993 *Oregonian*, reports that Julian Simon, an economist at the University of Maryland, states that the average immigrant family pays $2,500 more in taxes than it takes in from government services. And this does not even include the immigrants' broader economic activity. Yet, Wilson, whose letter was immediately supported by the religious Right, states that immigrants cost his state $3.3 billion each year. The net result is that the public is falsely led to believe that immigrants – in particular, people of color – are the source of our economic problems.

Increasingly, people of color, in one way or another, are blamed for our economic woes. No one is focusing hate rhetoric and ballot initiatives against those rich white men who made millions off the Housing and Urban Development and Savings and Loan scandals of the 1980s – which taxpayers are now paying for. Also little notice has been given to such things as the Medicaid prescription-drug fraud. Ironically it is popular opinion that people of color are the main recipients of welfare and the perpetrators of welfare abuse. However, columnist Jack Anderson writes on Aug. 16,1993 *Arkansas Gazette* that this fraud is perpetrated by "physicians, pharmacists, patients and other Medicaid middlemen who collude to loot a program intended to serve the poorest of the poor." Here are some examples he notes: "A doctor wrote 2,000 prescriptions a month; a pharmacist billed for more than 30 prescriptions a day for a single recipient; one recipient had the same three lab tests five times in four days at three labs and six prescriptions for Zantac in the same four days at six pharmacies. Medicaid shelled out more than $3,000 during an 18-day period for this recipient." Why then are low income people of color being targeted for blame for the cause of our economic problems?

The wolf is at the door trying to pit racial groups, as well as women and gay men and lesbians, against one another in its drive to put in place its authoritarian, fundamentalist vision of domination. For the religious Right, group must turn destructively against group, and chaos must reign so that it can instill its fundamentalist Christian solution of church-based authority and rule. It is engaged in a "holy war" that calls first for destabilization and then for domination. It develops the chaos and fear that can lead a populace to engage in "ethnic cleansing." Jonathan Hass in "The Causes of War" (March/April 1992 *Bulletin of the Field Museum of Natural History)* gives two lessons from his archaeological studies of ancient warfare: 1)"If ethnic differences don't exist before a war, they are sometimes made up to justify a war," and 2) "The causes of warfare are not to be found in ethnic differences but in the economic and demographic conditions at the time."

In the U.S. at this moment in history, we are in hard economic times, where the disparity between the rich and poor grows greater, and our new young president is given the impossible task of creating a fair and workable economic system out of the years of greed-based policies he inherited. We live in a failing economy in which the loss of manufacturing jobs from overseas relocation has hurt people of color disproportionately. It is also a time when the demographics of our country are rapidly changing through immigrants from around the world seeking economic and political asylum. Widespread economic stress and hardship make this time fertile for discrimination and injustice. Certainly, it is easier to blame people of color, women, and gay men and lesbians for our economic problems than it is to examine the motives of those corporations and businesses that close down shop in this country and go to Asia and Latin America to exploit workers there. Those corporations do not have a face. The person of color on the street does – where easier to put the blame than on targets of racial resentment?

The wolf is at the door, taking advantage of these ripe conditions. He carries a *Bible* and wears a good suit and tie. As he teaches people to hate one another, all in the name of morality and getting ahead, we must never forget that he has a ravenous appetite for discrimination and exclusion, and he will consume anyone in his way to reach his goal.

5.

Racist Politics and Homophobia

1993

No one can say that the leaders of the religious Right are not smart.[1] Indeed, they are brilliant in their strategies that move people toward their goal of an authoritarian regime dominated by a Christian fundamentalist vision. Perhaps the most stunning display of shrewdness is their ability to use deception, secrecy, and confusion as tactics. We see this in their much-promoted victories of stealth candidates, their ability to persuade voters to focus on a single issue rather than the Right's entire agenda, and their attack on lesbians and gay men as a way of diverting people from grasping their overall agenda of dismantling the gains of the civil rights movement and democracy itself.

Among the most disturbing of the religious Right's tactics is their use of racial politics wherein they deliberately omit discussion of race in their overall agenda yet use coded racial language to win the support of the white population and use religion and homophobia to win the support of communities of color. In their vision of social control, race becomes the bedrock that discrimination is built on, and racist fears are the motivation for the religious Right's movement to reject inclusive, participatory democracy.

We must never forget that their vision is one of exclusion, not inclusion. We need to take a look at that vision and then think about how race fits into the hidden agenda.

---

1. Originally published in the July/August 1993 issue of *Transformation* (Vol. 8, No. 4), the Women's Project newsletter.

Simply put, the religious Right wants to impose an extreme, fundamentalist Christian vision, with a political agenda to achieve it. That vision, which excludes the beliefs and participation of Jews, Muslims, Buddhists, and most Christians, is based on a belief that God gave man power and dominion over the earth and all its peoples. That means that God (thought of as white) gave man (who is presumed white) authority over women, children, people of color, and nature. The *Bible,* read in this literalist and selective manner, has been a powerful weapon in the hands of the Right to defend slavery and segregation, the subordination of women, and condemnation of those who love others of the same gender.

For the religious Right, this line of authority is rigid and provides order. Those who get out of line must be controlled. When people seek to have authority over their own lives, such as people of color in the Civil Rights Movement and women in the women's movement, the religious Right reacts by setting forth a political agenda that opposes any gains that promote self-determination and full participation in society. Thus we see a 30-year effort to dismantle the gains of the Civil Rights Movement, and systematic attacks against women's reproductive rights, publicly funded childcare, pay equity, and women's anti-violence programs such as battered women's shelters.

To sell their vision during this time of intense social and economic chaos, the religious Right pointedly appeals to a nostalgia for an ordered life that most people have never even experienced but have been shown in television shows and movies. They ask us to return to the 1940s and 1950s when times were more prosperous, and young white men returning from the war were able to get jobs or go to college on the GI bill. On the financial front, cities were not yet broke, discount stores had not destroyed the commerce of small towns, and farming was still a viable occupation. Socially, the mood of the country was patriotism and McCarthyism. What the Right calls the "traditional family" was given widespread publicity in advertising consumer goods, on radio, tv programs and movies, and in popular literature.

But let's think carefully – not in tv images of nostalgia – of what that time was like for many people. Segregation was legally and rigorously enforced. African Americans lived under Jim Crow laws and were subjected to persistent violence and intimidation. Almost all people of color experienced economic deprivation. Male authority was unchallenged by women, and domestic violence, incest, and rape were kept secret in the "traditional family." That family, of course, was not thought to include lesbians and gay men because it was too dangerous to be openly visible.

Also, people of color were not considered part of that "traditional family." For example, without mercy or compassion or respect for family units, slavery assaulted African American families through dividing them according to individual workers or "breeders." African American families have survived against terrible oppressive odds, developing new definitions of family and bonded relationships. Many of these families in their inclusiveness are not considered proper "traditional families" by the religious Right. Instead, the Right stereotypes and condemns African Americans along with Native American, Latino, and Asian families as fostering illegitimacy, criminality, and welfare dependency.

Because all of us feel the effect of the current social and economic chaos, the religious Right is able to appeal to some of us with their rigid vision of law and order, male control, and white supremacy. Our fears combined with our prejudices give them fertile ground for organizing.

"Special Rights"

The religious Right, in attacking the lesbian and gay liberation movement, puts forward the argument that lesbians and gay men should not have minority status or receive rights such as affirmative action or quotas nor should there be specific anti-violence laws to protect us. What we have here is a deliberate scrambling of categories. Minority status – currently granted to those who have known historic discrimination based on race, religion, sex, disability, and age – gives those groups access to the tools to fight discrimination in employment, housing, public accommodations, and through anti-violence laws. Affirmative action and quotas, on the other hand, are not rights or laws but programs designed to redress a history of discrimination which prevented equal access to education and employment. As Jesse Jackson says, it is an attempt to level the playing field.

The "special rights" argument is designed to appeal to both white and people of color communities, but in different ways. With the white community, the Right plays on racist fears and uses coded language to call them up. For their anti-gay organizing and constituency building, they depend on the complex fears white people have about the current economic depression and the changing demographics of the country, along with a lack of knowledge about sexuality in general and homosexuality in particular. That is, they build on the factual information that the population is shifting gradually from predominantly white to increasingly people of color, and on the myth that white men are losing their jobs because people of color are taking them through affirmative action. Then, to stop the gay and lesbian civil rights movement, they call up the specter of yet another group that is trying to take away jobs. To enforce this argument emotionally, they consistently characterize lesbians and gay men as undeserving of any rights at all because we are sick and evil. Discrimination, then, becomes a matter of job protection as well as a social necessity.

It is the racism encoded in the "special rights" language that makes this argument work so powerfully.

The religious Right argues that *everyone* was given the same rights by the original framers of the *Constitution*, and that anyone seeking any rights or protections beyond that original document is seeking "special rights." That was the argument they used against integration and the 1964 *Civil Rights Act*, that they used to defeat the *Equal Rights Amendment* (ERA), and are now using against lesbians and gay men. The Civil Rights Movement, however, was built on the idea that certain groups had no voice or legal standing when the Constitution was framed and therefore must be included at a later time when the public is made aware that the effect of discrimination against any group is to prevent their full participation in democracy. Because the Civil Rights Movement made such a compelling argument that there can be no true democracy without justice and access to full participation, other groups such as women and gay men and lesbians followed their lead and created movements inspired by this model.

Since the early successes of the Civil Rights Movement, which gained some integration but not necessarily its goal of equality, there has been a constant backlash against it from the Right. It has tried to block continued efforts for equality. The central point of this backlash has been that anything gained by people of color in this country must inevitably take something away from white people – that there simply cannot be enough jobs or education or even rights to go around. It is the *myth of scarcity* played on a racial theme. In the 1970s, the focus became affirmative action, the program that sought equality as well as integration. It was interpreted by the white community as an unjust program that took jobs away from talented and skilled white men and gave them to "unqualified" people of color and white women. By 1990 when David Duke talked about "special rights" in his gubernatorial campaign, everyone knew he was talking about the so-called threat to the white race by people of color. It took only a short step in 1991-92 to build on this perceived sense of white loss by using the "special rights" argument to suggest that lesbians and gay men would be just one more undeserving minority group trying to take away "deserving" white men's (and in this case, all heterosexuals') rights.

The "special rights" pitch to communities of color is of course different. This time it is the myth of scarcity played on a homophobic theme. The religious Right delivers the message that lesbians and gay men are trying to get some of the same economic pie which people of color fought so hard to get, and there is not enough to go around. They suggest that people of color were clean and upstanding and through their goodness earned their rights during the civil rights struggle whereas lesbians and gay men are evil and sick and are merely trying to take advantage of the history of that movement.

Wait a minute. Are these the same people who developed their base during the Barry Goldwater campaign in response to the Civil Rights Movement and then strengthened it during the George Wallace campaign? Are we now to think that they were longtime supporters of civil rights for people of color and to this day are out there promoting equality? Are these many of the same people who supported David Duke? Is not one of their major spokespeople Pat Buchanan who suggested that M-14s would be an adequate solution to the uprising in L.A.?

They suggest to people of color communities that civil rights should be granted only to those whose differentiating characteristics are immutable, such as race or sex or age. They say that sexual identity is a matter of choice, not a matter of who one is. First of all, we do not know how people acquire their heterosexual, homosexual, or bisexual identity, but we do know that people have a sexual identity, and currently homosexuals experience extreme discrimination and violence, and deserve rights and protections. Still, the religious Right returns to the argument that sexual identity is choice of behavior, though they do not choose to argue that heterosexuals then must also choose their sexual identity and consequent behavior. To make this argument work, they have to dehumanize and demonize lesbians and gay men as sexual predators, just as they have characterized African American men since slavery. Lesbians and gay men become "pedophiles;" African American men become "rapists."

Also, the religious Right does not discuss choice in another area of major civil rights protections: religion. Many of the early white immigrants to the U.S. came in search of religious freedom, and protection of that freedom has always been a basic tenet of this country's beliefs and legal system. That freedom means that people may choose their beliefs and forms of worship, whether it be in synagogue or cathedral or storefront church, whether speaking in Latin or speaking in tongues. It is a matter of choice and is covered under both the Bill of Rights and civil rights protections. We believe in that freedom so strongly that we grant religious groups tax exempt status, even when they use that status to raise money to mount campaigns of hatred and discrimination.

That is not to say that homosexuality is the same as either race or religion; it is different. Like religion, however, sexual identity is invisible and similar to religion, is attacked where practiced. Along with women, people of color, people with disabilities and religious minorities, lesbians and gay men have experienced historic discrimination, and the methods of discrimination have an identifiable kinship with those of other oppressions, as do the results. We see the same tactics used again and again, from oppression to oppression. They all lead to one group of people being able to define another group and have power and control over them and their lives. They all lead to exclusion from equality and full participation in democracy.

The white leadership of the religious Right depends on the concern people of color have for their families who are under attack both economically and socially and on their share in the homophobia that is rampant throughout all of U.S. society. They suggest that homosexuality is only about white people and is threatening to their families and lives. Lesbians and gay men of color are treated as nonexistent or rare aberrations.

The religious Right is particularly active in fundamentalist churches within people of color communities, using the same arguments against lesbians and gay men that were used against African Americans in my own conservative rural church in Georgia in the 1950s where there were no African Americans. Discrimination requires such vicious stereotyping and dehumanizing. The religious Right works to make the church a place of exclusion and condemnation rather than a place of liberation and acceptance. Their appeal is not to people's social conscience but to their sense of self-protection.

What the Right does not talk about in communities of color is their opposition to affirmative action for *anyone,* to welfare, to government funded programs that support families, to immigrant rights, to equal access to public education, to multicultural education, to HIV/AIDS education that would prevent the dramatic rise in deaths of people of color.

To people of color communities, they scapegoat lesbians and gay men as the cause of economic problems. To white communities, they scapegoat people of color as the cause of these problems. For example, in California, Asian and Latino immigrants are attacked as a "burden" on health services, school systems, and welfare, causing them to break down. While attacking affirmative action as a critical economic problem, the religious Right of course does not talk about who is really taking the jobs of working class people – those who make obscene profits by going to countries of color to pay subsistence wages for the manufacture of goods which are then brought back here to sell to those who are daily losing their jobs from this practice. Affirmative action is not closing down plants and businesses in the U.S. Unrestrained greed is.

Focusing our attention on the civil rights effort of lesbians and gay men is a shrewd way of diverting our attention from the real social and economic issues of our times. While the religious Right talks about morality, I believe they oppose HIV education because they consider the people currently most affected by AIDS as being dispensable: homosexuals, women, and people of color. If they care about the well-being of communities of color, why are they not spending an equal amount of time working for universal, government-funded health care? When the Right talks about families, I believe they care about only certain kinds of families, narrowly defined. If they care about families, why are they not mounting a national campaign against violence against women and children and against alcohol and drug abuse, the most destructive issues in family life today in both white and people of color families? When the Right talks about crime, through coded language they suggest that it is committed primarily by people of color. If they care about the effect of crime on our society, why do they support the creation of more jails rather than crime prevention through job training and jobs development? The solution to our economic and social problems is not the promotion of increased discrimination.

The religious Right is expending an enormous amount of time and money in its fight against the extension of civil rights to lesbians and gay men. It is clear to almost everyone that there is a larger agenda than just the repression of a small percentage of our society. Why else so much effort to dehumanize and scapegoat one minority group? What is the larger agenda? If it can be established that any one group of people in this country does not deserve civil rights and therefore can be legally discriminated against, it calls into question whether other groups *deserve* civil rights. If civil rights can be put to the vote for one group of people, then it follows that they can be put to the vote for other groups. This trend suggests that by the end of this decade, current civil rights laws will be put to popular vote for reconsideration. If civil rights can be defined as "special rights" and the original Constitution held up as a sufficient, all-inclusive document, then not only civil rights for people historically discriminated against, but the *Bill of Rights* itself, will be in the line of attack.

Public Schools

I believe the religious Right has set out to destroy public schools and replace them with private schools that they more closely control. To achieve this goal, they attack the schools from two directions. From without, they work for a school voucher system which will require that public funds be used to finance private education. From within, they run campaigns as stealth candidates to gain seats on school boards so they can control the curriculum.

The idea of universal, free public education is an idea that supports the principle of participatory democracy and a movement for equality. Rather than private schools for the wealthy or for those of a particular religious faith, public schools have worked to offer all citizens a common entry point into society. Struggles around inclusivity in public schools, such as desegregation, have been part of the continued development of the dream of democracy. Those struggles have been met with strong resistance from the Right. We can mark its battles against integration, Head Start, and now multi-culturalism, to name a few.

For the past three decades the Right has supported a private school movement that is now represented in the promotion of a school voucher system. The argument is that people should be given vouchers so that they can choose to spend their portion of school tax dollars on private schools if they wish. While presented as providing greater choice, this program is designed to bolster private schools and break the backs of already ailing public schools. Whether private schools are for Catholics, Protestants, or the secular rich, they are all generally known to be segregated schools, despite minor inclusion of people of color. In fact, "private school" is virtually coded language for "segregated school." The private school movement will segregate schools even further, leaving underfunded urban public schools to people of color and a few poor whites and moving the majority white children into church-operated schools.

If a theocracy is being created in this country, where one religious group will dominate both religious and secular life, what better way to advance it than with the takeover of public schools.

Schools controlled by the religious Right would be characterized not by the expansive number of things children could learn but what they would not be allowed to learn. We get a view of their plans for schools by looking at what they are currently doing on the school boards where they now occupy seats throughout the country. They support English-Only, banning books, school prayer, creationism; they oppose sex education, HIV education, school-based clinics, evolution, values clarification, multi-culturalism. They support the control of minds rather than the development of critical thinking and freedom of thought and judgment.

One of the most talked about school battles has been in New York over the Rainbow Curriculum which proposed the introduction of multiculturalism, a very small piece of which was discussion of lesbian and gay families. The larger part was focused on teaching about the different cultures which are represented in the city. The religious Right was so successful in diverting the public's attention by causing a flap over the possibility of talking about lesbians and gay men that people overlooked the rest of the curriculum. The curriculum included lesbians and gay men because they are parents of children who attend the public schools and because a portion of the children in the classroom are lesbian and gay. For the same reason, different cultures were included because New York is a multicultural city. In the heated debate that ensued, all those who were different from the dominant culture risked loss.

The idea of multiculturalism in the public schools strikes terror in the hearts of the religious Right. It is for that reason that the Christian Coalition opened four offices in New York in preparation for the school board elections. Multiculturalism is a linchpin issue in the struggle between the politics of inclusion and the politics of exclusion. If multiculturalism were not presented in a tokenized way (a month of Black history, a month of women's history, a week for Asians, etc.) and instead different cultures were presented as having equal value with European cultures, then our schools would become academies of freedom. Students of different cultures would be given an equalized entry point; that is, children of, say, Asian or African descent would enter on the same footing and pride as those of European descent. They would not have to try to persuade the dominant culture to value them and their people's history.

As schools are now, domination and prejudice are built into the curriculum and inequality is established from the first day a child enters. Rather than being the proverbial melting pot, schools force all children to study and obey European dominance in literature, history, and even ways of thinking. For example, the religious Right-supported English-Only movement serves as insurance to make sure that Latino and other immigrant children cannot carry the pride of their culture into the schools or receive information as easily as English-speaking children. Language is culture, and to forbid its use is ultimately to crush the culture.

However, the greater terror for the religious Right is critical thinking. Multicultural teaching mandates critical thinking. For example, if children are taught the European history of the "discovery" of America and indigenous peoples' history of the invasion of their land, then students are required to think about the differences between them. The equally respected and balanced presentation of different cultures – their history and literature – requires students to select among them, make comparisons and judgments, see things from varying points of view, and decide for themselves what they believe. This is the very essence of critical thinking and freedom. *And critical thinking is the greatest known enemy of authoritarianism and fascism.*

Most of the publicity the religious Right has received about its school board work across the country has been its opposition to anything related to sex education: HIV education, dispensing condoms, school-based clinics, discussions of dating and sexual behavior, etc. Obsessed with sex, the religious Right has taken a hard line: one must not talk about sex (because talking makes it happen), and abstinence is the only answer to any sex related problems such as unwanted pregnancies, sexually transmitted diseases, homosexuality, and I suppose, sexual abuse.

It is in this area of whether or not to talk about sex that ACT UP's "Silence Equals Death" is directly to the point.[2] If one assumes, as I do, that children learn most about sex not from their families or schools but on the street and from the media, it simply does not make sense to think that discussions of it in schools will increase children's activity. To not talk about it in the places where adults have responsibility for children is to deliver our children over to street misinformation and to prevent them from having the means of protecting themselves. Given the high incidence of sexually transmitted diseases, this abdication puts them at risk of sickness and death.

The religious Right targets people of color communities to get support in opposing sex education and HIV education, suggesting that sex education is a means of promoting abortion and HIV education is a scheme for promoting homosexuality. It is true that gay men are a primary targeted group for HIV infection, but they are not alone. The other extremely high risk group is people of color, especially women. To let homophobia prevent HIV education because gay men are not considered worthy

2. ACT-UP: The AIDS Coalition to Unleash Power.

and valuable human beings is to support the racism that prevents the work necessary to prevent AIDS among people of color. Homophobia and racism share the same belief: that certain groups of people are not as valuable as others and do not deserve health and happiness.

White Gay and Lesbian Racism

The religious Right has had some success in penetrating people of color communities and getting support for carefully framed pieces of its agenda. It has employed those constituencies in its electoral campaigns. It is important to analyze some of the reasons for this success, since they are dividing what should be natural allies in pursuit of an inclusive democracy. In addition to those already discussed, I believe there is another: the racism in the white lesbian and gay community and the Right's ability to play upon the racial divisions that already exist.

For the past two decades, the lesbian and gay community has characterized itself as white and, indeed, mostly male, despite outstanding work on the part of people of color and lesbians. Because that community has not given leadership and visibility to lesbians and gay men of color, worked openly against sexism and racism, nor supported them in their work in their own people of color communities, there is a racist legacy that is now heightened in the glare of the current attack. If lesbians and gay men of color had had their share of leadership and support, communities of color would now recognize the lesbians and gay men among them, and there would be natural bridges built between the issues of racism and homophobia.

Instead, homosexuality is often perceived as a "white thing." This means that lesbians and gay men of color get rendered invisible by both the lesbian and gay community and their own people of color communities. It means that when the Right picks up a small economic marketing survey of middleclass lesbians and gay men and then characterizes all as being well to do, communities of color say, how can those rich white people compare their oppression with ours? Why should they be concerned about discrimination in employment or public housing when they can buy their way? It begins not to matter that the assumption of wealth and race is false.

It also means when white gay men ask for support for lifting the ban on homosexuals in the military and compare the lesbian and gay movement to the Civil Rights Movement, that African Americans in particular are often resentful. Not often identifying their own people as lesbian or gay, and not having had gay visibility in the 1960s movement (despite the presence of closeted gays), African Americans now ask, where were you? Why this sudden interest in the Civil Rights Movement? And how dare you say that race and sexual identity are the same when one can be hidden? The lesbian and gay community is seen as making sweeping generalizations and broad analogies in its desire to get support in the face of this current attack. Communities of color are saying in return, why should we support someone who just discovered us? The central issue that everyone deserves civil rights gets lost because of unchallenged homophobia in communities of color and because of persistent white racism.

An interesting twist comes from the legacy of sexism. Because lesbians experience sexism and invisibility in the movement, our contributions are often overlooked. Of all the white people doing anti-racist work in the U.S. for the last two decades, white lesbians have done the most consistent and pervasive work. The disregard for lesbian politics continues as the major civil rights focus of the gay and lesbian leadership has become not employment, public housing, or public access. Instead, ironically, it has focused on the military, that male bastion, where once again women are not seen as central to the issue.

Community by community, the religious Right works skillfully to divide us along fissures that already exist It is as though they have a political seismograph to locate the racism and sexism in the lesbian and gay community, the sexism and homophobia in communities of color. While the Right is united by their racism, sexism and homophobia in their goal to dominate all of us, we are divided by our own racism, sexism and homophobia.

A Call for Dialogue and Coalition

We can no longer afford single issue politics that look at the small picture and miss the big one. We have to recognize that fascist development in this country is moving like a steamroller, and in its path it does not selectively choose specific groups to put under its authoritarian control: it is rolling toward all of us. Our only chance for defending the democracy and freedoms we now possess and creating the inclusive world we want to live in is to join together in our efforts. This will take recognizing how oppressions and oppressed people are interlinked – and then how this linkage necessitates mutual solutions.

First, there is internal dialogue. We cannot understand the issues of other constituency groups until we understand them internally. That means, for example, that the lesbian and gay movement must have serious discussions about race and gender, and people of color groups must talk about the role of women and lesbians and gay men within their own organizations and communities. And it means that people of color have to address homophobia within their own fundamentalist churches, and white progressives have to deal with the homophobia and racism in the white churches that are the major organizing base for the religious Right.

Once we understand these issues and take action on them internally, then coalition with other groups becomes much easier and our divisions are narrowed. We understand what is going on, what the issue is, without having to be brought up to speed because our vision is limited to our own particular area of social change work. *Coalition work* is hard because we are taunted and baited and set off against one another by the Right who keeps drilling the message that exclusion is necessary, that there is not enough to go around, that one person's gain is another person's loss. There is plenty to go around; the problem is that the method of sharing has not been equalized. We have to understand that if any group can be left out, then reasons can be found to leave any other group out.

It is coalition work, the long-term work of relationships, where we recognize the big picture and our connectedness, that will make it possible to build a progressive movement in this country that includes everyone, where power and resources are redistributed, and everyone gets a fair share. Certainly, everyone has the right and obligation to use discernment in determining social and moral values, but it is general discrimination against any group as a whole that we must work against. Full inclusion and acceptance of differences without stereotyping and dehumanizing are issues of morality because they lead to justice evenly distributed. When justice is evenly shared, then everyone wins because the world becomes a better place – where everyone is secure in the knowledge that basic rights are not to be earned or "deserved" but are generally applied as the safety net for everyone.[3]

3. Original author's note: "This is article #6 in an ongoing series on the religious Right."

6.

The Battle for Public Schools

1994

When Mrs. Daisy Bates walked the Little Rock Nine through crowds of jeering white people, police and National Guardsmen to integrate Central High School in 1957, she knew they were walking through the doors of democratic participation.[1] If there were not equal access to education for African Americans, how could there be equal access to jobs? To the courts? To governing bodies? To the creation of the laws of the land? She knew that the way to shared power was through shared information and that the worst shackles of all were those put on minds.

Mrs. Bates and hundreds like her risked their lives to integrate public schools so that this country could move a little closer to the dream of democracy.

No one has ever claimed that public schools were perfect. Mass education is not a simple thing. For the past half century there has been a lively debate about how to improve public education. Now that debate has turned to the question, not of improvement, but of whether there should be free, accessible-to-all, public schools. This debate is framed and led by corporate and religious leaders who seek the destruction of public schools. The discussion's heat is fueled by race and class concerns.

Corporations

In the mid-1980s, Arkansas Governor Bill Clinton convened the Business Council (locally known as the Good Suit Club),

1. Originally published in the September/October 1994 issue of *Transformation* (Vol. 9, No. 5), the Women's Project newsletter.

which was made up mostly of multi-millionaires, to provide guidance about the schools. At this time, Arkansas was ranked 48th in teacher salaries and 49th in per capita income, but was listed in the 1988 Forbes 400 as having 12 multi-millionaires, more than anywhere other than the Upper East Side in New York City. Many progressive people wondered what interest chicken baron Don Tyson had in improving public education for his thousands of low-paid assembly-line workers working in health-threatening conditions to cut up chickens for market. Or what interest Sam Walton had for improving the education of his low-paid workers who sell goods made by even lower-paid workers in other countries to low-income people in Walmart discount stores here.

What we are learning is that with the expansion of capital and production into countries along the Pacific Rim and South America, both labor and the environment can be exploited with few restrictions, so corporations here have little need for large masses of educated workers. Instead, they require an educated elite providing management and a small corps of workers providing high electronic skills. Indeed, as they downsize, many highly educated and trained workers are being dismissed along with those who provided less skilled labor. Those jobs now most readily available to poor people – in the service industry and tourism – do not require much education to flip hamburgers, clean rooms, or empty bedpans. Capitalism, in its current international, unchecked movement, no longer needs public schools to provide a large, educated, skilled workforce.

Their interest now is in the *privatization* of public services, so that they gain from reduced taxation as well as new business outlets through managing schools, the postal service, park lands, and the private development of their resources.

The Religious Right

It is no accident that the religious Right has chosen public schools as a central battleground for winning control of U.S.

culture and politics. It is a deliberate choice of a core issue, vital to the development or the destruction of democracy

If you wanted to change people's beliefs and behavior, to shape people to welcome unquestioned authority or to be independent critical thinkers, to lead people to tolerance or intolerance, to create the citizens who would change society, where would you begin, most hopeful of success? With adults or with the young?

The Right is directing its energies and resources at the young by attacking one of this country's largest institutions, the public school system. If this system can be destroyed and education of citizens put in the hands of religious groups and corporations, then U.S. culture and politics can be dramatically altered.

We are living in a time of social, cultural, economic, and political conflict in which many values are shifting and being redefined. It is a time of upheaval and change. Much of the conflict centers around what we believe the U.S. should be: a pluralistic (many ethnicities, religions, cultures), democratic society that finds a place for everyone – or what the Right envisions: a more monocultural, authoritarian society that limits participation and the ability to share equal access to resources. Should we have a society that uses its resources for the common good, or a two-tiered society with increased economic stratification and poverty? It is a conflict between the politics of inclusion and sharing and the politics of exclusion and selfishness.

At stake is the historical dream of this country and the values we have held onto in the ongoing struggle to try to make that dream real: that this country is open, providing a place where people can come in search of freedom, where people can find a place to be who they are and to live peacefully, where people can be equal partners with each other in the creation of family, community, and government, where people have hope and resources to meet their basic needs.

Generally, the religious Right is attempting to replace democracy with theocracy, merging church and state so that authoritarian leaders enforce a fundamentalist vision in this country's public and private life. This vision, developed from a narrow and literal interpretation of the *Bible,* is of one white God who gives authority directly to man to have power and dominion over the earth, its people, and its material resources.

This system requires a rigid hierarchy in which white men dominate women, people of color, and nature. Consequently, any strides toward autonomy and independence and full participation in society threaten this hierarchy. Therefore the religious Right works to dismantle the gains of the Civil Rights Movement for people of color and women, tries to prevent lesbians and gay men from achieving equality, and opposes efforts to protect the environment. Its work is done in the name of morality, law and order, and free-market capitalism.

The religious Right emerged as a contemporary phenomenon around 1972, at the same time that conservative strategists were also shaping racist backlash to the Civil Rights Movement, especially affirmative action and busing. The religious Right would focus its energy on issues of sexuality and gender (i.e., homosexuality, abortion, feminism) rather than directly on race. Through campaigns against "secular humanism" and in favor of prayer in the schools, the religious Right also opened up an attack on a public school system struggling to meet the challenges of racial integration. The religious Right also generated a network of private religious schools, many of them all-white. Both thrusts – the overtly racist Right and the religious Right – began to provide scapegoats for the national malaise at a time of declining standard of living and a tax base eroded by government giveaways to Fortune 500 companies in the form of massive tax breaks.

What better place for the Right to further its antidemocratic agenda than in the schools, which are the gateway to inclusion or exclusion in the public life of this country. For this reason, in the 1990s it has set a goal to infiltrate and ultimately control every school board in the country and to destroy the financial structure of schools through reduced taxes and depletion of funds through vouchers and expensive lawsuits.

Through control of the schools, the Right can limit information through censorship, shape narrow ideas and views of the world, and enforce a rigid and authoritarian hierarchy. With no accountability to the public, they can restrict entrance into the school system to those of their own choosing, rather than making schools available to all children. Religious observance can be enforced. Minority voices and dissent can be easily extinguished. Rather than being granted the right to education, children will have to earn the right through adhering to an authoritarian, antidemocratic ideology. The schools will not be accountable to the general public but only to those who own them.

Race and Class

The attack against the public schools comes at a time when race and class lines are becoming more tightly drawn. Currently, there is popular sentiment, reinforced by the media and the analysis of the Right, that, despite hard evidence to the contrary, people of color are responsible for the economic and social crisis because they have taken white people's jobs through affirmative action; overextended the welfare system through fraud, illegitimacy, homelessness, and huge numbers (focused on immigrants); saturated the country with drug traffic and drug abuse; and broken down the social fabric with violent crime, violating everyone's sense of safety and overburdening the courts and jails. Though studies show that people of color are not primarily responsible for these problems, the popular belief embedded in racism nevertheless persists.

What is true, however, is that the policies of the Reagan/ Bush administrations have increased the numbers of poor people, and because of historic racial discrimination and injustice, there are disproportionately large numbers of people of color who are poor. Those policies benefited the rich through deregulation of greed, allowing, for example, vast amounts of money to be made through land and housing development, leaving in its wake a massive savings and loan bailout for the taxpayer and hundreds of thousands of homeless people. At the same time, federal tax revenues to support cities were being drastically cut, reducing services and making their infrastructure begin to crumble.

Two resulting legacies being experienced in the 1990s are

1. Resentment and mistrust of the government, taxation, and spending for human needs;

2. A growing suburban white middle class, resentful, self-serving, and seeking insulation from social problems.

There has been major white flight in this country since the desegregation successes of the Civil Rights Movement and the loosening of immigration laws in the 1960s. Now, increasingly, cities are made up of people of color and are ringed by white suburbs where business has relocated. Despite 20 years of busing, schools are still generally segregated.

A renewed form of white flight is through support of the movement for private schools. There has been a long tradition of Catholic schools and secular private schools established to educate the children of the affluent. However, after the initiation of integration of schools in the 1950s, private schools were built across the South to serve the children of people who did not want their children schooled with African American children. Most of those schools were and still are church-operated. In fact, "Christian school" in the South is simply a code word for "racially segregated" school, despite the slight racial mixing in a few of them. Soon, these schools spread across the country and have increased steadily ever since.

Disturbed by the struggles public schools are undergoing, the white middle class deserts them in two ways:

1. By opposing tax increases to support them, thereby increasing their problems;

2. Supporting privatization as one more means of white flight.

The basic message is, "If you're going to mix our kids up with kids of color and treat them the same, we're going to take our money and create our own schools." The same white-supported Right that fought integration is now fighting for privatization, except this time it has the massive resources of a highly organized religious Right movement and corporations to increase its power.

Some of Their Strategies

There is probably consensus in this country that our public schools are in trouble. They are plagued by decreases in funding which result in elimination of extracurricular activities and pieces of the curriculum such as music, art, languages, and in poor teacher-student ratios. They also experience all of the ills of society at large such as increased violence in the homes of their students, against them in the streets, and recently, in the schools themselves. The schools sit at the center of this nation's conflicts and divisions concerning class, race, gender, geographic location, physical and mental ability, etc.

There is not, however, consensus about how to solve the problems of public education. It is into this shared concern and lack of consensus that the Right moves with handy simplistic explanations and solutions. As they see it, it is the secular, liberal nature of public schools that is the problem – a lack of uniform belief, a lack of single-minded authoritarianism, a tolerance of too many different points of view, an acceptance of too many different kinds of people and their ideas. The solution: eliminate public schools and replace them with religious schools that can choose their students and are accountable to religious leaders, not the community.

The Right uses a two-pronged attack: to destroy public schools' economic base from without, and to control their curriculum from within.

First, from without. Since the tax revolt began with California's Proposition 13, the Right has worked to reduce the tax base that supports public education. More than ever before, schools are fighting for their economic lives among a populace that is suffering from economic distress and is resentful of almost all public expenditures. Another strategy has been the attempt to get the public to approve school vouchers, which would provide tax money for families to send their children to private schools.

In most areas, school budgets have already undergone massive cutbacks, and this final assault on their funding base would no doubt destroy their ability to survive. A third strategy is to support corporate takeover of the schools, to run them like a business by a corporation, or to support charter schools, so that in effect we have private schools paid for by public dollars. And the fourth strategy is to sink the schools with expensive lawsuits that deplete their funds through prolonged litigation.

The attack from within is directed toward the curriculum. From religious Right school board members and an organized constituency, based primarily in churches, there has been a focus on three primary areas: health and family issues, religion, and nationalism. In each of these areas, not only is there an attempt to censor spoken ideas in the classroom but a highly successful effort to remove books from the curriculum. Thus, for example, a teacher may not be openly gay or lesbian, talk about homosexuality as a sexual identity, or give children books that are written by gay men or lesbians or present their culture. Or Beverly Sheldon (wife of the Rev. Lou Sheldon, director of the influential Traditional Values Coalition) can single-handedly get the California education department to remove an Alice Walker short story from their statewide assessment test because in it a rural Mississippi woman who is married to a Muslim is "anti-religious and will change students' beliefs and values."[2]

Under health and family issues, they have opposed sex education, HIV-AIDS education, school based clinics, parenting classes, and distribution of condoms. For the most part, their opposition is based on the notion that becoming educated about sexual matters leads to having sex outside of heterosexual marriage, which they apparently believe protects people from the harm of disease, abortion, and violence, as well as the "development" of homosexuality. Their focus is consistently upon marriage, as evidenced in their current effort to require identification of paternity for babies and mandated marriage as

2. The story in question was Alice Walker's "Roselily," originally published in *In Love and Trouble: Stories of Black Women*. United Kingdom, Harcourt Brace Jovanovich, 1973.

qualification for welfare benefits. Marriage and ownership are at the center of their male-controlled hierarchy.

The Right's advocacy for the inclusion of religion (Christianity) in the school curriculum has focused primarily upon school prayer and upon the teaching of creationism rather than evolution. Creationism is another core issue because if one believes in the inerrancy of the *Bible* and the hierarchy of power from God to man, then one has to believe that God created the world in seven days, that God created man in his own image and gave him power over all that had been created. It only follows that the Right would oppose anything that deals with differences in belief: values clarification, what they call "secular humanism," and even physical activities that include some yoga positions – because yoga comes from a religion that does not follow their *Bible*. Much of their current attack is focused on Outcome Based Education that meets not only basic education goals but attempts to help children be better prepared to function in the world by developing self-esteem, self-reliance, group skills, and critical thinking.

Promoting the need to preserve the "real America," the religious Right has supported English Only laws, which require that schools use English only in their curriculum even in those communities where English is the minority language. Their nationalism and biblical inerrancy lead them to oppose multiculturalism in the schools. Multiculturalism, which assumes that all cultures are of equal value, not only leads to comparative religions but to comparative values. It promotes the idea that people are of equal worth as well. For the Right, multiculturalism poses grave dangers: it does not produce a single hierarchical religious vision, it does not necessarily promote male dominance nor white dominance, and its comparative nature mandates critical thinking and choice. Critical thinking is the greatest enemy of authoritarianism and of fascism itself – and it is the most essential element of autonomy and freedom.

Organizing Pro-Democracy Forces

Public education has fallen upon hard times and is fighting for its survival. However, the conflict surrounding it offers great organizing opportunities around the basic principles of democracy. This is a time when people can be motivated to speak out for what they believe in – for the creation of a society that offers fairness and equality to everyone.

Public education defense and reform offer an opening to create strong coalitions of groups that have a critical interest in inclusion in the processes of democracy. There are many groups that can be brought to the table – labor unions, religious institutions, nonprofit groups, and certainly poor people – but I want to focus in particular on identity groups: people of color, women, people with disabilities, lesbians, and gay men. Not only do these groups understand the moral imperative of working against discrimination and injustice, they often hold in common basic principles: a belief in a multicultural society, the necessity for the inclusion of everyone, and the importance of equal access to participation and opportunity.

However, these groups have had an imperfect history of sitting down at the same table together, so the question is: what is it that might make them recognize their common ground and the importance of making coalition? The answer can be found, I believe, in the interlinking of the issues.

Access

The issue of private schools links everyone in these groups because it goes directly to the concern of who gets to be there. As stated before, many of the private schools, especially church-based, have been racially segregated. Female students are not necessarily kept out of these schools but women, along with people of color, lose in the public accountability arena: discrimination in faculty and administrative positions and salaries, as well as in the curriculum that does not speak to the worth and inclusion of every person. For people with disabilities, there is the continued problem of physical access, which is costly and at this point has to be enforced in public schools by the government through the *Americans with Disabilities Act* (ADA). For lesbians and gay men, the fight for inclusion becomes even greater because private schools can discriminate more comprehensively and openly. For poor people, there is even further diminished hope of adequate educational opportunities.

Health

Under health issues, people can find common concern around HIV / AIDS education. While gay men have found this to be a core issue for more than a decade, women and people of color are now understanding its effect on their lives, as their numbers of infected people have become the fastest growing. For example, in New York City, AIDS has become the leading cause of death among African American women. As the virus has spread, all sexually active teenagers have become increasingly at risk, yet the Right has been effective in preventing AIDS education or the distribution of condoms. Their primary argument has been that these preventive measures will condone and increase heterosexual sexual activity and increase the numbers of homosexuals. AIDS education requires talking about the most at-risk groups, and gay men are among these. Without a grain of supporting evidence, the Right fervently believes that talking about homosexuality creates lesbians and gay men. Consequently, homophobia becomes a weapon of death as they refuse to give young people the information that can save their lives.

There is common ground to be found on another major health issue, sex education. It is from sex education that teenagers learn to be knowledgeable about sexual activity, i.e., what causes pregnancy, how to use good hygiene, how to prevent sexually transmitted diseases, etc. And it is there that they learn about responsibility, i.e., dating norms, family planning, parenting (which, ironically, the Right with all its traditional family values rhetoric does not support). It is where they learn about sexual differences, such as heterosexuality, homosexuality, and bisexuality, and that people with disabilities are as sexual as the general population. It is where they learn about the consequences of their choices. Adequate information could help prevent the hundreds of thousands of unwanted teenage pregnancies in this country each year. These pregnancies are a major health concern for both the mother and child due to the increased poverty that usually accompanies teenage single mothers and the consequent inadequate health care. Sex education, whether about the prevention of pregnancy or sexually transmitted diseases, is a life and death issue for all of us.

Multiculturalism

This is the core issue that most frightens the religious Right because it is here that control of monoculturalism, nationalism, and white male supremacy can be lost. It is here where there is the most likelihood of bringing together people of color, women, lesbians and gay men, and people with disabilities into coalition but also where there can be dramatic divisions along race, class, gender and sexual orientation issues. It is here where there is hope of forging inclusive, participatory democracy or enforcing a narrow nationalism that calls for white dominance. Multiculturalism does not call for a black or women's history month but for equal presentation of black and women's culture throughout the curriculum. With true multiculturalism, we learn as much about American Indian culture as we learn about the white Europeans who moved into their lands. We learn that there is lesbian and gay literature and history, and the same for people with disabilities, long kept invisible. Multiculturalism presents not one point of view but many, and children are taught critical thinking that leads to informed discernment. People cannot have genuine freedom without authentic information and choice. And we cannot have a society of equal opportunity until we believe in the equality of all people. Multiculturalism is a stake driven into the heart of racism.

We cannot make true coalition around the shared principles of liberty and democracy until we understand the necessity for the inclusion of everyone and the common ground shared by those who represent the vital minority voice. When Mrs. Daisy Bates worked to integrate Central High School, she had to fight the forces of exclusion who said that we cannot have black children sitting next to our white children because our white girls will be raped. When women entered the academy, the message was not only that women were too foolish and frail to go to school but their very presence would destroy the morale of men and cause them to do sexual violence. Children with disabilities were told that they did not have the capacity, that they were a public disgrace and should be hidden away. And lesbians and gay men are told that they are an immoral public danger because they will prey upon children sexually. A major part of our common ground is that we understand that the methods are always the same: stereotype, dehumanize, marginalize, divide, and conquer. If we allow ourselves to be divided by the forces of exclusion, then we risk losing a place for ourselves, as well as others, in a world that offers access to full participation and opportunity.

Organizing

There is much long-term work to be done. Perhaps the greatest is building a coalition that is based on establishing good relationships, understanding the interconnection of oppressions and their methods, determining common ground, and developing shared strategies that move beyond simple self-interest and benefit everyone over time.

Coalitions grow strong through doing specific, goal-oriented work together. Here are some possible organizing areas for preserving public education:

- Organizing to promote fair and accountable taxation, so there is a strong tax base for financing the schools.

- Working for equal distribution of tax resources, so that there is not such inequity among schools, some rich, some poor. Also: a program for assignment of teachers into underserved areas, such as remote rural or inner city, perhaps through work credits toward payback of student loans.

- Promote and support progressive candidates for school boards. Identify, expose and oppose stealth candidates.

- Create incentive programs for diversity among teachers, i.e., increased scholarships for people of color, people with disabilities, etc., to prepare for teaching.

- Join the PTA. Work together on solving problems such as violence in the schools. Educate others about the principles of democratic inclusion.

- Organize the community to oppose school vouchers, school takeovers.

- Support the local teachers union. Be a voice against the Right's anti-teacher messages ("they're the most pampered workers in the country, working part-time and getting paid full-time"). Work against union-busting as the Right takes on the nation's largest union.

- Organize around specific issues such as multiculturalism, book banning, sex education.

- Monitor the activities of the local school and its board.

- Get involved in the school. Be a bridge between it and the community.

Final Message

We must take the attack against public education seriously. It is at the heart of the debate about what politic we will live by. We must keep this question before us: is it possible to grow toward genuine participatory democracy and equality without free and accessible-to-all public education?

7.

Violence in Houston

1992

In late July when I returned from six months of working against the religious Right in Oregon, I told my co-workers at the Women's Project that I was afraid that people had begun to think I had gone over the edge, becoming obsessed and exaggerated in my sense of the growth and influence of the religious Right.[1] Then, in August, I went to Houston to work with national strategists who were gathered together by the National Gay and Lesbian Task Force (NGLTF) to put lesbian and gay issues before the Republican National Convention and the general public. I returned from Houston feeling that, prior to the convention, I actually had been too low-key about what I knew was happening on the Right; I had not been outspoken enough.

What changed my mind was witnessing first-hand the broad systematic attack that the Republicans, as they capitulated to the leadership of the religious Right, made against feminists, people of color, lesbians, and gay men. What some of us had observed in seemingly unconnected parts of the country, now was laid out in the Astrodome and the streets surrounding it as a national agenda of bigotry and discrimination, and a climate of violence was intensified. Homophobia, sexism, and racism that had once been more covert were made clearly overt. The Right's carefully designed religious/cultural/political war was brought into the open and battle lines were drawn.

1. Originally published in the November/December 1992 issue of *Transformation* (Vol. 7, No. 6), the Women's Project newsletter.

For me, the first day of the convention, Monday, August 17, 1992, mirrored the further shift to the Right by the Republican Party. My day was divided into three political scenes, each related to the other.

Early Morning: Operation Rescue

At 4 a.m., Ruth Finkelstein and Tim Sweeney of Gay Men's Health Crisis, B.C. Craig of AIDS Coalition to Unleash Power (ACT-UP) New York, and I awakened to join women and men from Houston in a 5 a.m. training for clinic defense. The clinic defense team had developed a highly efficient process for incorporating people into the work of keeping abortion clinics open and safe. By mid-morning, Operation Rescue (OR) and the more radical, violent Lambs of Christ had selected their targets from among the fourteen clinics, and hundreds of clinic defenders were moved from their training areas to prevent attackers from hurling their bodies through the lines of human defense and into the clinics. Legal observers were in place to record the events by camcorder and written notes.

Despite the tight defense, five OR members broke through the first lines but did not reach the more thoroughly defended clinic doors. Then the Houston police took over, moving the defenders away from the clinic, separating them from OR crowds, and establishing their own lines of defense.

The use of police defense rather than the voluntary defenders left the volunteers at loose ends, unclear about their role and eager to be involved to a greater degree. While the greater goal of keeping the clinic open was achieved, there remained a question about the tactic of using police for the major defense. What, then, happens to citizens' sense of empowerment and involvement? Ironically, by the end of the week, these same police had arrested sixteen clinic defenders at another clinic because the landlord who rented to the clinic operators objected to the clinic defense.

Afternoon: God and Country Rally

The most popular Republican event of the week outside the Astrodome was the God and Country Rally, which showcased Dan Quayle, Pat Buchanan, Oliver North, Phyllis Schlafly, and (can you believe it?) Pat Boone. Along with the Gay Atheists, ACT-UP, and Queer Nation, who were protesting outside the hotel, B.C. Craig and I attended to hand out fliers to the press and to support the four ACT-UP New York members who went inside the rally for an action to call attention to the AIDS crisis.

This event was standing room only in a ballroom filled with adults and children dressed in red, white, and blue, many wearing the red cowboy hats given out by the Eagle Forum with anti-abortion stickers on them. Some carried signs that said, "Family Rights Forever – Gay Rights Never!" Except for the local gospel choir, it was an all-white crowd. Just outside the doors of the ballroom were rows of tables presenting anti-abortion and anti-gay literature, as well as a table full of little plastic fetuses. On the street outside, a Texas Republican leader, wearing a plastic face shield (to prevent catching AIDS), was giving away a flier that was in hot demand. In bold letters at the top, it read "NO QUEERS or BABY KILLING." In the center there was a women's symbol that had a face with a Hitler-style mustache drawn in the center, and instead of the usual vertical line with a crossbar, there was a swastika. In bold type at the bottom was "FEMINAZIS."

The four ACT-UP members who stood up during Dan Quayle's speech and held signs to call attention to AIDS were not arrested but were tackled and roughed up by people in the audience and then were escorted out by security. It was not until Wednesday, when they stood up in the Jerry Falwell rally (another white crowd), that they were assaulted by his son and other participants and arrested by some of the more than 150 police (state, county, and city, as well as undercover cops) on hand to control the fewer than 100 lesbian and gay protesters outside the motel.

Evening: AIDS March

Urvashi Vaid and Robert Bray of NGLTF, B.C. Craig and I joined approximately 2000 people in a two hour march sponsored by ACT-UP and Queer Nation to raise consciousness about AIDS and to protest the Republican administration's lack of response to the crisis. When we first arrived at the pre-march gathering, I noticed and commented on how the number of police on horseback had been doubled to 20 or 30 for this event. Laughing about police hysteria, we then went on to join the high-spirited and good-natured assembly of lesbians and gay men and people living with AIDS; for two hours the march was the usual fun, with rowdy chants, drumming, whistles blowing, friends greeting friends. At the end, which coincided with dusk, we were maneuvered by the police into a street near the Astrodome made narrow by a hurricane fence that had been erected along either side. Police on horseback then blocked the street and the march's forward motion. Protesters began milling around, not knowing quite what to do with a march that had no formal ending, no closure. Some of us participated in a die-in; others began burning an effigy of Bush – time-honored street theatre and acts of protest. Soon others put their protest signs on the fire, and someone burned a flag. A broken police barricade was placed on top.

At that moment, with no order to disperse, the police on horseback charged the crowd. Fortunately, B.C. and I had just said to one another that the police seemed dangerous and we had grabbed Urvashi to reposition ourselves about ten to twenty feet away from them, and this little bit of lead saved us from being trampled in the charge. We at first called for people to be calm and not run; then we saw what was happening and yelled, "Run like hell!" Just in front of the horses' hooves, the three of us held hands and ran with pure adrenaline speed across a field. As we ran, we saw that suddenly in our midst there were scores of police in full riot gear, knocking protesters down and beating them with their batons. Overhead, the police helicopter we had been watching during the last half hour of the march was now strobing the field with a searchlight.

There were many members of the press at the march, and there is full documentation of the police brutality on video, including the short clip shown on "Nightline" in which a man's voice can be heard shouting, "Don't kick them when they're under the lights! Don't kick them when they are under the lights!"

As I ran with Urvashi and B.C. and then tried to get people to safety, find Robert Bray, who had been separated from us, and give testimony to the legal observers, images of the 1968 Chicago Convention and Kent State kept coming to me. I thought about how there comes a historical moment in a people's pursuit of justice when the very people who are supposed to ensure justice turn to kill – literally – the voice of dissent and protest.

Little did I know what the Republicans and Houston had planned for us or I would have been even more frightened. In a syndicated column by Jack Anderson published the next day, August 18, 1992 he reported on the planning contingency documents of the Texas National Guard that delineated the streets of Houston between "enemy forces" and "friendly forces." They defined "enemy forces" as the "citizens and special interest groups" that "have been authorized to conduct demonstrations during the Republican National Convention." Anderson went on to quote the document as warning: "Members of our staff have attended briefings by the Secret Service, the FBI, the Department of Public Safety, the Houston Police Department and numerous other agencies on plans for the convention. Our primary concern surrounds those demonstrations that could trigger violence by gangs and dissident citizens."

Thinking back to my amazement at how instantly the riot-geared police appeared, seemingly out of nowhere, I berated myself for having been uncharacteristically naïve as I read on in Anderson's column:

Although a premium is put on keeping a low profile, the Texas National Guard is armed to the teeth, poised to mobilize about 2,500 troops on the streets within 16 hours. If need be, they would arrive with M-16 rifles, shotguns, .45-caliber pistols and more than 1,000 hand and smoke grenades. Each guardsman would carry seventy one rounds of live ammunition. In addition, to help maintain command and control, forty cellular telephones would be rented. Moreover, the Texas Air National Guard is ready to provide C-130 airlift support. Nearby Rice University football stadium would be used as a staging area if forces are committed. If required, city buses would be taken over for military transportation.[2]

Should we consider ourselves lucky that only six people were arrested, three hospitalized, and the walking wounded managed to stagger away into the night? We did not understand we were in the middle of a war zone and the extent to which the Republicans and Bush's hometown would go to stifle dissent and alternative voices at the scene of the Republican National Convention. We are lucky to be survivors of what we at first thought was a police riot but now know was a planned response and could have become a killing field.

The Politics of Exclusion

As we were attacked by the police on the streets, inside the Astrodome this day's demonstration of power by the religious Right was brought to a fitting crescendo by Patrick Buchanan who was chosen by the Republican National Committee to make the first major prime-time convention speech that would set the tone and themes for the week.

And what a tone it set. Buchanan, who represents the party's perfect fusion of the religious Right and the Far Right, came out swinging at feminists, lesbians, and gay men, veiled references to people of color as the cause of social problems, and punctuated his speech with references to God and country. His speech left no question about the religious Right's goal to merge church and state.

By the end of the convention, it was clear that the Republicans had become dominated by the agenda of the religious Right. Moderate Republicans in attendance were squirming as speakers repeatedly referred to "family values" and brought roars of approval from the crowd when they spoke negatively of lesbians

2. "If Things Turn Ugly, Houston is Ready." *Arkansas Democrat-Gazette*. August 18, 1992.

and gay men or feminists. The mood from the podium was both sanctimonious and falsely hearty. Even the traditional fiscally conservative Republicans faltered when trying to find a positive response in press interviews.

By Thursday, through the outstanding work of Robert Bray, public information director of NGLTF, in all of the national print media there were references to the attack upon the lesbian and gay community and writers were beginning to characterize the Republicans as wanting to exclude those different from them, while the Democrats were struggling to figure out how to include those of diverse views. By the end of the week, for any who thought that the President might not be in accord with Buchanan and his ilk, he erased those doubts by leaving the convention to go straight into the deep South, where he attacked the Democrats for leaving "God" out of their platform.

The Republicans, failing in their efforts to address domestic problems and to revive the economy from its Depression woes, forged a partnership with the religious Right to develop a message of "morality" that has inherent within it the immoral teachings of bigotry, intolerance, discrimination, and exclusion. Through using their party platform to define themselves as the "good people" who believe in order, they gave notice that anyone using the democratic process to request inclusion was an outsider or "bad person" calling forth chaos.

The Republicans introduced the idea of a war within the U.S. – a cultural war, a religious war – and divided the country into "us" and "them," 'friendly forces" and "enemy forces." The "enemy forces," those of us who dissent and demand justice and liberation, were targeted as scapegoats in these economic and social hard times which this administration has failed to address with remedies. Establishing scapegoats and dehumanizing people is an invitation to violence against them.

Domination and Liberation

My brooding over the events I witnessed in Houston has led me to think of lessons to be learned from them. There are several.

It seems to me that all offensive violence (as opposed to that used to defend oneself) serves a political end. It maintains the politics of domination in a society, and it is domination that is at the heart of all oppression. Hence, when the police, who were never endangered in their work, charged the AIDS protesters, the message was sent that people are not allowed to dissent from the dominant political culture that tells us to ignore AIDS because those who are dying are expendable anyway. Likewise, the biased violence of sexism, racism, and homophobia played out in the streets and our homes every day serves the purpose of keeping entire groups of people controlled and suppressed. When police brutalize people of color and poor people, when we kill each other in our communities, when a man beats a woman, when a gay man or lesbian beats his/her partner, when adults beat children, oppression is served through maintaining the politics of domination.

Domination is at the heart of Christian fundamentalism, and a basic premise is that one must not question authority. In the fundamentalist's view, authority has been given by God to man, who then must dominate the earth and all its peoples. What we have seen unfold over the past two decades in the rise of the religious Right, culminating in their political success at the Republican National Convention, is that any group who demands justice, participation and liberation is seen as questioning authority – the authority of certain passages in the *Bible*, the authority of white men to dominate the earth. Hence, anyone involved in a liberation movement is seen as an enemy to be suppressed by legislation to control behavior and restrict rights and by police violence, if necessary.

The question facing us as targeted groups is what strategies do we use to combat the forces of exclusion, violence, and domination.

Exclusion

We work against exclusion by increasing our visibility. For the lesbian and gay community, this means we must be out and visible every place that oppression, against us and other targeted groups, exists. The more we are told to disappear, the more we must be present and vocal, no matter what the occasion and who the players are. As we move into the fall campaign of hatred and scapegoating, we have to be talking everywhere we can find an audience – about our lives, our humanity, our rightful place in the American family, our part in the political process, our unceasing demand for civil and human rights. A part of this work will have to be with our local press as we help them understand and shape the stories of this campaign. This attack against us comes as a gift of sorts because it opens opportunities for us to educate a population that is basically ignorant about lesbian and gay issues. However, we must remember that we are in a time of social change, and there are millions of moderate people who are struggling with ideas of inclusion, equality and justice. We need to speak openly and directly to them.

Violence

We must expose in careful detail all of the violence that is brought against us and our communities. We must report it, write about it, analyze it, and bring it constantly to the conscience of this nation. When, for example, the offices of the Campaign for a Hate Free Oregon were vandalized and members of the lesbian and gay community began getting vicious, life-threatening phone calls, it was important to talk about how the political purpose of this violence was to suppress and intimidate, all as a part of the climate of oppression created by the Oregon's Citizen's Alliance and their ballot initiative to destroy all rights and protections of homosexuals. Our response to the violence against us must be non-violent, I believe, because non-violence also serves a political end: to create, step by step, a liberation movement that eliminates the politics of domination and creates the politics of justice and equality. Our tactics have to reflect the vision of the world we are seeking to create.

Domination

By dissenting, by questioning authority whenever it does not serve liberation, we give notice that we refuse to be dominated. Questioning authority is at the core of critical thinking, which in turn is the greatest threat to the growth of fascism. Those of us who question and dissent serve the interest of freedom everywhere. The mere physical presence of lesbians and gay men, feminists, people of color and Jews is a *major* question mark in the face of Christian authoritarianism. Then, when we join together as targeted groups and speak on behalf of our rights and freedom, we become the force that can dismantle domination and replace it with liberation.

The final message of Houston for me was that despite the Republican hype about family values and morality, it was those whose issues were excluded from the convention – people of color, poor people, feminists, lesbians, and gay men – who had the force of a true morality on our side: inclusion, tolerance, equality, and justice. It is our continuing job to speak to that morality, loud and clear.

8.

The Oregon Campaign

1993

At the Republican National Convention held in Houston, TX in November 1992, Pat Buchanan announced that this country is in a "cultural war."[1] However, I do not think we are in a war but are in a time of massive social change that is bringing about new forms of power and new participants in our society. For many, now unable to rely upon old systems of social control, this is a frightening time, and it is this fear that the religious Right has seized upon to promote their agenda to gain religious domination over the political and social life of this country.

To increase the fear and to polarize the country into "good" and "bad" groups of people, the religious Right frames this multi-faceted, complex shift in our society as a "war" which must be won by godfearing people or else all is lost. For the purpose of media sound bites and fund raising, the metaphor of a war is clever indeed.

During eight months working in Oregon against the Oregon Citizens Alliance (OCA) – a rightwing religious group who sponsored a constitutional amendment to make homosexuality "abnormal and perverse" – I was able to witness the characteristics of their attack that make it perhaps similar to a one-sided, religious war in which the troops are armed with *Bibles* and funded by churches and the well-heeled Christian Broadcasting Network.

While rejecting the framing of this moment of social change as a war, I think in the interest of understanding rightwing thinking

1. Originally published in the January/February 1993 issue of *Transformation* (Vol. 8, No. 1), the Women's Project newsletter.

and strategies it might be helpful to look at the Oregon campaign through this metaphor. As in war, the aggressor almost always proclaims that "God is on our side." These rightwing Christians are fueled by a belief that only they are qualified by God to enforce their narrow vision of morality for all people. To them, Oregon was one strategic battleground in their nationally proclaimed war against women, people of color, gay men and lesbians, and people who practice religions other than Christianity.

As in most wars, there was an aggressor who tried to impose its will against a group that was then forced to defend itself. This particular attack ostensibly was launched against lesbians and gay men. But in the style of wars, there was the highly-charged, emotional public focus of the assault, defended in moral terms, and then there were the behind-the-scenes less popular and more base motives. Was World War I indeed fought to make the world "safe for democracy" or was it fought for economic gain and world domination? Was the Gulf War fought to liberate Kuwait or to protect our oil interests and maintain domination? While the public attack in Oregon was against lesbians and gay men, defended on their moral terms (these people are the "abomination of God" and threaten families and children), the larger design was to gain control of the public agenda by the religious Right. The ultimate goal was to gain "territory" in a war that seeks domination over women, people of color, lesbians and gay men, all who are different from dominant groups yet desire autonomy and freedom.

As in war, the violence was both physical and psychological. The terrain of physical violence was scattered with firebombing deaths of a lesbian and gay man, random attacks by racist skinheads, desecrated churches, vandalism of gay and lesbian organizations, sabotaged cars, and assaults. The psychological violence sought terror through name-calling, hate graffiti, and countless hate phone calls and death threats. The OCA even more effectively used a propaganda of lies and distortion to attack core values and self-worth among lesbians and gay men and to undermine their standing within the larger community. This was done using the classic fascistic tactics of scapegoating and dehumanizing. In this assault, lesbians and gay men were described as "animals," "abnormal and perverse," "unnatural," "an abomination of God," people who "eat feces," "spread disease," and "prey upon innocent children."

As in war, those defending themselves and protecting their terrain had to do so in an atmosphere of fear and crisis. It was a state of tension and high pressure that brought out the best and worst in people as they struggled to survive and resist. The very best could be witnessed in people reaching beyond their ordinary selves into the extraordinary behavior of courageous risks, of grace under pressure, of strong friendships and bonding in the face of attacks designed to fragment and alienate. In Oregon, ordinary people performed extraordinary acts of liberation every day of the campaign. However, the worst comes when the war without creates a war within. Then people experience paranoia, betrayals, horizontal hostility, and divisions that subvert their work and relationships. In both Oregon and Colorado, the casualties of individuals and the community fell both at the hands of the religious Right and at the hands of people working to mount a defensive campaign. Outrageously, in wars we call this "friendly fire."

As in war, people engaged in defensive electoral campaigns can develop a kind of amorality in which they come to believe that the crisis is so great that the end justifies the means. Thus, in Oregon and Colorado, decisions were made to keep lesbian and gay presence and issues away from the forefront of the campaign, using polls to substantiate that victory could not be reached if there was too much visibility. The process of inclusion of people of color in all stages of the campaign was sacrificed to the strategy of expediency which called for the more comfortable use of white people in leadership roles. Rural areas were ignored or treated shabbily because they were not seen as vital to the victory since they held so few votes compared to urban areas. The end seemed to justify falling back on the most entrenched forms of hierarchical decision making and uses of backroom power.

And finally, as in war, this campaign to save the few rights and protections of lesbians and gay men drained off community resources, both human and financial. This is a goal in all of the rightwing attacks against our communities: to spend us to death. For a year and a half, the lesbian and gay community and most of the progressive community gave their energy to the defense of freedom and were forced to give scant attention to other compelling social issues such as homelessness, hunger, violence against women, HIV infection, neo-Nazi hate crimes, breast cancer, joblessness, the welfare of children and teenagers. The Oregon No on 9 Campaign and other PACs raised $2.8 million to spend on advertising and get-out-the-vote, and no one knows how much was spent by other organizations and individuals around the state during this 18 months. The total was undoubtedly several million. A positive reading would be that it helped the Oregon economy, but it was as false as a military-based economy, requiring continued aggression and violence to sustain it.

Despite the phenomenal expenditure of resources, on November 4, 1992 lesbians and gay men awakened in Oregon with not one additional civil right than they had prior to the election: the victory was that justice-loving people had stayed an effort to divide the state and to dehumanize and disenfranchise a people. Though extraordinary organizing had led almost every person in the state who had a public forum to speak out against the initiative, in a state with a population of only 2.5 million, there were still more than a half-million people who voted in favor of eliminating rights and protections. Further, Lon Mabon, the head of the OCA, when conceding defeat, said that they would be back in January seeking signatures for a new constitutional amendment fashioned after the successful Colorado amendment. In this one, they would employ what they had learned from this campaign and omit words like "abnormal and perverse" and "pedophilia," and it would be on the ballot in 1994.

Thinking themselves in a war of "family values" and "no special rights," the OCA, as part of the religious Right, no doubt viewed the Oregon campaign as just one skirmish or battle in a major war for which they have bountiful resources and people. And as fundamentalist Christians, they feel they have plenty of time – until the end of the world.

The Struggle for Cultural and Social Change

While the Oregon campaign, through the manipulation of the OCA, had some of the hallmarks of a war, for those of us who participated in any way in the effort to protect rights, it was not a battleground of good and evil but a very intense and dramatic time to sort through values: who we are as responsible humans, how do we want to relate to one another, what kind of community do we want to live in, who gets included, who excluded. It was a fierce moment in an on-going debate about this country's ability to be fully democratic and the meaning of democracy. Because the OCA forced this debate to take place in a cauldron of hatred they had created, many people were hurt but many found themselves made stronger and clearer in their individual lives and in the life of their community.

Additionally, all of us received intensive training on the strategies of the religious Right, the ins and outs of operating an electoral campaign, the ways hope and optimism can be assaulted when hate and violence become central to everyday life, and the wonderfully creative ways people can respond to vicious attacks. The lessons we learned are critically important for shaping the response to the religious Right, proactively advancing our rights, and developing our vision for a more fully inclusive, democratic society.

In many ways I left the Oregon campaign with reaffirmation of what I knew when I went there in January 1992, now tested:

- That the issue was larger than the lesbian and gay community, larger than Oregon; that this was a national test site of a strategy to further the religious Right's goal of merging church and state, destroying civil rights and, ultimately, the *Bill of Rights*.

- That the campaign could not be managed like the campaign of a candidate or of typical referenda; that the expediency of the ends justifying the means could not be employed; that traditional polling methods alone would not be helpful; that a numerical victory would not necessarily mean an overall victory for the lesbian and gay community.

- That as well as acting defensively to protect rights, we had to work during the campaign to create relationships and strengthen organizations so that after the vote, no matter which way it went, the community would have gained from the attack against it

- That this unwarranted attack by the religious Right was both a crisis and a remarkable opportunity; that there was an unparalleled chance to educate an entire state as the OCA forced it to consider lesbian and gay issues; that there was a perfect moment to forge deeper alliances with other oppressed groups, all of which are under attack by the religious Right.

Many of my hopes for the campaign were not met. Expediency often won over movement building. I learned that when the campaign management in Oregon and Colorado too closely followed the pattern of traditional electoral campaigns, the lesbian and gay community was hurt in the process.

However, there were successes that went beyond my greatest hopes. Never have I seen so many people who were not natural allies come together to support a single issue in a state. Thousands of people donated time, talent, money, food, equipment, flowers, and emotional support to the No on 9 Campaign – all the things, large and small, that make people able to work beyond their usual limits. Consequently, there were people on the staff who worked under tremendous stress and difficult working conditions to create daily miracles.

I learned that a campaign cannot control a people who are under attack; they will not be prevented from fighting for their lives and for the quality of life in their state. In Oregon, the campaign was strengthened by people and organizations all over the state who were not directly affiliated with the No on 9 Campaign but were determined to do the difficult and loving work of trying to educate ordinary people about a group of ordinary citizens within their midst, those who call themselves lesbian and gay.

There are a few in particular that stand out as shining examples of hope:

- The Walk for Love and Justice was a weeklong walk by lesbians, gay men, and their allies from Eugene to Portland. They were housed by churches, synagogues, a farmworkers organization, and fed by other groups and individuals along the way. Each night there was a community meeting filled with music, poetry, and conversations about justice.

- Over 100 people in Speak Out Oregon received training on all the ballot measure issues and then covered the state, speaking to organizations, doing radio talk shows, participating in debates, writing letters to the editor, and assisting local groups in getting the information they needed.

- The Rural Organizing Project (ROP) organized over 20 communities, bringing together people from all sectors of the community – people of color, lesbians and gay men, religious minorities, women's anti-violence workers, labor unionists, etc. – to develop organizations and strategies to work against bigotry during the election period and beyond.

- The statewide newspaper, *The Oregonian*, under an absolute commitment to making sure the public understood the immense danger of Ballot Measure 9, printed over a dozen editorials (entitled "Inquisition I," "Inquisition II," etc.) that taught us about the history of injustice and scapegoating. Never has the lesbian and gay community had more eloquent representation from the non-gay press.

- People of Faith Against Bigotry, representing people of all faiths, organized people all over the state to reach "those in the pews." They led discussion groups of social principles, invited lesbians and gay men to speak in their churches and synagogues, held days of reconciliation, distributed packets of materials targeted for specific faith groups, held candlelight vigils, and published a full page ad that read "The OCA Does Not Speak for Me," signed by hundreds of people of all faiths.

• At great personal risk, countless lesbians and gay men came out to their families, religious leaders, co-workers, neighbors, and talked about their lives. They put a human face on the ballot measure. Because of them, the OCA was deterred in its attempt to demonize and dehumanize the lesbian and gay community.

A big lesson of Oregon and Colorado for me was that this is not a series of strategic battles that will be won or lost from ballot initiative to ballot initiative, from lawsuit to lawsuit. Though lesbians and gay men, women, and people of color will be attacked at the ballot box and in the legislatures, those of us under attack cannot spend all of our time and resources simply defending ourselves and being diverted from creating a place of justice tor ourselves in our communities. What is important in this post-campaign season is how we use the lessons we learned from these attacks from the religious right to advance our movement.

Until now, the religious Right has succeeded in dominating public debate and framing the issues of multi-culturalism and democratic process as a conflict between right and wrong, a cultural war that pits what they consider to be the moral against the immoral. They have moved into a vacuum created by our lack of strong leadership and conviction and visibility and filled it with their own misleading definitions of issues and supporting misinformation. I believe we must reject this entire framing of what is going on in our society as being a war, cultural or otherwise. We must be creative, not merely reactive, and therefore name our own reality and morality and our own terms for living.

Rather than accepting the religious Right's declaration that we are in the midst of a cultural or religious war, we need to acknowledge that we are in the midst of a Civil Rights Movement that is under such attack that it sometimes feels like the conditions of war but is instead steadily moving forward, creating fundamental social change. It is an ongoing movement that we create every day. One could say that this Civil Rights Movement has a 500-year history in the U.S., and certainly its many streams began to collect into a river in the 1950s when African Americans initiated a unified struggle for justice. That river, made up of people of color, grew to encompass women and then lesbians and gay men and people with disabilities. It is an ongoing movement, flowing toward justice still, that place of moral being. Seeking control, the religious right wants to dam and divert this river.

While resisting attacks, our task as targeted groups is to find our place in this broad Civil Rights Movement. I do not believe we will succeed as separate groups, if we consider our issues as distinct and different from those of other oppressed peoples. *We have to put our lives with each other, understand our connectedness, and act in solidarity.* The work is not short-term: it is for the long haul. We will always have immediate crises, but liberation will come from changing the hearts and minds of people, changing institutions, changing laws.

We must remember that most of those more than one-half million who voted for ballot measure 9 were simply people who are afraid, people who have been fed misinformation, and people who are yet to be educated about lesbian and gay issues. Some of the best work of the Oregon and Colorado campaigns occurred when people were educating about civil rights. At the victory party for the Oregon No on 9 Campaign, the campaign manager announced that she was told that there was a militant homosexual agenda, and she wanted to affirm that, indeed, this was true. At that moment, No on 9 staff and volunteers unfurled an enormous banner bearing the agenda. It read: **EQUALITY. NOTHING MORE, NOTHING LESS.**

We must provide leadership and education in bringing the nation to understand the morality of justice wedded to equality and inclusion.

The religious Right will be successful in reaching its long-term goal if we wait for them to control the public agenda and set the timetable for our activities, all centered upon defending ourselves from their attack. Long before there is a direct attack, such as a racist or homophobic or sexist initiative placed on a ballot, we must be working on issues of inclusion and democratic process in our organizations and communities. We must create statewide networks that include rural people and those who experience the extremes of economic injustice. People of color, women, lesbians and gay men, poor people, religious minorities, and people with disabilities must begin standing side by side to counter injustice and create systems of justice. We do not need coalitions and alliances only when under attack; we need them all the time because our issues are interrelated and ongoing.

Our work is now, not some time in the future. Through attacking us, the religious Right has put all of our issues smack in the middle of the public debate. It is our work to use this debate to educate the public about justice and injustice and the ways to bring about change that includes the well-being of all people.

For the first time since the 1960s, I sense there are rising expectations among those from whom justice has been withheld. Major movements are built on this kind of hope, not despair. Our historical moment is upon us. If we join with and bring together those who experience injustice, we have the hope for building a mass movement that will achieve the dream of people from biblical times until the present, a world where justice will "flow down like a mighty river."

9.

Seeking the Promise of Equality

1996

In my time of working against the Right I haven't found anything so difficult as trying to find ways to warn people of the danger of Promise Keepers.[1] Here is a mass movement of Christian men which began in 1970 and has now grown to over one million men in 1996 – a movement that brings men together to talk about their lives, to acknowledge their faults and to take more responsibility in their families and communities. In a time of community and family destabilization, whatever could be wrong with such a movement?

Haven't I as a feminist been longing for men to share more responsibility, to be more of a presence in their homes and communities, to show more emotion and sensitivity? Haven't I been wanting them to find some way to be whole so they could stop standing in the way of women's wholeness?

Because it addresses some of these issues in partial ways, this movement has mass appeal – for both men and their wives. Wives of Promise Keepers (some of whom are organized as "Promise Reapers") have been quoted as saying they are thrilled that their husbands have joined this group. It has helped the men become a presence in the marriage and the home where they were often absent emotionally and physically before. Men are quoted as saying they feel connected to other men for the first time, feel able to be more complete, more of a contributing member of society.

I want to acknowledge some of these positive results of these meetings. I think many of us are desperately seeking

1. Previously unpublished. Portland, OR.

solutions to very difficult societal problems, and I have to appreciate people who are reaching out to find some way to improve themselves and their communities.

What, then, is it that so profoundly disturbs me about Promise Keepers?

Perhaps it is because they were founded by former Colorado football coach, Bill McCartney, who is an outspoken supporter of the anti-abortion organization, Operation Rescue, and was one of the forces behind Colorado's anti-gay and lesbian Amendment 2 (now declared unconstitutional). And their major backers are the rightwing James Dobson of Focus on the Family, Bill Bright of the Campus Crusade for Christ, as well as Pat Robertson of the 700 Club and the Christian Coalition.

Perhaps it is because they use the language of war in so many of their speeches, because they boast of organizing along a military model, because they use former military personnel as leaders, because they recruit within military installations through military chaplains, because they say men must be "committed to the blood," and "stand in the blood." Their heavily centralized operations branch out from the national leadership through ambassadors and "key men" whom they hope to install in all of this country's 400,000 churches, leading small groups of Promise Keepers to work together to accept hierarchical authority and exert leadership in their churches and families. Each of these men – using the Alcoholics Anonymous model – is paired with another man for support.

Perhaps it is because they describe their work as a war to take this country for Christ, to make it a Christian controlled nation in twenty years. There is no place in their vision for Jews and other people of faith. There is no place for denominations that "divide us." There is no place in their vision for a secular government that reflects a pluralistic country of diverse races, beliefs, and religious practices. There is no room for democracy – paltry thing as it may be – as we know it. Their vision is of the complete merger of church and state, dedicated to Jesus Christ and his now political, fundamentalist practitioners.

Perhaps it is because they call for the "leadership" of men over their wives and families, for the submission of women to this leadership that holds no shared decision-making, no shared power, no equality. They base their authoritarian vision on one verse of the *Bible* that suggests that as Christ is to the church, man is to woman – that is, she must look to him (worshipfully, I assume) for guidance; she must obey his rules. This notion of righteous hierarchy is taught to young men as they are organized into the "Promise Seekers."

Perhaps it is because they exhort men not to be effeminate and sissy that leads their leadership and major backers to organize people politically to oppose lesbian and gay civil rights, indeed the very existence of homosexuals in this society. Their huge merchandising outlets promote the organizations (such as Exodus International) that have formed to convert homosexuals to heterosexuality. They have been leaders in the demonization of lesbians and gay men as sexual predators, disease carriers, and destroyers of the "traditional family."

Or perhaps it is because their program of racial reconciliation that spends millions of dollars in outreach to men of color to bring them into the stadia for "feel-good" experiences with white men. White people certainly need to apologize for our past racial injustice but we cannot erase that history or eliminate current inequality simply through patting backs and hugging people of other races. This is a gesture of atonement without one substantive effort to make systemic change for people of color in this country such as efforts to support affordable housing, health care, and child care, immigrants of color, job training and affirmative action, youth programs that offer recreation and employment as ways to prevent crime. "Racial reconciliation," practiced as momentary emotional catharsis, provides the Promise Keepers with legitimization of their over 90% white male movement, offers a way to get men to bond around gender alone rather than issues of justice and injustice, and gives them serious inroads into communities of color to advance the "one holy race" of white domination.

So the question is how to say these things to men and women who have experienced the corporate takeover of America and found their jobs, families and communities radically affected – and have been told by the likes of Pat Robertson and Rush Limbaugh that their problems resulted from the Civil Rights Movements (people of color, women, lesbians and gay men) having created discrimination against them and chaos in our society? How to voice these concerns to people who are desperately seeking solutions to their personal and community problems? These are people of good faith, innocent before a sophisticated leadership that has a rightwing agenda awaiting the mass numbers to gather before it is put into action.

I don't believe it will work to tell people that this is either the largest evangelical tent revival in history or indeed the mass movement the new fascism has been waiting for. People's current needs run so deep that we must find ways both to describe the dangers lying beneath the surface of Promise Keepers and to offer a workable vision of a world that gives us economic and social justice and true equality. It is worth our time to talk with those people of faith who are drawn to this movement. Perhaps we could pose this question: why is it Promise Keepers never mention the Biblical concepts of economic and social justice and genuine equality? Our discussion of authoritarian dangers and of the promise of a just and equitable world could begin there.

10.

Deregulating Women's Lives and Regulating Greed: An Open Letter to the Conservative Right

1990

I am writing this letter to express my concern over the obsession you have developed about regulating women's lives, using as your agents the clergy and elected officials.[1] You have taken a stand as major proponents of preventing a woman's right to choose an abortion – that is, to have control over her own body – and also of the deregulation of big business so that there is no control over greed and economic injustice. I wonder why the regulation of one and not the other?

To each of us we are given only a body – it is all that we bring into the world and all that we take out. If we cannot have control over it, if we cannot have privacy where it is concerned, if we cannot make decisions about our own best interests, what is there left to us that we can call our own? You propose a world where those men who lead the anti-abortion forces such as Operation Rescue (OR) and those men who make up the majority of the courts of the land will have decision-making power over women's bodies and thereby over women's lives. You are saying that no woman should have control over her own life: it should be controlled by government regulations.

You say the same for gay men and lesbian women. One should not be allowed to live out the sexual identity one is given;

---

1. Originally published in the November 1990 issue of *Transformation* (Vol. 5, No. 6), the Women's Project newsletter.

you say that people should not have the right to choose who they love. In fact, you advocate for laws to control the lives of gay men and lesbian women. Who are the chosen few, then, who should be allowed control of their bodies and their lives?

I find it strange then to see how you fight the control of the government in almost all other areas. Aren't you the same guys who fight against gun control and for the death penalty? Your anti-abortion troops call themselves pro-life and yet your forces are on record everywhere as being overwhelmingly in favor of these agents of death: guns and lethal injections. And aren't you the same ones who support the likes of Ollie North of the Iran-Contra scandal and financial and military support for regimes that have the worst human rights abuses and killing records – i.e. the Contras, the white government of South Africa, and Saddam Hussein up until the day Iraqi forces invaded Kuwait? Would you please explain to me again your stand on life and death issues?

It seems to me that you're always talking about wanting to save the "unborn child." Well, what about the children already born and those policies you promote and support that lead to their early deaths or diminished lives because of poverty? What about the regulation of greed that leads to poverty for the many and obscene wealth for the few? I believe you are the fellows who scream about no new taxes on the rich and then seek a balanced budget by cutting benefits to the elderly, assistance to farmers, and social programs that provide that fine, vulnerable screen that keeps most people in this country from falling off the edge into total disaster. You're the same ones who supported the deregulation of the airlines and jumped transportation prices out of sight, the deregulation of the Savings & Loans that promoted so much unbridled greed that the taxpayer is now sacked with a bill in excess of $100 billion. With waving flags, you support our entrance into Saudi Arabia and this bogus war for oil and greed that will quite likely end up taking the lives of countless adults and children, along with depleting the monies here at home that help keep people alive. And you continue to fight a national health care bill that would ensure the health of children and adults who cannot afford to purchase the high free market rate of competitive health care.

I keep forgetting. You say that your domain is moral issues and these I mentioned are not moral; they're only economic. And you quote the *Bible* to me about the domination of women and the abomination of homosexuality. Well, I beg your pardon. It seems to me that many of you on the Right tote that *Bible* around a lot, talking about "this Christian country" (not acknowledging our religious diversity of Jews, Muslims, and man other religions), holding prayer breakfasts that are fronts for political meetings, and naming yourselves the gatekeepers of Christian morality. In fact, you talk about Christian morality as though there were no other. Inspired as you say you are by Christ and his words, where do you find among those words attributed to him (not the words of the misogynist Paul, for instance) one word about the domination of women and the abomination of homosexuality? What you find are statements again and again about economic justice and about the acceptance of all persons because they are equal in the sight of God. Nowhere is there a directive asking you to stand in God's place as the judge of humans and the controller of their lives.

It is no wonder that many people now think of conservative politicians and clergy as being Bible-thumpers who exhibit moral bankruptcy. They are waiting for you to speak out in support of the Christ you extol and to help lead the country to a time of economic and social justice. You concentrate on controlling the lives of women and protecting children while remaining silent on the issues that would save the lives of children and adults (here is a radical idea for you: the lives of adults are as precious as those of children), and that silence reeks of immorality because it supports the destruction of life.

Why are you not roaring with rage from every pulpit and from every politician's favorite media spot about the destruction of women's lives through battering, rape, incest, and murder? Why do you support with your silence and your policies a war zone for women and children? Why are you not insisting upon such a high taxation for U.S. companies exploiting cheap labor overseas that those companies would willingly return to this country and institute fair labor practices and provide decent employment for the increasingly underemployed here? Why aren't you supporting anti-discrimination laws and economic development in rural and people of color communities? Why aren't you crying out for free prenatal care, childcare, and health care for all our people so the children born into this world could have a chance to live productive lives? And if you are so obsessively focused on abortion, why don't you work on prevention and fight like hell for the development of simple, effective, accessible birth control for both men and women?

You have the power to be a part of a general movement to bring about good, especially those of you who are clergy and leaders in religious settings because, at least, once a week you have an audience as well as an established organization to work from. I am asking you to bring about a change in focus – from the destructive one of attempting to control people's lives to the creative one of attempting to make a world where people's lives are livable. It is a high moral calling.

11.

Rightwing/Whitewing Christians: Hel-lo, Operation Rescue

Original Author's Note: I make a distinction between rightwing Christians and fundamentalist Christians. I understand that fundamentalist Christians use a literal reading of the Bible to create a moral vision for themselves and their church community, whereas I believe rightwing Christians are political activists using the Bible and church in conjunction with the government to promote an agenda for social dominance and control. Progressives are political theorists and activists, both religious and not, who promote an agenda for equal distribution of wealth, equal rights, and liberation for all peoples.

—

1991

The *Arkansas Gazette* brought us the news: Operation Rescue is considering Little Rock among five cities (Baton Rouge, L.A.; Asheville and Fayetteville, N.C.; Fargo, S.D.) for its next onslaught against women's right to choose abortions, and they might arrive as soon as November.[1] Whoaaa. Is this a gift or a curse? Should we be depressed or excited? Is this our chance to be on national news, and should we begin dieting and experimenting with new hairdos now to get ready for the cameras?

Frankly, I've been looking forward to this moment because it gives us a chance to discuss our issues right out front and highlight the essential differences between those who are pro-

---

1. Originally published in a 1991 issue of *Transformation* (Vol. 6, No. 6), the Women's Project newsletter.

fertilized-eggs and those who are pro-women-and-children. Or more central to the larger issues at stake here, those who are pro-social-control and those who are pro-self-determination-and-freedom. I look forward to this debate and to telling Operation Rescue firmly why they are not welcome, despite our long tradition of Southern hospitality, in a town where there has been a major struggle for freedom since 1957 when Mrs. Daisy Bates and her compatriots walked with the Little Rock Nine to Central High School through the crowds of jeering white people who were united in their efforts to maintain this country's schools as bastions of white privilege.

Here in the South we know what it's like not to be free because we live forever with the memory of a group of white people who enslaved Africans to meet their own agenda of need and greed. This playing out of social control was demonstrated again in the twentieth century by the Nazi concentration camps and by apartheid in South Africa. We have etched in our memories what it means to control a people's lives by using laws, violence, and imprisonment to prevent self-determination and to impose a social agenda that meets the needs of those who control the land and the institutions. That deep memory is going to make Little Rock a most unwelcome place for Operation Rescue because we understand the connection: we see clearly their agenda for social control to meet needs that are not our own.

There are at least two kinds of Southerners who just can't bring themselves to have any use for Operation Rescue and their desire to control lives. One is the African-American community who during slavery daily witnessed women's bodies being controlled by their white owners – through rape and forced breeding. Indeed, everything about the lives of men, women, and children was controlled by the slavers: self-determination is antithetical to slavery. The other kind is the poor Scot-Irish immigrants who hit this soil running – running from a tyrannical British government that indentured them through unrecompensed labor, exclusive voting laws, unjust taxation, lack of religious freedom, and imprisonment – and running toward the hills of the South where they sought to be free of the tyranny of government and its control of their freedom to have their own lives. Both groups, Black and white, have it ingrained in them to be suspicious of any one, any group, (and especially the government) that wants to impose repressive demands upon our freedom to make decisions about our lives.

Now here's our deepest suspicion. We just can't help noticing that Operation Rescue's leadership – like all its brother rightwing Christian groups – is made up entirely of white males. Is there a clue to something here? Whose agenda is being served in this massive campaign to save fertilized eggs and embryos?

Women have been aborting embryos since we first learned where they came from, yet there has been no major outcry against the practice (using the *Bible* as a weapon of authority) until the late 1970s and 1980s when women began to gain power through the women's movement, when civil rights advances began to be dismantled and racism rapidly worsened, when the white supremacist movement began to strengthen, and this country's government took a strong turn to the Right and increased support of rich, white men of the western world. Is there some coincidence here? I think not.

And have you noticed another suspicion of ours is being clarified in the press these days? For some time now we've been thinking that the anti-abortion troops were connected to the organized white supremacists: that the Christian Identity churches of the white supremacists were the most radical, militant religious arm and that the rightwing Christians of Operation Rescue were from the more socially accepted fundamentalist and conservative Christian churches. All, of course, promoting a similar agenda, some with fatigue dress and guns, others with neckties and pictures of dead babies: social control of everyone who is not a white male, and what's more, even control of the bodies of their white women as the producers/nurturers of the white race.

Then what happens to confirm these suspicions? Enter Ralph Forbes, one of the main neo-Nazis in Arkansas, and it's suddenly out in the open. First, he successfully brought a lawsuit against the University of Arkansas Medical Sciences hospital to prevent it, as a state funded institution, from providing abortions except when necessary to save the mother's life. His lead was followed by Arkansas Right to Life, Family Council, Christian Civic Foundation, and the Unborn Child Amendment Committee in a subsequent lawsuit on the same issue. And then more recently, Forbes joined Operation Rescue demonstrators in Wichita, KS, was arrested and spent two days in jail. According to the *Arkansas Gazette* (September 1, 1991), it was then that Forbes suggested to Operation Rescue leaders that they choose Little Rock as a site for activism.

Our suspicious nature leads us to think that these rightwing Christians who oppose women's right to choose are merely one piece – the religious arm – of a larger agenda of social control designed to limit the lives and freedom of people of color, of women, of lesbians and gay men, of the unemployed and working poor, so that the great movements of the 1960s and 1970s, along with the labor movement, are squashed and power remains in the hands of a few rich, white men. Rightwing Christians and the white supremacist movement are both part of the grassroots front for the political agenda of Ronald Reagan and George Bush – the grassroots activists for a conservative, repressive government that serves the continuation of white male power and domination.

There are some real questions here. Why of all the enormous social issues facing this country is the Supreme Court nominees' conservative stand on abortion and attitudes toward civil liberties the litmus test for Bush and Reagan? And why is the rightwing Christian issue of abortion so major in the nominating process of a judge to serve all of us when poll after poll indicates that the majority of Americans are pro-choice? And why are the men of the white supremacist movement and the men of the Bush administration united in opposition to affirmative action, the second litmus test for Supreme Court nominees?

Clearly these issues are connected in a larger agenda that limits peoples' right to control their bodies, their lives, their communities, and ultimately, their government.

For those who believe government is necessary, there are two positions to take about its role: for government to control people's lives – or for government to support programs that enable people to control their own lives. The power is either in the hands of the state or in the hands of the individual. Rightwing Christians promote a politic and an activism that takes away the right of an individual to control her/his own life, thereby supporting the government's, or the state's, right to control our lives – though they, along with white supremacists, promote the right of the individual in the racial politics of anti-affirmative action, school busing, etc.

Anthony Lewis, writing in the *New York Times* (September 9th, 1991) about the Supreme Court, notes that the Court is now "bent on building up the centralized power of the President... weakening the protection of individuals from the power of the state," even though this is what the framers of the Constitution most feared – centralized government power.[2] He gives as an example the Court's gag rule on doctors in federally funded clinics mentioning the word abortion or referring the patient to an outside doctor for discussion, thus violating the doctor's right to free speech, and "indicating the remarkable doctrine that whenever the government aids an institution it can dictate what anyone there may say." Lewis gives another example: in 1971 the Court held that employment tests were suspect under civil rights laws when they produced racial disparities. The ruling, known as the Griggs case, was generally applied and accepted in industry. The Reagan administration successfully challenged it in the Supreme Court, and since 1989 Congress has tried to pass legislation restoring it but Bush vetoes it each time. Lewis ends by stating:

> President Bush and his right-wing supporters say they want 'strict construction' of the law by judges. It is a transparently cynical claim. What they want, and what they are getting, is a Supreme Court that will increase Presidential power and carry out the political agenda of the radical right.

There are very large questions here. Such as, who controls our lives, who sets the parameters of our freedom? Though it

2. Lewis, Anthony. "Abroad at Home; A Royalist Court." *The New York Times,* 9 Sept. 1991, www.nytimes.com/1991/09/09/opinion/abroad-at-home-a-royalist-court.html.

is part of the rightwing strategy to get us to view abortion as a single and moral, not political, issue, it is misleading to look at the abortion issue in isolation. Perhaps it will be helpful to look at the rightwing Christians' participation as grassroots activists in the larger agenda of those who want a conservative, centrist government that controls our lives by eliminating individual freedom and to compare it to the progressive agenda that seeks self-determination and individual choice, with government supporting our independence.

Rightwing Agenda – Progressive Agenda – Or – Pro-Life Compared to Pro-Women/Children

Abortion

Anti-abortion advocates ask that the state intervene to control women's bodies and to protect the development of fertilized eggs. They ask that information about the range of options be withheld from women through a gag order placed on doctors who receive any kind of federal funds. The leadership is male. Pro-choice advocates ask that the state stay out of women's private lives and not intervene in their decision to nurture or abort a fertilized egg. We believe that women should be given as much information as possible about all options available so that they can make informed decisions. The leadership is female.

Children

The rightwing believes that "traditional family values" will save children but they do not support programs that support families and children. For instance, a study done by Catholics for Free Choice of congressional voting records points out how the pro-lifers in Congress voted against issues affecting children: establishing standards for child care, requiring companies to grant unpaid leave to parents of newborn or seriously ill children, funding for health programs, minimum wage increase, etc. The pro-women-and-children agenda includes advocacy for programs that enable all children – not just those of the upper classes – to be healthy:

- Free pre-natal and post-natal care;

- A nationalized health program;

- Free and/or affordable childcare;

- Parenting classes in schools so that skills for raising healthy children can be developed;

- Free medical and dental care for children to age eighteen;

- Parental leave;

- Provision of beds for women in drug and alcohol centers so that mothers can produce drug-free children;

- Development of effective, safe, affordable means of birth control so that unwanted pregnancies do not occur;

Education

The Right believes that schools should be restricted in what they may teach so that citizens of uniform, unquestioned values are produced. They believe in the elimination of choice that comes from exposing children to the teaching of critical thinking, values clarification, sex education, and humanistic values. They believe in banning books that do not agree with their view of the world, and they support Christian prayer in schools.

Progressives believe that the most important thing to be learned in schools is critical thinking so that one can gain the skill to make informed decisions in any situation. Believing in choice and individual freedom, we do not believe in the banning of books or subject matter. Because children of many religions attend schools, progressives do not support Christian prayer in schools. We also believe that children cannot make informed decisions about sex unless they are provided sex education, as well as the means for preventing pregnancies.

Life and Death

The Right supports the life of a fertilized egg and the state-enforced continuation of life for brain-dead patients, the terminally ill who wish to take their lives, and those who wish no longer to live, for whatever reason. While they oppose people's right to take their own lives, they support the state's right to take lives through employing the death penalty. (Because of their belief in "traditional family values," they persuaded Louis Sullivan to suppress a government study on teen suicide that showed evidence that concern about being gay or lesbian and pressures concerning sexual identity was a major factor in teen suicide. On the other hand, they have had a rabid response in opposition to Final Exit, the best-selling self-help book on being in charge of ending one's life.)

Progressives support people's right to choose their deaths through establishing "living wills" that spell out how they want their medical life and death decisions made and through obtaining information about how to be responsible for ending their own lives if circumstances necessitate. We oppose the state's use of the death penalty.

Sexuality, love, and marriage

Under the catch-all term, "traditional family values," rightwing Christians oppose

- Sex outside of marriage (and consequently access to birth control information and materials for those who don't have a marriage license);

- Single parent families (referred to as the "breakdown of the family," "absence of male authority, role models," etc.);

- Love and sex between people of the same sex (while also opposing lesbian and gay marriages);

- Pornography, not for its violent content but for its sexual content;

- Prostitution, not because of the abuse of women by men but because "bad" women use their bodies for sex outside of marriage.

Their definition of "traditional family values" is a heterosexual marriage in which the male has authority over his wife and children, an authority given him by God. They believe the state should control areas of sexuality by laws preventing sex education and availability of contraceptives, so-called "sodomy" laws designed to prevent the sexual practice of anything other than penis/vaginal sex and to give the impression that homosexuality itself is illegal; laws to punish prostituted women; and laws that ban sexual expression.

Progressives believe that people have a right to their sexuality and the enjoyment of it among consenting adults; that teenagers are sexual and should be provided sex education and safe means of contraception; and that families have many configurations, including single parents and children, several adults living together, lesbian and gay couples with or without children. Some oppose pornography because of its violence against women and children, while others find a blurred line between pornography and erotica, and there is heated debate about the most effective strategies for protecting individual freedom while providing protection for women and children. Our definition of family is two or more people who are connected to each other through love, trust, commitment, shared goals and responsibilities. Progressives believe that the right to control one's own body is primary: that everyone has the right to love persons of one's own choice and to use one's sexuality in ways of one's own choosing that are not destructive. Believing in the right to privacy, we support the right of the individual to live without the interference the state in the private domain.

Violence

It is in the area of violence that so many contradictions arise that the "pro-life" position is laughable, but we cannot afford to laugh because this small, church-based movement of radical rightwingers is having such a destructive effect on the lives of people struggling to live in peace and freedom.

As far as I can tell, judging from their response to Operation Desert Storm (all these "operations" – "Operation Rescue," "Operation Desert Storm," – do these names come from the same think tank?), Christian right-to-lifers are adamantly pro-war. Operation Rescue spent weeks and thousands of dollars (their own and the city's) and thousands of people hours (both protesters and police) attacking the Wichita clinic and saving, as Keith Tucci boasted, "Thirty-one babies unjustly sentenced to death." At the same time, a Harvard medical team was reporting that Iraqi infant and child mortality had doubled compared to the prewar period: more than 50,000 children had died since the war and another 170,000 are estimated to die before the end of the year. So, once again, the rightwing Christians support state initiated violence and their right-to-lifer President, this time against women, children, and old people in addition to soldiers. They do not lie down across the steps of the White House to protest the deaths of these Iraqi children.

Most shockingly, these Christian "savers of babies" are resoundingly silent, both in their pulpits, in the White House, and in the chambers of the legislatures, when it comes to speaking out against violence against women and children. These preservers of traditional family values do not acknowledge the number one cause for the destruction of the family is violence against women and children. Those who wish to save babies and the family do not speak out against battering, rape, and incest, and they accuse those who provide shelters and services for victims of being "destroyers of the home." Highly organized protesters, they do not lead their "operations" to stage protests over the acquittal of the white "running boys" who sodomized a young Black woman at St. Johns University. Or, in Arkansas, lead congregations to mourn the deaths of the sixty-eight women murdered by men in our state last year.

The progressive agenda opposes war staged for greed and supports the Iraqi people maimed by a high technology war that left all of their public health systems destroyed. Opposing bias violence in all its forms, progressives consistently speak out and take action against violence against women and children, religious minorities, people of color, lesbians and gay men. We believe that everyone has the basic human right to live a life free of violence.

Conclusion

Because of our reputation for hospitality, Operation Rescue has been misled to think they will find a warm welcome in Little Rock. Though we are a mixture of Southern and Southwestern (and certainly people think of both of those areas as archly conservative), that particular blend has led us to be independent minded and full of belief in self-determination while recognizing the absolute necessity of living as good, caring neighbors to one another. Consequently, we have a history of struggling to create a progressive agenda, supported by a long line of progressive to moderate governors – Republican Winthrop Rockefeller and Democratic Dale Bumpers and Bill Clinton, for example – and U.S. senators and representatives.

In our state, we have strong advocacy and organizing groups seeking social change that will give people self-determination and control of their lives and communities. Our people are on the front line when it comes to working to end violence against women and children, saving Black farmland, creating innovative ways to prevent teenage pregnancy, working out private and public partnerships for low-income housing, preventing school drop-outs, addressing community drug problems, fighting the toxic wastes being dumped and burned in the state, promoting people before bombs, establishing Black/white dialogues. Though often falling short in the struggle during hard economic times imposed upon us by the policies of our government, we seek to create a progressive agenda that will enable all our people to live well.

We see the rightwing Christian agenda as regressive, where they drive toward the twenty-first century looking only in the rearview mirror of their car, trying to recapture a time that eludes them as it recedes into what has been, not what is now. Their nostalgia that feeds their passion for reclaiming "traditional family values" is for a time when races were segregated and white people could benefit from the social and economic subjugation of Black people; when silence surrounded families and women who were beaten and children who were sexually molested had nowhere to turn for help; when abortion was not debated because it was done illegally and in secret and women lost their lives; when lesbians and gay men were living closeted lives that imprisoned them; when there was not a Civil Rights Movement and a Women's Liberation Movement to stir up the social unrest that called for a change on behalf of freedom.

We have a broader view. We see a future of "social unrest," and we call it good because it brings the social change necessary to accommodate the very different kinds of people who now make up our small world. We are hearing new voices asking for recognition of different needs, different ways of life from those times when the white male establishment was secure in its power before the great movements of the 1960s and 1970s. We are still working on the dreams deferred from those movements: we are dedicated to struggling with the issues of true multi-culturalism and of economic and social justice.

Because of our commitment to solving community problems within the community and our belief in people's right to control their own lives, we think the Operation Rescue question becomes simple. Do we want to participate in creating an agenda that calls for state control of our decisions, both individual and community, or do we want people to have self-determination and responsibility for their own lives and the life of their community? We've seen the alternative: we'll choose freedom.

Operation Rescue, we're putting you on notice.

12.

FED UP

1991

You may have noticed that it's very popular to create organizational names that are acronyms, such as ACT-UP (AIDS Coalition to Unleash Power) or Kansas City's own FIRED-UP (Freedom Involves Responsibly Exposing Decadence & Upholding Principle).[1] Some of these organizations, such as ACT-UP, have thousands of members, others have only one or two but give the impression they have hundreds. My newly formed organization probably falls in the latter category because it has only one member, and its name – which looks like another acronym – actually is only a group of letters standing simply for the words they make together. Mine is called FED-UP.

And what is it I'm FED-UP about?

I am fed up with rightwing Christians preaching against lesbians and gay men and upholding heterosexuals as those chosen by Christ and an anthropomorphic god called "Father." I and many others have searched through the New Testament for a single word about homosexuality that is attributed to Christ himself, and there is not one on this subject by the man who kept the company of men and held them dearest to his heart. So I want to know where rightwing Christians get off drawing this hard line between heterosexuals whom they see as normal and good, and gay men and lesbians whom they see as perverted and evil.

---

1. Originally published in the May 1991 issue of *Transformation* (Vol. 6, No. 4), the Women's Project newsletter. Written for a speech given to the LGBTQ community in Kansas City, MO in May 1991.

I am fed up with this strange, relentless, hysterical, strident attack on lesbians and gay men. I've been thinking about what the rightwing Christians are supporting with heterosexuality and what they (probably appropriately) fear about lesbians and gay men. And that's the subject of my talk today: how odd it is that rightwing Christians should be so all-out supportive of heterosexuals, and given that peculiarity, how right it is that that they should fear lesbians and gay men.

Just what is it that rightwing Christians see as so admirable about heterosexuals as a class? Now, I must admit that some of my best friends are heterosexuals, and so are all of my favorite family members, but to embrace them generally as a class? I'm sorry, but I think there needs to be major improvement across the board before I can do that.

For instance, in 1990 there were sixty-eight women killed by men in Arkansas. Those murders were extremely brutal: women stabbed over 100 times, women dismembered with specialized instruments, women abducted and raped and killed, women shot in the face with a shotgun, women mutilated, etc. Almost all of those women were in some kind of relationship with their murderer: he was a husband, ex-husband, boyfriend, ex-boyfriend, etc. As far as we know, every one of those men was a heterosexual. Can I embrace that? No, I'm fed up with heterosexual men killing thousands of women each year.

The Department of Justice reported in March that there were over 100,000 reported rapes in the U.S. in 1990. They figure that only one in ten rapes is reported, so you figure out for yourself how many rapes there really were. These were acquaintance rapes, date rapes, family rapes, stranger rapes and of course, what is so seldom mentioned, marital rapes. And guess what? Probably 99% of these rapes – including men raping men in prisons – were committed by heterosexuals. Do we want to support these people?

There is now a remarkable body of documentation showing that there is violence in over 50% of marriages; that domestic violence accounts for more injuries to women than mugging, rape, and auto accidents combined; that the number one cause of homelessness for women is domestic violence; that the 1,100+

U.S. battered women's shelters cannot begin to accommodate all the victims of violence. Domestic: that means husbands, boyfriends, lovers, family members. We're talking heterosexuality here – men and women, women getting beaten by men, their children witnessing it as a way of relating, as a way of life. No, thank you. After fifteen years in the battered women's movement, I'm fed up. The body count is too great, and it never ends.

And then there is child sexual abuse: rape, molestation, incest. Diana Russell's studies indicate that one in four girls will be sexually assaulted before she is eighteen, and one in six boys; 38% of all women will be sexually assaulted in their lifetimes. And these are conservative figures. I think it is so morally wrong for anyone to sexually abuse a child – anyone – and here again, I have to wonder what group of people is being offered up as an ideal, as the preferred norm, when the Department of Justice tells us that 95% of those who sexually abuse children are heterosexual men? As you know that includes those who abuse boys; with few exceptions, they too are heterosexual men who are in positions of trust: family members, teachers, ministers, coaches, scout leaders, etc. Doesn't this make you sick? Should we be thinking of some way to keep them away from children? If rightwing Christians want to hold up these heterosexuals as normal and good, they can have them. Me, I'm fed up with the whole lot of what I would call perverts and am happy to be dissociated.

And then there's a billion dollar pornography industry, forced prostitution, and the physical abuse of children. There's the KKK, the Aryan Nations, the Savings & Loan scam and the Housing and Urban Development (HUD) scandal, the Iran-Contra affair, war games, and the destruction of the environment by big business interests – all led by visible heterosexuals, I'm afraid. I may have to create yet another group called WORN-OUT because listing these heterosexual achievements is wearing me down to a nub, emotionally and physically.

I need to pick myself back up and get on to my second point: why rightwing Christians probably should fear lesbians and gay men.

Of course, there are some murders, some battering, some child abuse, some pornography, etc., in the lesbian and gay community – because we inherited the ills of heterosexual society, I'm afraid (you can't escape the dominant culture) – but our numbers can't even begin to compare. We can't get into the same ballpark of destructive behavior with heterosexuals. However, rightwing Christians aren't preaching sermons about heterosexuals or launching major campaigns to wipe them out through conversion techniques (sexual deprogramming) or incarceration. But they spend an incredible amount of time attacking gay men and lesbians for simply loving people of the same sex.

So why are rightwing Christians so obsessed with lesbians and gay men? Because they fear the possibilities of change we bring to society. This is probably a legitimate fear for those who want to preserve the old order of domination and control, of violence and abuse. This particular variety of Christians is really into social control: what people read, watch on TV, who people love and how they love, what people do with their own bodies, etc. There are rules and regulations for everything, and vague biblical references to justify censorship and suppression of people's right to be in control of their own lives. These people prefer for the world to be controlled by men, and white men, at that. In order for all of the abuses I just listed to exist, that is, in order for women and children, people of color, and the earth itself to be dominated and controlled by men, a fairly rigid hierarchal order must be maintained to support male power. Heterosexuality is a major piece of that order. It is, in fact, a linchpin.

To be lesbian or gay is to threaten that hierarchal order of male power and control. Let me explain.

First, lesbians. Lesbians are not "real women" because we live outside ownership by men. "Real women" know their place, and that place is to be subservient and subordinate. We lesbians at our best drive a stake right into the heart of male power and control because we offer an alternative to living emotionally and sexually dependent upon men. Lesbians construct whole, complete and satisfying lives in the company of women. We then are free to pursue friendships with men when there is a willingness to work at peer relationships. We offer an alternative, radical vision that posits this possibility: that if all women, heterosexual and lesbian alike, could work to bring an end to their dependency upon men, then perhaps gender equality and liberation could be realized. This independence of women would be the wedge that breaks open the male ownership of women which leads to social and economic dominance.

Gay men are especially hated because they are not part of the male system of ownership of women. Those who are visible – out of the closet – are a serious threat to male power and control because they make a clear break from traditional power and privilege that comes from heterosexuality. Those who are closeted of course still seek and receive heterosexual male privilege and in this way collude with our oppressors. It infuriates our rightwing friends to see an open gay male who offers an alternative to the ownership of women and even goes so far as to offer a vision of female qualities within males. Both gay men and lesbians show us that there can be a blend of female and male characteristics within either gender, and in a better world, we would encourage the qualities of both in each person. Such a world would not have gender roles, and if we didn't have gender roles, how would it be possible for one gender to dominate the other? It is this possibility that puts terror in the hearts of rightwing Christians.

If there is one social territory that rightwing Christians think they *own,* it is the family. Here again is where they no doubt have good reason to fear gay men and lesbians, for we offer a vision of family that has the power to change the world. The traditional family system that the Fundamentalists still promote is man, woman, child – in that order – with the man being the head, the ultimate authority over the family. Any other configuration signals societal breakdown to them. And what is our vision? We say the definition of family is two or more people who are connected to each other through love, trust, commitment, shared goals and responsibilities. And any combination of people can fit into this definition: blood relations such as a mother living with her children, two men with or without children, several people of the same or different sexes, a father and his children and his friends, two or more women with or without children, the traditionally married, divorced men and women with their new spouses and their exes and the various children of all concerned, adult brothers and sisters – the combinations are endless. What is important is the *quality* of what connects them into what can truly be called family. We need to stop using the word family to describe just those ownership connections where so often controlling behavior and abuse destroy the lives of those caught in a legally defined configuration of people.

I guess there is one other area where rightwing Christians also feel some strong ownership: that's the area of love. On their radio shows, in their writings, at their anti-Choice rallies, etc., I hear them talk about love of one's fellowman, love of Christ, love of the unborn child, love of one's neighbor, and yet amidst this abundance, I also hear such restrictions. That is, we are to give our genuine, full love to the right kinds of people; to others it should be very conditional – I would say patronizing – based on the recipient's willingness to change. Rules and regulations are everywhere about who is worthy of love and how and whom one should love. For instance, lesbians and gay men. We would be worthy of love if we would simply change our sexual identity – rip it out, annihilate it, become something we are not, a heterosexual. And then there is the issue of who and how we love. It simply is not permitted to have such deep passionate, erotic love for someone of the same sex, to make family with them, to create a life of fullness and completeness.

No wonder they fear us on this score. Our vision is totally in opposition to theirs because we say it is okay, in fact it is really very good and wonderful, to love any adult in a passionate, erotic, or platonic way. What is important is not who you love – their gender, or race, or class, or religion – but how you love. What is wrong is imbalances of power, where one person dominates and controls the other, where there is physical and emotional abuse. So much of the violent abuse I named earlier in my speech was done in the context of what some call love: child rape and molestation, child physical abuse, date rape, marital rape, the battering of women. Who needs it? Maybe the larger question is, is love enough? Are heterosexual pairings enough? No. It is behavior that counts, the daily acting out of kindness, trust, honesty, peerness, commitment and responsibility. We lesbians and gay men are on to something: we know that figuring out the how of loving people of every variety is necessary to bring about the massive social change to make this world livable.

These are just a few of the ways that lesbians and gay men threaten the world order of rightwing Christians who are trying their best to hold on to the old miserable violence-filled ways of traditional male hierarchy. They yearn for that world where women and people of color lead restricted lives serving a world view where they are allowed little power. Me, I'm fed up with that world. My craw is full. Or to change my animal metaphor here, I'm fed up but I'm beginning to chew my cud and think more and more seriously as I gaze out at the world beyond the restrictive pasture fence. I'm yearning for freedom. I love the vision that lesbians and gay men provide; I love the visions of races and religions and cultures that are outside the dominating class; and I want to find more and more effective ways to bring all of us together – in all of our grand differences – to act out our vision for a better world. For each of us, that will mean getting the courage, no matter what the opposition, to act out blatantly the truth of who we are. For me, that means being as clearly and unmistakably lesbian as I can be.

Maybe I could dissolve my new FED-UP organization and create a new one that has potential for more than one member. What do you think? Shall we call it ACT-OUT and bring to it our best Outness? Our most honest and true-to-ourselves selves? I ask you to join me tonight in acting out your most free and total selves. There's a new day of freedom coming in this land. The rightwing Christians ain't seen nothing yet.

III

Missed Connections

13.

The Battered Women's Movement: A Brief Retrospective – and a Call for Action

1990

Southern families – perhaps all families – can get downright ornery when someone from outside criticizes one of us.[1] We circle up and lay out the defenses in what appears to be a united front. However, from the inside, we can lay out all our problems and talk them to death, or in good times, to a solution.

In the spirit of that tradition, I am writing about some of the problems and failures I have witnessed as a participant in the battered women's movement since 1976. For more than a decade I have written articles to document or analyze or strategize or criticize the work of this loosely knit, varied group of us (numbering thousands) who have worked to end violence in the lives of women and children. This is the first time I have taken something of the long view, looking back over time, to give a personal assessment of that work.

I write this article as a daughter of the battered women's movement because, though I had been involved in other movement work in the 1960s and 1970s, it was the battered women's movement that gave me a chance to grow as much and as fast politically as I was capable. It was here through working alongside extraordinarily diverse women and learning the ways that violence worked in our lives that I found all women's issues converged and were connected. It was here I learned that every woman was a

1. Originally published in the September 1990 issue of *Transformation* (Vol. 5, No. 5), the Women's Project newsletter.

battered woman. It was here that I learned from battered women an ever-growing analysis of the many forms of oppression. It was here that I grew up.

Because I have such deep love for the battered women's movement, because it gave me the women I call my closest friends and chosen family, because it is the place I have so often felt the sense of genuine and lasting worth in our work, because for so many years it was home and community, I find it now painful and profoundly disappointing to witness its failures – and to write about them. I write now because I still believe there is no more important work than our efforts to end violence and because I maintain hope for radical change. I write as part of the dialogue that must take place to find the strategies, the solutions that lead to lives of safety and wholeness for all women.

The early days of the U.S. battered women's movement were filled with the heady air of rebellion and creation, of women's power and control over our lives. Battered women opened their homes to house other battered women. Women broke the silence of centuries and spoke out to say they had been beaten, raped, terrorized. Ordinary women took extraordinary steps of courage to leave their homes and all means of financial support to seek safety for themselves and their children in the company of other women.

Thousands of women joined this movement – some were recently battered, some battered years before, and some not currently experiencing violence in their lives – all seeking hope for safety and a better world. As shelters began to be opened and staffed, it was a grassroots movement, a popular movement – that is, one created from the populace, not the government or already established institutions – and it was radical.

As P. Catlin Fullwood, the founding chair of the National Coalition Against Domestic Violence's (NCADV) Women of Color Task Force, used to say, most of us were not radicals when we entered the battered women's movement; we were very ordinary women and it radicalized us. How did it do that? By chance or by design, it followed some long established steps of popular movements. With the understanding that all women share the common oppression of sexism and its attendant violence, the movement offered a place to every woman who was willing to share her life. It broke the isolation that keeps people from being able to recognize common problems and organize together. From that beginning, the steps were simple but life-changing:

- Women broke socially enforced silence by telling the stories of the violence they had experienced, and they found safety together;

- Together women reflected upon those stories, coming to realize that each individual was not unique in her story but that they all shared common elements.

- Analysis of those common elements led women to stop blaming themselves for the violence and instead to look at the source of the violence. In time, it was necessary to look beyond the individual abuser and to analyze the institutions that support domination and violence.

- And finally, women recognized that action was necessary, and that it had to be more than individual; it was essential for women to join together to confront and change institutions – in fact, the entire fabric of society. (It was in the confrontation of institutions that women were radicalized, Fullwood said, because we never thought the institutions would be so entrenched, still so woman-hating, once we showed them the full extent of violence against women.)

So far, so good. What more could one ask of a movement? Perhaps that it be not just a radical movement, that is, one that goes to the root of the problem, but also a liberation movement? A movement that offers power and leadership to all its people, equality of access and opportunity, a new way of being with one another? Liberation for all? Power to the people?

Paulo Freire points out that the difference between liberating work and domesticating work is that liberating work confronts and changes institutions (or creates new ones) so that oppression is overcome and the people have power, while domesticating work seeks to make oppression more bearable to the people who experience it. Domesticating work most closely resembles charity, or doing for people rather than working with people to have control over their own lives. It was in choosing between these two points of view that decisions were made that led to the major failure in the battered women's movement.

By the early 1980s, battered women's activists had slammed right up against entrenched institutions that supported male dominance, centuries of social conditioning for women to be "nice girls," the Reagan years, and a job market flooded with social workers. The coded words for the pressures for domestication placed on women were "institutionalization, credibility, and professionalism."

Institutionalization

When women confronted institutions about their covert or overt support of violence, we were told that the best way to make change was from within, that the goal of the battered women's movement should be to get shelters incorporated into already existing institutions, thereby ensuring their respectability, their continuity, their economic survival. Consequently, many women made the decision to try to make their shelters a part of – or at least accepted by – the very institutions that had historically oppressed us, the institutions that were the embodiment of, the enforcers of, our oppression. Battered women's organizations began to be in the position of the chickens trying to win the approval of the fox. The power began to move from women's hands into the hands of parenting institutions – churches, YWCAs, county governments, Salvation Armies, alcohol and drug treatment centers, etc.

Credibility

From the beginning, there was tension between the idea of a movement and the idea of service delivery, empowerment and charity, social change and social work. Some people argued effectively that it could be a movement and still provide the services of safety, housing, childcare, support. However, the idea of a movement was frightening to many women because it called for reflection, analysis, confrontation, and change to a new, previously unknown, way of living; that is, it called for behavior that for centuries had been called unwomanly, unladylike, unnatural for women. To gain credibility, we were advised to create boards that were filled with powerful members, both female and male, from the community's established institutions. Those who followed this advice, created boards that were made up of representatives of business or institutions with no history of supporting women's empowerment – and constituents (battered women and those with a history of working on behalf of women) were left out. Many battered women's organizations then developed into something that resembled businesses whose products were service and public relations.

Professionalism

In the early years of the movement, battered women helped one another, created shelters, raised money, and worked to get their communities to understand this thing called male violence. Then came the pressure for legitimacy, for credibility (in the dominant culture's terms, of course), there was a call for trained, "professional" people to administer programs, for advocates to be replaced with counselors, and suddenly formerly battered women and movement women, were not adequate to provide leadership. This call for professionals coincidentally came at the same time there was a glut of social workers on the job market. Women who would not get near us in the early years of our struggle to get established now applied for the highest level jobs. Let me not be misunderstood: some of our most brilliant and radical workers in the movement have been degreed social workers, and they moved beyond their training to develop strategies for lasting social change. But hundreds of other social workers entered this work for a job, not for a place to work to change the world. Domestication is at the very core of much social work training – finding ways to make oppression more bearable, providing services and charity.

By the end of the 1980s it had become almost unheard of for a shelter director not to have a MSW (or a degree in business administration), individual counseling had replaced most group work, and some shelters began hiring men as directors.

And where did this decision (or these many small decisions that add up to the same) lead us? We have suffered two enormous losses:

- A widespread, united effort for radical social change. The drive for institutionalization necessitated moving away from social change work because it is not in the interest of the dominant culture's institutions to seek true social change – only to make oppression more bearable. Shelters have continued doing the critical work of providing safety for women, a place to talk about their lives, and support for living lives free of violence, but most have not gone beyond service delivery. The major risk-taking work of organizing with battered women to confront institutions and create alternatives often takes second place to service delivery or does not happen in any significant way. As far as I know, there has been no reduction in battering since 1970, but there has been an enormous increase of shelters providing services. In Arkansas, for example, since 1980 we have grown from four shelters to eighteen, many operated under the umbrella of conservative institutions.

- The promise of liberation. The decision to seek credibility and professionalism brought with it traditional hierarchical structures (what else does the dominant culture respect, what else serves it?), and the elevation of those people already closely aligned with the community's established institutions. Hierarchical structures, by their pyramidal design, severely limit leadership development, collective work and empowerment. Even in supposedly feminist institutions such structures still reflect those of male culture in salary differentials and decision making power. Generally, those most acceptable to the dominant culture are hired into the top positions. To gain credibility, battered women's organizations, in a sense, had to leave behind those women the dominant culture does not traditionally honor or think worthwhile: visible lesbians, women of color, poor women. These women have been relegated to the lowest paid or least visible jobs or in fits of liberalism, they often have been tokenized, but in general, there has been a low ceiling placed over their leadership and advancement in hierarchical structures. Consequently, issues of race, class, sexual identity and gender have been removed from the forefront of the analysis and work necessary to bring about the liberation of women and end male violence.

We have done a good job getting the public to understand that woman abuse exists but a bad job of getting them to bring about the change necessary to end it. We have a great proliferation of shelters and direct services and relationships with the criminal justice system, but women are being beaten, raped, terrorized, and murdered every day. In Arkansas alone in the first seven months of this year, forty women have been murdered by men in horrible circumstances where robbery was not the motive. The majority were killed by husbands and boyfriends, present and former.

Clearly we need a new strategy to bring an end to violence against women. Our failures are pressing us on. We have witnessed the battered women's movement become fragmented and part of the system that oppresses us; the mass murder of women engineering students in Montreal; and the passage of a national hate crimes bill that deliberately excluded women from coverage. Yet it is females who are the most viciously attacked, abused, and killed across all cultures; it is women who are consistently victims of the cultural crime of woman hatred. We have exposed the crimes, we have exposed the nature of the hatred, but no rescue, no solutions are forthcoming from major institutions and certainly not from the perpetrators and supporters of male violence.

We must enter a time of intense reflection and analysis; we must examine anew the issue of violence against women. It is time for women to represent all of our variety and differences to come together in large groups and small, in think tanks and strategy meetings, in political retreats and in overnights in women's homes, to intensify the dialogue of bigoted hate violence against women and the discussion of stronger, more effective strategies to work locally and globally to bring it to an end. This work must take place now to end this war zone of assault against the female gender. It is time to take strong, courageous action to save the lives of women.

14.

White Male Supremacy: Hate, Bias, and Discrimination

1991

I can't seem to get this idea out of my head: that it was wrong for women to be left out of the Hate Crimes Statistics Bill. Wrong, wrong, wrong.[1] It's not that I think the killing and maiming of women would have been significantly reduced if we had been included, or that we could trust the men of the criminal justice system to collect statistics faithfully about attacks against us. However, I do think that the inclusion of women would have sent a societal message that the terrible sexist violence we experience is at least on a par with racist, religious, and anti-gay violence. And I guess that this is what still galls me: that the violent destruction of women (and our numbers of victims are legion) is consistently minimized and not taken as a serious threat to the health and moral well-being of this society. That was the message sent by those who crafted the Hate Crimes Statistics Bill.

Since those who worked on this bill were people of good will, I simply have to assume that women were omitted because there was a limited, skewed, or wrongful analysis of hate crimes and hate criminals. At the time of its passage, the bill represented some of the best political thinking of the male progressive left, and there was considerable self-congratulation on the success of including gay men and lesbians in the bill. As a lesbian, I am also profoundly grateful for this inclusion. However, it still leaves a gaping omission that fails to address the incessant, destructive,

1. This previously unpublished commentary was written in February of 1991.

violent assaults against women every day. I am first and foremost a woman, and where in this bill or in this society is my safety sought? Are the crimes against me and my gender not those of hatred?

That very question leads me to consider the possibility that the current definition of hate groups and hate crimes might be incomplete. This definition limits hate groups to those organized white supremacist groups who use rhetoric and violence to terrorize and control people of color, Jews, gay men, and lesbians. We do not use the term hate groups to describe street gangs who use rhetoric and violence to terrorize people of their own race or religion. Again, we use hate crimes to describe the violent acts of individual white people, Gentiles, and heterosexuals against people of color, Jews, gay men, and lesbians. And we do not apply the term to other acts of violence between people of the same race, religion, or sexual identity. Yet, hatred exists in all of these cases. The question is this: what is the difference, if any?

On one level, there is no difference. Hatred is hatred. When young heterosexual men wait outside the gay bar in Little Rock and attack a gay man with baseball bats, when white young men rape and kill an African American woman in Dumas, Arkansas, and hide her body in a swamp, when neo-Nazi skinheads paint swastikas on tombstones in a Jewish cemetery, when Klansmen burn a cross on the lawn of an African American, or when African American street gangs kill an African American youth in a drive-by slaying, when Asian American gangs terrorize Asian American women, when a man of any race or religion abducts and rapes a woman, when men or women kill each other in jealousy, competition, and passion – each incident is filled with hatred. It is a hatred that destroys and kills.

Clearly, we mean something more than hatred when we talk about hate violence and hate crimes. I was helped to understand how inaccurate and inadequate the use of the word *hate* was by Debbie Lee of the Family Violence Project in San Francisco who recounted a conversation with her co-worker, Leni Marin. They pointed out that hate is a psychological term that describes a raw emotion, something that many or perhaps all people experience in all kinds of circumstances. Hate can be grounded in many different things. Debbie and Leni believe, as we do here at the Women's Project, that the real issue is systemic oppression. To use *hate* as the defining term calls up serious questions about strategies. As Leni said, if *hate* is the problem, then what is the strategy for eliminating it – *love*? Love the Klan and the Aryan Nations and they will go away or convert to loving individuals?

We need more accurate language to describe what we mean when we talk about crimes by those who have institutional power and support against those who do not. Our language must come from an analysis that includes the systems and the institutions of this society that foster bias, bigotry, and discrimination. There is always an element of hatred in the politics of systemically-fostered violence, but it is more accurate to call this overall violence biased, or institutionally supported violence, and whenever possible, to include the specific systemic category: racist violence, anti-Semitic violence, homophobic violence, sexist violence. In this way, we see that it has societal roots, and is not just any violence or hatred that occurs.

Those groups who monitor organized biased hate groups have perhaps created a strategic error by focusing so much time and attention upon these groups, when the majority of the acts of biased violence are committed by individuals who do not belong to such groups. Though there is compelling reason for all of us to be deeply concerned about the presence of such overtly violent, terroristic groups as the Klan and the growth of fascism in this country, they are only the most visible layer of the strata of biased violence and oppression. They do not exist in a vacuum; indeed, their terrorism is supported by the bedrock of systemic racism, sexism, anti-Semitism, and homophobia that pervades the institutions of U.S. society. While the Klan and its brother organizations terrorize and/or kill some hundreds each year, hundreds of thousands are terrorized and/or destroyed by individual acts of biased violence (i.e., the rape, battering, and homicides of women by men) and their lives controlled and limited by social policies of bigotry and discrimination. The violence of both organized supremacist groups and individuals is given tacit permission by institutions that maintain racist, sexist, anti-Semitic, and homophobic policies.

The organized supremacist groups need always to be seen in this context, not separately. Otherwise, we could get into the untenable position of thinking that the existence of such groups causes the oppressions (racism, anti-Semitism, etc.) of society instead of their being an outgrowth of socially supported bias, bigotry, and discrimination. It is the policies and beliefs of our institutions that make fertile ground for the growth of biased violence.

When the organized supremacist groups are seen outside of this context, then it is easy for them to be seen as the bad guys of society, thereby letting all others out of their responsibility for sustaining institutions that create the climate for this violence. This problem was clearly exhibited in the Phil Donahue show that dealt with white supremacist parents who teach their children the politics of hatred. It was one of Phil's lowest moments when he brought together five doughy neo-Nazis with their very young children sitting at a play-table in front of them. It took a concerted effort by all concerned to get the children to pay attention enough to spew forth a little evidence of the hatred they had been taught. But most appalling was the audience who yelled at the Nazis, telling them how terrible they were and how they (the audience) were free of such feelings and behavior. One would have thought that systemic racism had died except for a dim life among a few people such as these five and their children. The holier-than-thou sentiment was thick in the room. No one was taking responsibility for participation in colluding with a society that creates such racism that moves along many avenues before it reaches the heart and mind of a Klansman.

Isolating the organized groups from the continuum of institutionally supported violence and labeling them as the major problem leads those opposing them into a limited vision of biased violence. Anti-violence organizations find themselves focusing on support for only people of color, Jews, gay men, and lesbians because the supremacist groups name them as the enemy, and the supremacists get to control the agenda. These are the people most often mentioned in hate literature and also those targeted for biased violence. Where, then, are women? Are we not targeted by these groups, and if not, does that mean that violence against women cannot be classified as biased hate violence?

Women are not named as direct targets of supremacist groups because of gender alone. Women are also targets for some other aspect of ourselves: because we are women of color, Jewish women, lesbians, etc. The issue of female gender by itself is critically important to the men who form these groups because women's subordination is the cornerstone of male domination and control. Much of their rhetoric is focused on the necessity of keeping the white Aryan race pure, and of course this purity depends upon the control and consequent purity of white women. Maintaining this purity becomes justification for destruction of people of color (particularly men), Jews, gay men, and lesbians. Women fall into two categories: those who are devalued (women of color, Jewish women, and lesbians) who can be used for white men's pleasure or vengeance, and those white women who are necessary for bearing the seed that ensures the continuation and dominance of the white race.

To be considered a real target of supremacist groups, people have to experience terroristic attacks against them, such as cross burnings, destruction of religious property, gang attacks against gay men. One way that women experience these terroristic attacks from the rightwing is through the bombing of abortion clinics. These are performed by newly created white supremacist groups who seek the control of women's lives while saving white children for the perpetuation of the white race. The leadership of these groups is white male, and their concern is for stopping white women from getting abortions, from having control over their own lives. The anti-abortion groups do not have people of color in any numbers in their ranks, and they do not present any concern for children of color or for their mothers: their focus is on white women. The religious fervor of this crusade against reproductive choice is the same that is found in Christian identity churches that promote white Christian domination.

An examination of attitudes toward women within the organized supremacist groups helps us to put together a more complete analysis of what these groups have in common and how they operate. Even a superficial examination will show that these groups have three things in common: they are made up of white people; they are created and operated by men; and they desire supremacy over those not like them. Hence, to name them accurately, we must call them exactly what they are: white *male* supremacists. In almost all the writing about these groups, the word *male* is left out or not emphasized. Indeed, there are a few Klanswomen, a few Aryan women, a few female racist skinheads but with one or two rare exceptions they are not in major leadership roles; indeed, their roles are of the traditionally subordinated female: support roles, sex partners, caretakers. These are men's groups.

When the mostly male-led anti-violence and human rights organizations name the white supremacist groups as the enemy and omit an analysis of individual acts of biased hate violence, a battleground between the polarities of the left and the Right, or good and evil is established, and the strategy becomes one of confrontation between male warriors. Individual warriors on both sides can get into competitive roles of risk-taking and bravery while both groups have shouting matches at marches where the white supremacists of the Right parade before the crowds of the left. Here again, as on the Phil Donahue show, those who help to create the systems that foster white male supremacy are not forced to look at their own participation: the focus is on the extreme, on the symbolic poles of good and evil.

What does it mean, for instance, that many of the male-led organizations of the progressive left reflect the same relationships to women that the white male supremacist groups have: that men lead and women are in traditionally subordinate roles. Again, as in the white male supremacist groups, women's issues are not targeted by male dominated groups on the left; indeed, it is extremely difficult to get women's issues even put on the agenda for separate consideration or action. Other than feminist organizations, what progressive group has ending violence against women as a major part of its agenda for social change? Anti-violence groups such as Klanwatch or Center for Democractic Renewal (CDR)? No. Human rights groups such as Amnesty International or Worldwatch? No. Civil Rights groups such as the National Association for the Advancement of Colored People (NAACP) or Southern Christian Leadership Conference (SCLC)? No. Gay and Lesbian groups such as National Gay and Lesbian Task Force (NGLTF) or Human Rights Campaign (HRC)? No. Organizing centers such as Highlander? No. The Communist Workers Party? No. What does it mean for the perpetuation of discrimination and violence against women when even progressive groups do not put women on the agenda?

The question of why women were left out of the Hate Crimes Statistics Bill comes down finally to this: to have included women, men would have had to face more directly the violence they perpetrate or collude in perpetrating. *Male* would have had to be placed in *white supremacy*. The white male warriors of the left would have had to look at their role in supporting white male supremacy. And men of color would have had to look at how their sexism does not, in the end, support a male supremacy which is inclusive of them in the institutions of this society: instead, it supports the ultimate institutional goal of white male supremacy. With women placed at the agenda table, the polarities of good and evil would not have been so easy to establish as a battleground and strategies would have had to be reconsidered in the recognition of the complexities of biased hate violence. What is the continuum of violence? And who is the enemy?

With women, as with people of color, Jews, gay men, and lesbians, the majority of violent attacks are not from organized supremacist groups but from individuals who believe in the inferiority, the lack of value for the life of the victim. What these acts of violence have in common is that they grow out of institutionally supported oppressions: racism, anti-Semitism, homophobia, sexism. When states have sodomy laws or institutions have policies that deny visible gay men and lesbians jobs, medical care, etc., then the climate of discrimination, bias, and hatred is set up. When all the major institutions of society are controlled and dominated by men, and women suffer overt economic disparity in hiring, pay, and promotion, then the climate for violence is created. The policies of racism, sexism, and homophobia send forth the message that these people are inferior, they do not have great value, they are not to be afforded honor and dignity in their daily lives.

When institutional policies of discrimination are mirrored in progressive organizations, women are led to anger or despair. What does it mean when on both the left and the Right women's leadership is not supported and women's issues are not included, when violence against women is seen only as a private or domestic problem? Women are left with no place for wholeness between either extreme, no place for our lives to be valued as independent, autonomous, and of worth except as adjuncts to men and their concerns. Devaluation of lives is the beginning of the road to violence.

There has been strong resistance from progressive men to including women in any hate crimes legislation, and they provide lengthy arguments for why women do not fit into the definition of biased hate crimes. Women, on the other hand, as I've talked with them in meetings around the country, understand immediately that crimes against women are biased hate crimes of the first order. They also talk about men's resistance stemming from a refusal to face men's responsibility for violence.

Perhaps most galling to women is the argument that violence against women cannot be classified as a biased hate crime because in the majority of the cases, the perpetrator is related to the victim: a husband, boyfriend, neighbor, family member. This argument suggests that because a relationship is involved that the victim is also somehow responsible for the violence. Or put another way, she in some way has brought it on herself. Violence in relationships between men and women is considered interactive: that is, there are no "innocent victims," despite the centuries of history of men's domination and control of women. Because of this history of men's ownership of women, there is a reluctance on the part of institutions and individuals to intervene until there is a homicide. This lack of intervention and appropriate punishment clearly implies the right of the perpetrator to be violent.

With stranger violence in the instance of racist, religious, or anti-gay violence, there is the assumption that violence does not occur because of personality or behavior but because of who one is as human being, and therefore the violence is the more terrible. In this case, stranger rapes and homicides of women would fit into a definition of biased hate crimes, though the courts are still reluctant to acknowledge "innocent victims." However, women state that just the opposite is true: that the violence is all the more terrible when the perpetrator is known through relationship, when the contract for love and safety is demolished with violence. This violence, despite male definition to the contrary, is also biased violence, for it grows out of a societal belief that men are of greater worth than women, that men have the privilege of controlling women, and that the toll of violence on a woman's spirit, productivity, or life is not a great loss to anyone. There is societal permission, supported by lack of intervention and minor punishment, to batter, rape, assault, and kill women. By definition, the oppressions of racism, sexism, anti-Semitism, and homophobia are formulated on institutional power plus prejudice. In this way, the institutional power interacts with personal prejudice to classify certain categories of people to be subordinate, inferior, excluded from full participation in society. The power of institutions to control the lives of people of color, women, Jews, gay men, and lesbians is maintained through the use of economic sanctions and violence employed both by the state and individuals. The violence that occurs in the lives of women comes from the same source as racist, religious, and homophobic violence; the only difference is the bias is gender-based rather than race or religion based, and the perpetrators are those of the dominating gender, not the dominating race or religion.

To leave women out of a definition of biased hate violence is to refuse to see the whole of the societal system of violence and how all of the violence is connected to serve the purpose of sustaining white male supremacy. To eliminate all the forms of biased hate violence requires the building of a major movement that brings all oppressed groups to the organizing table to place their issues in equal weight on the agenda for social change. It will take more than waging battles against the organized white male supremacist groups each time they raise their Nazi heads because each time one is put down, our fertile soil of systemic oppression grows another group that is more clever, more acceptable, such as the David Dukes or the anti-abortion leaders of this land. Their faces become harder to recognize on our school boards, in our legislatures, in our pulpits.

We have to integrate our analysts and vision so that we come to see that the firebombing of an abortion clinic and a letter bomb to a civil rights judge are of equal importance, or a man stabbing a woman dozens of times and then raping her dead body is of equal importance to a white man killing an African American man and stuffing his genitals in his mouth, or that the violence of pornography sends a terroristic threat to women in the same way as the painting of Nazi graffiti in a Jewish cemetery. In our work to make a movement for social change, we cannot minimize the importance of any lives or the effect of violence on those lives to control who they and their people are in the world.

If women do not have an equal place at the strategizing table for the movement, if our issues, our lives are not considered of equal value to all others, then the effort to end biased hate violence is doomed to fail. Success in saving the lives of people of color, Jews, gay men, and lesbians will be an incomplete victory because it will still leave over half of the population targeted for brutal violence, not because of our race, religion, or sexual identity but simply because of our gender.

This is the work of the progressive left: to begin now, this day, to examine and acknowledge how it colludes through sexism – through the devaluation, subordination, and exclusion of women – to support the system of white male supremacy that creates a continuum of violence from individuals to institutions to organized biased hate groups. A partial answer is not enough; we have to figure out the whole, or no one is safe from the violence that grows so vigorously and freely in this country.

15.

The Rise of Mean-Spiritedness & The Gay and Lesbian Movement

1995

For weeks, calls were crisscrossing the country to me: "You need to know how people are attacking Melinda on America Online."[1] It took me a while to get around to it, but finally I read the 112 entries posted about Melinda Paras, the new executive director of the National Gay and Lesbian Task Force (NGLTF). It was a daunting and exceedingly depressing task. What bitterness, what rancor, what viciousness, vindictiveness, and anger from a small group of gay men leapt from the screen. When an occasional voice offered a few words in Melinda's defense or identified as a woman or person of color, then that person became the object of attack. I'm new to these on-line postings, and frankly, it took my breath away to see so much venom on screen.

This experience made me reflect on the mean-spiritedness that is on the rise across the country which expresses itself in attacks against women, people of color, Jews, poor people, immigrants, lesbians, and gay men. It is carried by a defensive and aggressive anger that is infecting even the liberation movements for various identity groups. It sometimes seems we are going to eat each other alive as conflicts erupt along the fault lines that run through issues of race, gender, class, and sexual identity.

Consider the attack against Melinda and NGLTF. As one of those people who signed a letter in support of Melinda, I had

---

1. Originally published in the May/June 1995 issue of *Transformation* (Vol. 10, No. 3), the Women's Project newsletter.

to wonder what in the world could have led to such outbursts of passion, such vehemence, such shrillness in these online messages that came from "our" people, not the anti-gay and lesbian bigots. The primary charges against Melinda were concerning her financial management at Shanti, her left politics, her not having a "true" disability. Yelling "Commie" seems strange at this time in history. So Melinda, like many of our leaders, was at one time a Marxist and probably still uses some Marxist analysis to good purposes in her politics. So she worked to defeat Marcos, a despot – are people suggesting that she should have been on the side of Marcos? So she is a female, a woman of color, and her disability is chronic fatigue – does this mean she cannot provide leadership in the work against HIV/AIDS along with all the other many issues NGLTF takes on? As a woman of color can she not also represent men and white people? And how many times must people be told that no one absconded with any money at Shanti?

What is really being talked about here?

Frankly, I think some of this mini-cyclone circling Melinda is about fears concerning Melinda herself (and anger at her) but I believe most of it is about other things that represent the conflicts taking hold of this society. I am reminded of Hillary Clinton and the relentless attacks against her for everything from bad hairstyles to power-mongering among the mighty. Hillary is a lightning rod for the hatred many people in this country have against women (especially smart, liberated ones), against feminists, and against progressive people. The same is true for Melinda: a lightning rod. Even Mother Theresa would be having a hard time these days in either of their positions because her work among the poor would be seen as seditious anti-capitalism, I'm sure, and her clothes as self-damning poor taste.

The general mood of many people in this nation at the moment is to destroy, not to build. We see this at every level of society but nowhere any greater than in the attack against elected political leaders, people who are victims of historic injustice (poor people, women, people of color, Jews, lesbians and gay men, etc.), and the leaders of organizations whose job is to work on behalf of oppressed people.

The sad truth is that mean spiritedness is being nourished by talk shows and politicians and is growing across the nation. After the 1980s decade of focusing on *me, me, me* during which time we plunged deeper into debt and economic crisis, there is now a cry for getting *mine,* for not getting left out, no matter who has to be hurt. The individualism of the 1980s has run amuck, and the backlash is vicious and coordinated against those seeking justice and equality for everyone, not just the few. It is a nasty mood that seeks to attack and destroy anyone who gets in the way or differs in politics or opinion.

Tragically, this vicious mood and conflict has taken root in many of our progressive organizations. Rather than being united in our commitment to people-centered liberation politics which stand in opposition to the Right's agenda, we find that within our movements we have people who join in the ranks of the Right in their political vision of a world that excludes almost everyone but "people like me."

I would like to think that lesbians and gay men are exempt from this mean spiritedness, but unfortunately some of our people are major proponents of it. Leadership on the national and local level has been decimated by angry personal attacks that allow no quarter for past mistakes, for redemption, for change and growth. I believe that some of our rightwing attacks come from within. Let's face it: there are people who would like to see NGLTF destroyed if it embraces a multi-issue approach to social change.

Within the lesbian/gay/bi/transgender population we have the same conflicts that exist among heterosexuals. Despite our dreams of one movement, we probably share in common no more than the experience of homophobia and varying degrees of discrimination. We stand in very different places on all other issues. What we are beginning to comprehend is that we are gay, lesbian, bisexual, and transgender people, we are people of color and white women and men, we are Republicans and Democrats, and like the general population, we have a political left and Right and lots of middle ground in between. And at this moment, the Right seems to be in ascendency.

I think we need to face up to the current political moment and consider that part of the conflict displayed on America Online concerning Melinda and other issues is a reflection both of the conflict between conservative and progressive politics in general and, in particular, of the influence of the Right on gay and lesbian politics. The debate is often focused on whether the Gay/Lesbian/Bi/Trans Movement should be single-issue or multi-issue, and whether we should be conservative or progressive. But deeper within the conflicts the question of who has worth, who gets a share of the resources, who gets full participation, a question of queer supremacy (rights for queers alone) or of democratic participation and equality for everyone. NGLTF, along with other progressive organizations, will have to choose where it will stand in this conflict.

Here's where I weigh in. I believe in everyone's right to be represented and to have a part in constructing a platform for their issues, but I do not believe one or two national organizations can represent everyone's concerns. I would like to see NGLTF come out openly as a truly progressive organization that recognizes how discrimination against lesbians and gay men is intricately connected to the discrimination against other groups, how almost everyone in its constituency brings more than one issue of discrimination to the table (homophobia, AIDS-phobia, racism, classism, sexism, ageism, etc.), how we are all hurt when a nation scapegoats and disrespects any group of people, how we must build allies by supporting each other through reciprocal work. This focus will give NGLTF a solid place to stand as a liberatory civil rights organization with a varied agenda which focuses on the many facets of gay/lesbian/bi/transgender lives. And it will not have to try to serve lesbians and gay men on the Right.

To have such an organization does not preclude there being many other single-issue gay/lesbian/bi organizations, liberal or conservative. It simply clarifies the work of one of the national organizations and gives a framework for our expectations of it. It gives lesbians and gay men a clear choice. I hope NGLTF becomes an openly progressive organization that works to end violence against our community, to end the HIV/AIDS epidemic and all of the discrimination in its wake, to bring affordable and just healthcare to all our people, to win a civil rights amendment, to end the practice of racism and sexism in our organizations and communities, to end discrimination in the workplace and in the courts and in social services, to take a committed place in the effort to bring about justice and equality for everyone. And in doing so, I hope it takes the time to consider the complexity of every issue and, listening to many voices, applies complex, thoughtful answers to their solutions.

The leadership for such work requires the commitment of all of us who believe in multi-issue politics. It is time to do more than writing online. It is time to sign up for the long-term work of liberation.

16.

From Welfare Queens to Gay Marriage: the Path to Compulsory Heterosexual Marriage?

2006

A major icon of the Reagan era was the welfare queen, developed carefully in the media by conservative leaders to evoke taxpayer disgust and resentment.[1] This icon was female, Black, unmarried, drove a Cadillac, and had gangs of children whose very existence brought her great financial benefits from the government.

A major icon of the twenty-first century is the gay couple, developed carefully in the media by gay leaders to evoke sympathy and compassion. This couple is male/male or female/female, white, wants a wedding, drives a Subaru, and seeks benefits from the government. Both icons stand historically at the center of a swirling, culture-changing controversy about morals, values, money, and power.

The welfare queen arose from the 1980s, a decade dedicated to globalization, corporatization, the trickle-down theory of economics, union-busting, deregulation, anti-taxation, and privatization. It was a forceful and ongoing agenda to bring more wealth to the powerful and to destroy the social contract that was created following the Great Depression. The idea that we pay taxes because we live in community and must provide care for each other was replaced by the *myth of scarcity* and *meanspiritedness*: the idea that there is not enough to go around and someone is going to take "mine" from me.

---

1. Originally circulated in a 2006 issue of SisterSong's *Collective Voices* (Vol. 2. No. 5.).

The social contract was broken when human needs were successfully portrayed as racialized problems that people of color had somehow willfully created. The welfare queen was created by Reagan to represent the immorality, greed, and tax burden that are destroying our culture: a Black woman, under the authority of no man, who takes the money of good honest people who pay their taxes. The way to stop her and to save America was to eliminate those taxes and cut those benefits right out from under her.

The marriage-seeking gay couple arose from the culture wars of the past three decades in which sexuality outside of marriage was bad, family was narrowly defined as married couples with children, and allegiance to country was blended with belief in heterosexual, monogamous two-parent families. Good gay people increasingly became identified as those who passed and who sought ways to mainstream into a culture whose norm was white and middle-class. By the 1990s, not many LGBT organizations were taking on the broken social contract that was fracturing our society; instead, they were for the most part seeking equality in a vastly unequal world. It was then that the path of the welfare queen and the good gay couple began to merge. And the Right figured out how to combine racism and homophobia in its strategies to move both its economic and social agenda.

Their common road was displayed in 1992 in the two landmark ballot measures in Oregon and Colorado. These constitutional amendments called for prohibiting "minority status" and "quotas" for lesbians and gay men – that is, prohibiting something that no one in the LGBT community had ever called for. In their campaigns, they argued that "gay rights are special rights" and that only "deserving minorities" should receive civil rights, i.e., special rights. What they successfully accomplished in these campaigns was to redefine this country's understanding of civil rights to be special rights (as opposed to civil rights being constitutionally granted to all) and to make people think that one had to be deserving in order to receive them. And who became defined as not deserving? Why, of course, LGBT people, depicted by both the mass media and our own media as white, and Black people as "welfare queens."

These amendments, defeated in Oregon and passed in Colorado, prepared the groundwork for the Right to attack affirmative action as a special right and to send Black communities the message that white gay men and lesbians are challenging both their morality and their civil rights gains. These cultural, religious, and economic wars continue. The welfare reform act has virtually demolished welfare; no elected official dares to support increased taxation despite an enormous national debt, impoverished state governments, and diminishing human services; churches have become a major force in politics; and gay rights, abortion, and immigration remain the hot button issues of the media and elections. These conditions are the landscape for another shared path of the welfare queen and the gay couple. This time, there are two seemingly separate but connected agendas, and both promote marriage.

The right wing's "pro-marriage" agenda comes with $300 million from Bush for marriage promotion for those who receive welfare, initiating a distinction between good families (married) and single parents (welfare queen). For the last decade, the Right's web pages have been filled with concern about the breakdown of marriage, the need to keep gay marriage from weakening it further, and more importantly, with definitions of healthy families. They are set on a course to define narrowly what a legitimate family is and what support it can receive through church-based initiatives who deliver government benefits.

The path leads to compulsory marriage granted by the state, delivering the benefits of small social units held under the authority of men and easily identified and controlled. Such units fit in nicely with the massive identification and surveillance agenda of Homeland Security, whereas loosely woven, broadly defined families do not.

The "gay marriage" agenda seeks the full benefits of marriage at the moment when these benefits are disappearing through the loss of the social contract. The fight is for access to one's partner's insurance coverage at a time when insurance is dwindling, for access to one's partner's social security benefits at a time when social security is in complete jeopardy, for tax benefits when taxes are not the issue but services are. Framed as a civil right, this course seeks equality in a world that daily destroys economic justice and creates a fractured society. As does the Right's pro-marriage agenda, it calls for benefits, however few they might be, to be tied to legality and legitimacy, determined by the state. LGBT engagement in the battle for marriage as a single focus risks missing the larger issue that surrounds it: how family is defined and, through that definition, who is determined to be legitimate in this society, who has standing, privileges, benefits.

A narrow definition is based on state-determined legal status and includes who can adopt, who can provide foster care, who can retain custody, who can have in vitro fertilization, who is eligible for benefits – and ultimately, who has legitimacy as a full person in society. The Right's effort to restrict the definition of family far overshadows the agenda to enforce heterosexual marriage. Because the relentless constitutional amendment campaigns have opened every door for discussion of marriage, we now have a chance to use the marriage debate to move toward a larger goal.

We as LGBT people do not want to contribute to a more restrictive, authoritarian society, especially one that particularly targets African American single mothers. We can take this moment to move the debate from marriage to the definition of family and the social contract. What, then, are some ways the LGBT community can move in concert to achieve common goals in a time in which the focus by the Right and our own people is on marriage? We can seize the moment and use it to shape what we want. Because the television sits at the center of most homes, this discussion of marriage is going on everywhere.

There is no more silence or denial about the existence of LGBT people. Now is a rare moment of great opportunity to talk about every issue of importance to us. Those issues are many, but I would place family high among them. This is not an argument for saccharine images of couples and children or for nostalgic images of two adults and children in a small house with a picket fence. Instead, it is recognition that our strongest social formations are small and are found in the ways we are bound to one another by commitment, love, loyalty, responsibility, and sometimes, but not always, biology.

Worldwide, these formations are called family, tribe, clan – one's people. What we have called family in the U.S. has been fluid over time. Today, what we know as family (but is not necessarily legally recognized) includes many configurations: blended families of married couples and their children and relatives from other marriages; LGBT couples, with or without children; grandparents raising children; single parents and their children; unmarried people and their chosen families of committed friends; nuclear families; unmarried people living together; unmarried individuals and their children; old people living together for companionship and economics; married or single people with adopted or foster children; families who always have room for one more, whether blood related or not. What we have in common is that we all want recognition and respect for our relationships, the means to take care of each other, freedom from unjust authority, a legitimate place in our communities.

To achieve these goals, we will have to develop some strategies such as these:

- Use our skills, born of necessity, for creating chosen families (we are experts);

- Broaden the definition of family within state agencies;

- Gain legal recognition of a wide range of relationships;

- Separate benefits and privileges from marital status;

- Work to establish a strong social contract that guarantees universal healthcare, genuine disaster relief, affordable housing, etc.

- Build new cultural traditions for honoring relationships in ways that are not controlled by either the church or state;

- Join with others who face state opposition to their family composition and/or rights: immigrants, old people, single parents, former prisoners, battered women, and poor people. It makes sense that so many of us seek marriage because of our deep longing for public commitment or because of economic need.

While a marriage strategy meets some of our individual short-term goals, we have the opportunity now to build a movement strategy that includes everyone and gives us much more. As Kay Whitlock says,

> We can follow a strategy that permits us to build bold, new relationships across many constituencies struggling for the integrity, stability, and security of many kinds of families and households. Far from being a tactical retreat, this approach stakes out new ground that permits us to forge new approaches to shattering the power of homophobic and racist "wedge" politics. And it creates new terrain on which to engage countless faith communities that care passionately about economic justice. By its very nature, it deconstructs the lethal sense of 'us' and 'them' that has stalked the marriage wars.[2]

Our efforts for recognition of our lives and our right to be free and fully human are intimately connected with others who suffer injustice and who struggle for fairness and human dignity. Why not take this moment to go for what we want for all of us: a free and just society that is inclusive and provides broadly defined human rights based on equality and justice. Why not include it all in our vision: our individual and collective right to food, clothing, shelter, education, health, a clean environment, a living wage, safety, and relationships of our choice.

2. Whitlock, Katherine, and Kamel, Rachael. *In a Time of Broken Bones: A Call to Dialogue on Hate Violence and the Limitations of Hate Crimes Legislation*. United States, American Friends Service Committee, 2001.

17.

The Mercurial Face of Covert Racism

1988

As a white Southerner, I have no claim to being an expert on racism, but I have struggled with it, both within myself and within society.[1] The more I come to understand racism, the more all-encompassing it seems to me, and the more I see its connection with all the other oppressions. What do oppressions hold in common? Among other things, they hold in common the desire and ability of one group of people to exert power and control over the lives of those within a different group. Those who exert power and control define the limits of freedom, of wholeness, of possibility, and of hope for the other group.

Those who oppose oppressions support empowerment of individuals and groups of people. And what is empowerment? Empowerment is being able to speak one's own truth in one's own voice and having a part in making the decisions that affect one's life. That doesn't seem like asking too much, does it? And yet at the core of racism – and all the other "isms" – is the silencing of people and the systematic exclusion of people from decision-making in both social and economic arenas. Some examples:

- Congress recently passed legislation to create a Lower Mississippi Delta Commission to study conditions in a seven state area and prepare a ten year plan to improve economic conditions of the people who live there.
  Three of the most "progressive" young governors in the

---

1. Originally published in the December 1988 issue of *Transformation* (Vol. 3, No. 4), the Women's Project newsletter.

South govern the three main (and poorest) lower Mississippi Delta states – Arkansas, Louisiana and Mississippi – and they recently agreed in a much publicized meeting to work cooperatively to improve this region that has such fertile soil, such extreme poverty, such wonderful culture, such a large black population, and such limited educational and social service delivery systems. Who was appointed to serve on this new commission? Nine white men, three of whom are the young governors who appointed themselves. Not one Black person, not one woman. Black leaders from the Delta responded with outrage and despair. The response to their concern was one we've seen many times: these commissioners will set up an advisory group that will have Black people and women on it. That is to say, a group without power. An afterthought. An appeasement. When this idea was not met with overwhelming approval, Bill Clinton, the Governor of Arkansas, said the group would hire a Black executive director, if they *"could find a good one."*[2] And he went on to assure us, *"I'm sure we can."* When do we ever hear white people saying, "We'll hire a white man if we can find a qualified one."

- A local Arkansas foundation that has a commitment to educational change became interested in the diminishing numbers of Black teachers in public schools in the state. It organized a committee to examine the problem and make recommendations. Who was on that committee? Not one Black person.

- Two national organizations sponsored conferences to set national gay and lesbian agendas, one for gay and lesbian activism, one for work against homophobia. The organizing committee of the former was almost all white males. When confronted, the leaders said, *"We*

2. *Arkansas Democrat-Gazette.* December 10, 1988.

just turned our rolodexes out on the table to get a list, and these are who showed up." And guess who showed up at the conference? Primarily white people. The organizing committee for the latter was all white men. No people of color. No women. When confronted, their spokesperson said there was no ill intent. *"It was just your garden-variety racism. We called on who we knew."*

In each of these cases, the people in power – those making the decisions, naming the agendas – no doubt would say that their intentions were good, that they were trying to do what was best for people. That is the nature of *covert racism*. With *overt racism*, the intent is openly to hurt, to limit, to cause harm, but with covert racism, the intention is positively stated but the result is harmful. Needless to say, the latter is much harder to deal with because of its mercurial nature: just when we think we have identified and pinned it down, it slips out of our fingers. We name the injustice, and the perpetrator says, "Oh, no. That's not what was happening. I was doing this other thing. I was trying to help you." That is, what's wrong with you? Why are you always reading discrimination or injustice into everything?

This covert racism exists everywhere, even in social change organizations. So many of them work with communities of color, and yet the boards and staffs – where decisions are made – are made up of white people with a few (if any) "representative" people of color. So very often this configuration exists in direct service organizations such as battered women's shelters where many of the residents may be women of color and yet the vast majority of the staff and board will be white. As we know, those who make the decisions hold the power. Yet, among white people there is so often the lament that people of color just will not participate in the organization's events, no matter how much outreach they do. Is anyone surprised?

The invitation is to come take part in an event or a service where one has no voice, no power in decision-making, no place except as what so often seems an afterthought.

We get confused sometimes in our social change organizations: we begin to think that empowerment is naming someone else's power for her/him. Empowerment recognizes that every person's voice is important, that no one can speak for another as that person can for her/himself. No matter how much power and privilege we possess, no matter how good our intentions are, we do not know what is best for another person or another group of people.

Empowerment implies, demands equality. We have little hope for eliminating racism until we confront issues of equality.

18.

Do we want to play Faust with the government – OR – How do we get our social change work funded and not sell our souls?

1987

During the past two years, I have been front row witness to an organization and a movement struggling with the issue of government funding.[1] Now, I want to share some of the things we learned from that struggle in the hope that they will be helpful to the HIV/AIDS movement and other organizations that are facing decisions about government funding. If we can learn from one another, perhaps we will not be condemned to stumbling into the same pitfalls that impair our social change work.

First, some background. The part of the women's health movement I want to talk about is the battered women's movement. In that movement, since the mid-1970s we have dealt with women's mental and physical health issues. Our first concern has been to provide safety from physical and mental battering by establishing shelters, safe houses, hot lines, and information, referrals and support groups around the nation so that women can escape from those who want to destroy their lives. We have been successful in providing services that support the empowerment of women. We have saved women's lives.

Our second and equally great concern has been to create a movement that works to end violence against women and children. In this work we have developed an analysis of battering that is

1. Keynote address at the March 1987 National Gay and Lesbian Healthcare Conference held at the Los Angeles Gay and Lesbian Community Center.

about sexism and men's socially condoned right to power and control over women, which includes violence. In our movement building, we have recognized that violence affects all women, we have made connections among all the oppressions women experience (sexism, classism, racism, homophobia, anti-Semitism, ageism, ableism, etc.), and we have worked to include all women, no matter how unacceptable to mainstream society, in this movement that seeks the radical change of ending violence against all women.

Beginning in the early 1980s, there has been an increased institutionalization and professionalization of the movement, with fewer battered women in leadership and more social workers and therapists. Or, to put it another way, there has been a division between those who see themselves not as part of a movement but as simply providing services and perhaps reforming some institutions so that battered women get better treatment – and those who see themselves as both providing services which are inclusive and empowering women of color, lesbians, older women, differently abled women, and sex workers, while doing the risky work that goes to the very root of violence in our lives.

With this stage set for what could be creative tension and positive struggle, what happens next? The government enters from – where else? – stage Right. After years of struggling to get the criminal justice system even to take seriously the needs of battered women – that is, without making jokes – we are suddenly faced with funding coming to us through the criminal justice system.

I'm a Southerner, so of course I have to tell you a story. Here's how our episode with the government began. Lois Haight Harrington, Assistant Attorney General to U.S. Attorney General Ed Meese, developed a keen interest in domestic violence and in 1983-84 initiated the Attorney General's Task Force hearings around the country. The leadership of the National Coalition Against Domestic Violence (NCADV) worked closely with Harrington to organize these meetings and to ensure that battered women and battered women's movement workers as well as criminal justice people were heard. What emerged from those meetings was recognition of our movement's strength and leadership and a published Attorney General's Task Force Report on Domestic Violence. NCADV recognized that the report had gaps and often didn't go far enough, but we found it a helpful document to use in our work with local criminal justice people. It lent authority to the issue. Little did we know that the Attorney General's office would now consider themselves the ultimate authority – or worse, the owners of – all U.S. domestic violence work. But more about that later.

The Department of Justice (DOJ) began discussing the possibility of providing NCADV a small grant (around $50,000) to do a think tank or symposium in which we would bring domestic violence workers and criminal justice workers together. However, soon the offer from the DOJ was for us to apply for a large grant for over a half million dollars to do a national public education, training, and information and referral project. At that time I was co-chair of NCADV's lesbian task force, and I opposed the grant on the grounds that the DOJ was not a friend of women of color and lesbians and that they would control and subvert our work. However, NCADV had very little funding and a deep commitment to work for battered women, so the organization decided to take the risk and go ahead with the grant.

When the time came for the grant to be announced, it was delayed, and there was a media blitz from the rightwing, particularly the Heritage Foundation, arguing that NCADV should not receive the grant because we were a "feminist, pro-lesbian, anti-family organization." Well, they were right on the first two counts, because we have always been openly committed to feminism and to the inclusion of lesbians in the movement. And no doubt our views on the family differed from those of the rightwing. The lesbian baiting became a central issue. Our membership responded by getting members of the House and Senate to support the grant. It seemed almost an issue of pride at this point.

The DOJ then decided to go ahead with the project but changed it from a grant to a cooperative agreement under which they would monitor all our work, approve our hirings, and review all publications. They assured the Heritage Foundation that the work would not be pro-lesbian and against the policies of the

Reagan Administration. At this time, I vehemently opposed the acceptance of the grant, and the Lesbian Task Force requested that, since we were between meetings, our steering committee (representing 50 states) should be polled because the decision was so controversial. We saw no way the work of the grant could be done without sacrificing the safety of lesbians and without distorting the meaning of our work.

Our executive committee signed the grant, and we went into our September steering committee meeting in a state of chaos, with some people feeling they had had little or no information, others feeling that the process had been incorrect, some in agreement with the decision, and some feeling betrayed. We spent three consecutive 14-hour days trying to come to consensus on whether or not we would affirm the acceptance of the two-year cooperative agreement. The meeting was conflictual and highly emotional. Finally, we developed bottom lines for accepting the grant, listing out our policies and beliefs we would not compromise, and then moved to a painful consensus to accept the agreement.

At that time I was elected first vice chair, which placed me, as the person who had been most vocal in opposing the grant, in charge of overseeing it. I suppose you could say I entered from stage *left*.

During the year we worked with the DOJ, there were three benchmarks that signaled serious trouble for our relationship. The DOJ's first rejection was of a project director because she had been a member of the National Organization for Women (NOW) and had visited Nicaragua as part of a women of color group. The second was when we submitted plans for our first regional training: we thought we had an agreement with Lois Harrington (though we failed to get it in writing – a crucial error) that we could discuss racism and homophobia and their connection to violence against women. We were told we could mention them, but we could not discuss them. The third was when we submitted our first general brochure on domestic violence for approval. As well as objections to our analysis of battering, we were told that we could not talk about racism, sexism, etc., as connected to battering nor could we mention that lesbians were battered. Throughout our negotiations with the DOJ we were told that if something didn't appear in the Attorney General's Task Force Report, then it didn't exist. It had become final authority.

At our May steering committee meeting, after seven month's struggle, we decided not to go for a second year of funding (approximately $260,000) because we saw that the question was this: who is going to define who we are, what our work is, what our analysis is, and even what the issue is? After over a decade of developing an analysis of battering that indicates that it is about power and control, and after working for the empowerment and self-determination of women, we were now in a position to experience these same power and control issues at the hands of the DOJ with subsequent effect on our sense of empowerment and self-determination. We decided to stand by our politics: if a funder would not let us be who we defined ourselves as being and would not let us be openly committed to all women, then we would return to low-level funding and seek money elsewhere. We took the dangerous stand for integrity, knowing that there would be controversy.

We decided at that meeting to renegotiate the remaining months of the grant to find work that we and the DOJ could agree upon. We entered our national conference in July having negotiated a very difficult agreement, and found part of our membership in an uproar, fed by a letter sent by Lois Harrington to the membership asking us to reconsider our decision. In it, she not only made an argument for re-defining domestic violence in the DOJ's terms but named the past leadership that signed the grant as some of "the finest women" she's known and did a strong divide-and-conquer technique by lesbian-baiting the current leadership. Harrington wrote, "Some of your new leadership appear to have a hidden and very different agenda in an effort to gain acceptance of the choices of a very few women, they are willing to risk harm to all women. In effect, they have seized this issue of import to all women and limited the gravity of its impact by elevating the concerns of a small minority."

It was after the conference that we learned that the group of women she had named as "the finest" had organized a new national domestic violence group to accept the second year funding from the DOJ. At the end of NCADV's experience with the DOJ, we were left with a year of struggle in which our work was stopped, our movement was divided, and our leaders trashed. We are still reeling from our wounds.

So what have we learned from this experience that we can share with those of you who now face government funding for AIDS organizations? My strongest urge is to say, *DO ANYTHING – BEG, BORROW, STEAL – BUT DON'T TAKE GOVERNMENT FUNDING.* But I will resist and say, before you consider accepting government funding, you might consider these things:

- Be sure your organization/membership is strong in every aspect and is clear about who it is and what its work is. Develop clearly understood written policies and procedures.

- Hold organizational discussions about what is the best approach to service delivery, social change, etc. Discuss who controls and defines your work and how willing you are to give up that control. Seek unity.

- Have a clear, democratic decision-making process.

- Be open in all communication within the organization/ membership. Discuss beforehand the possibility that you may be played off against one another.

- Do trouble shooting and problem solving beforehand. Talk about the risk of cooptation and what you will do when faced with it.

- Have operational bottom lines solidly in place before accepting the money. Be clear with everyone involved that you will not be moved to compromise them. Be clear about organizational commitment and accountability to bottom lines.

- Negotiate hard for what you are willing to do for the funding. Get everything in writing. If necessary, carry a tape recorder.

- Don't accept government funding that is larger than your core operational budget. That is, don't risk your survival on government funding.

- Do not expect the government to support you in genuine social change work. Homophobic and racist to its core, the government does not find it in its interest to support the kind of change that would make it a fair government of the people, for all people.

These things I've listed may be helpful in protecting your organization but I would not trust that they would be enough. You must remember that you are dealing with one of the most repressive administrations in U.S. history, and our AIDS work must be seen in the context of all that they do, both nationally and internationally. Consider their actions toward voting rights, abortion, the poor, Grenada, Nicaragua, equal rights for women, affirmative action, and social security. You have to see it in a context larger than just your AIDS funding. The issue here is power and control – the unbridled power and control that suppresses all who are different. It is a gigantic force at work, one that manipulates people, events and the media to do its bidding.

I want to say in closing that if we, as lesbians and gay men, are to survive in the world, our work always has to be about more than service delivery; it has to be about the social change that transforms the world into a place where every one of us – no matter what age or gender or race or sexual identity – can live in freedom and equality. When we work, we are working for our lives.

19.

Funding Our Radical Work

2004

From "The Revolution Will Not be Funded" conference

In the early 1990s, I developed a growing concern about the funding of social change organizations. At that time I had worked for a dozen or more years at the Women's Project in Arkansas and in the battered women's movement locally and nationally.[1] My connections to social change organizations were extensive, and I had had many opportunities to observe their struggles with funding. Here are some observations that raised my concerns:

- It was a constant struggle for the Women's Project to maintain a left analysis that engaged the community in systemic change – and to receive funding that did not attempt to modify our work;

- The battered women's movement had moved from local, grassroots organizing to "professional" service delivery funded by government entities;

- Staff of nonprofit organizations were spending an extraordinary amount of time on fundraising and a rapidly decreasing amount of time on organizing;

- There was a dreadful competition among groups for fundraising and less cooperation in working together;

- There was a loss of political force and commitment to

1. Speech given at the 2004 INCITE! Women of Color Against Violence conference. The conference theme that year was "The Revolution Will Not Be Funded."

movement building;

- Very few organizations seemed to have an active membership base committed to organizing for change.

During this time, many people talked about the disorganization and weakness of the progressive movement. I came to understand this problem to be not the result of a failure in vision and courage but of the impact of prolonged attacks under McCarthyism and COINTELPRO (Counter Intelligence Program) – and of the effect of becoming a nonprofit "sector" controlled by the state.

As with all politics, these issues are complex. As part of this panel of speakers for The Revolution Will Not Be Funded, we cannot give a very nuanced analysis here, but we can lay the groundwork for a more detailed discussion. While I do not want to disparage the significant work that has been done by nonprofits (of which I have been a part) nor the work of those who have tried to reform philanthropy, I'd like for us to consider what we might do to fund a radical movement in a time of rapacious capitalism.

As an example of the impact of the 501(c)(3) (tax-exempt status) on our work, a brief history of the battered women's movement perhaps is helpful. This movement arose in the 1970s in the space created by the Women's Movement. Women in cities and small towns across the country came together to describe our experiences with male violence. Through those discussions we learned that there were great commonalities in the experiences and we were not alone nor unique in what we had suffered. Groups of women in large and small communities analyzed these common themes and then determined actions to provide safety and to end violence against women. We knew that we had to radically change the power relationships between women and men.

These beginnings were community-based and constituency-led – by women who had experienced violence. As programs were developed, women sought tax-exempt status for battered women's shelters and credibility in communities for financial support. The latter demanded hours of public education, often in hostile environments such as men's clubs and law enforcement agencies. When the goals of tax-exempt status and community credibility were achieved (albeit with considerable sacrifice such as being lesbian-baited, facing woman-hating jokes, and accusations of being home-wreckers), the funders from all sources – individual, foundations, and government – began making demands for certain policies and practices.

It was in this environment that what we call "the professionalization of the movement" began. We began seeing new standards set for the highest level jobs, i.e., a social work degree and a different, more business-like approach to working with battered women. Rather than a popular education approach – sharing stories of abuse, developing analysis, and taking action – where any skilled facilitator could be a leader, therapeutic groups and individual sessions were offered. Battered women's organizations began to reflect corporations in their structure and policies. Domestic violence was redefined as an individual mental health issue requiring therapists rather than a social justice issue that required organizing. Though some organizing continued, most organizations moved to service delivery, accompanied by advocacy. Some of us think that the last big act of autonomy and defiance by the first wave of the battered women's movement was NCADV's rejection of a $600,000 grant because the Department of Justice would not permit reference to lesbian battering, an analysis of racism, or promotion of organizing.

Though it is difficult to date particular changes, it seems that it was at this time that the movement split between those who thought we must work equally hard to combine service delivery with efforts to end violence against women – and those who thought that it was most critical to partner with government agencies and make necessary compromises to receive funding for service delivery and advocacy. Through the Violence Against Women Act, funding and partnerships became real, and battered women's organizations engaged in cooperative work with the Department of Justice, with funding available to maintain organizations in ways we had never experienced before.

Have the past twenty-five years of work to end violence against women been a failure because it has moved from a central focus of social change to one of social service? No. Many things have been accomplished: extraordinary public education, new laws and public policies, thousands of lives saved. However, the work was modified in ways that allowed some challenge to systems and to power – but only so much – in order to maintain funding stability. And there has been no indication that violence against women has diminished. The culture of violence remains to be changed. And this is a social justice issue, where the question is called, "How do we get to the cause of violence and change it so that women can be autonomous, self-determined, and safe?"

We also have to ask ourselves how much we have given up by being in the funder-controlled box. As the government was moving toward the right during the Reagan years, we were seeking relationships with government. They were writing the rules and we were doing our best to shape the work within those rules and to defend the achievements we had made. As Reagan was destroying the tax base and eliminating human services, we were concentrating on service delivery. As every social issue was being racialized by the Right, we were both taking on anti-racist education and excluding women of color from our professionalized, corporate-style leadership. As young feminists found fewer and fewer places to express their politics they came to battered women's programs and found that the new systems gave little space for shared power or advancement up the leadership hierarchy. At what cost did we get government funding and community acceptability?

It was this experience in this many-faceted battered women's movement (that I loved) that led me to dwell on the effect of chasing money through our non-profit status. I observed the impact of funding conditions bringing changes to the progressive nonprofit world in general:

- An increase of charity and volunteerism to replace the government's role in meeting human needs;

- An increase of service delivery, using low-paid workers (majority women);

- A decrease in organizing to confront and change power relationships;

- An increase in financial dependence on foundations and government funding for nonprofits;

- A decrease of membership organizations;

- An increase of professionalism;

- A decrease of constituency leadership;

- Organizations modeled on corporations, with executive directors (even when there's only three staff), CEOs, etc., and a focus on outcomes and deliverables;

- Nonprofits competing with one another for funding, limiting our partnerships and collective work for change;

- One to three year funding cycles leading us to short-term efforts instead of long- term vision and strategies;

- Reform efforts instead of radical work;

- Less public dissent;

- The creation of a non-profit sector which, by offering just enough services and advocacy to keep people mollified, makes the world safe for capitalism.

All of these, I believe, are linked at least in part to the 501(c)(3) and our pursuit of tax-exempt funding sources.

First, let me say that I believe the government should fund services. That's one of the reasons we pay taxes: to enable the human needs of all of us to be met. The questions for us at this conference are whether government-funded organizations and programs, in a time of rightwing control, will allow us to act in just and humane ways, will they support oppressed people to gain power, and will they initiate a revolution against the hand that feeds them? Do we need services? Yes, of course, and we need good liberals to make sure they are delivered justly to everyone. Will the provision of social services alone bring about true social justice? I think not.

Second, we cannot expect the government or foundations to fund our most radical work. The government or corporate entities will not fund us to change them at their core or to take them down. It is our work to bring about radical social change through demanding justice and fairness. It is our job to figure out how to support this work.

When I think of radical or revolutionary groups, I think of the American Indian Movement, the Black Panthers, the Zapatistas, the early U.S. labor movement, etc. Somehow I cannot imagine these groups going on a foundation visit or writing a large government grant. And yet their work has had a tremendous impact on the world we know today.

What do these groups have in common? They are radical groups that are built around either a membership or a group of people who closely represent people who have suffered injustice. They provide a place and way for people to express their passion, and they have constituency-based leadership. Their financial support comes from people who believe in them, and at the core of their work is organizing.

I think there are lessons to be learned from radical groups around the world: the African National Congress, the Landless People's Movement of Brazil, AIDS Coalition to Unleash Power (ACT UP), and our own INCITE! Women of Color Against Violence and Critical Resistance. We can learn, for instance, from the Black Panthers about adding service delivery to organizing – or in the case of many of our own organizations, adding organizing to service delivery. We can learn from the Zapatistas about how we must start small and local and build democratic units where people have genuine voice. And we can bring to INCITE! our question about how we do the work, how it draws people by its heat, how it appeals to the whole self, how it is imbedded as a way of life. For our radical work to be true to people's needs and the courageous actions they demand, it will have to draw funding from individuals who believe in it wholeheartedly. It will require no less a commitment than that which millions of people make every Sunday when they enter a place of worship and drop a check or a $5 bill in the collection plate. How will this commitment come about? Our victories will come through authentically connected membership and organizing. Collectively, we have to build a sense of possibility, grow muscles and courage and joy in the work, and stay strong together in the vision and practice of a transformed world.

20.

Reflections on Individual Change vs. Systems Change

1991

For most of 1991, I worked with a group of five people to plan a meeting of 30 women activists at Blue Mountain Center to discuss the escalation of violence against women and what could be done about it.[1] At one of the planning meetings for this gathering, we were in the midst of a discussion about what we hoped to achieve by having the group look at an integrated analysis incorporating sex, race, and class, when I suddenly balked like a Southern mule facing an unplowed field. Warnings went up in my head, I began digging my feet in, and it took a few minutes for me to be able to name my fears. It was the idea of discussing class that was stopping me cold in my tracks. As a result of that discussion, my co-planners asked me to write about my concerns.

One of my jobs at the Women's Project is that of lead organizer on the social justice project, which provides community education on issues of oppression and strategies for making social change. The project works to make connections among the oppressions and to avoid single-issue approaches. Consequently, workshops, whether on racism, sexism, or homophobia, begin with an economic analysis followed by discussion of the connections among the oppressions before addressing a single oppression.

One of the ways I learn about what is happening in the social change movement is by listening carefully to what people ask for

1. Originally published in the May/June 1991 issue of *Transformation* (Vol. 7, No. 3), the Women's Project newsletter.

when they call to request these workshops. For instance, fairly often organizations call requesting workshops on class, and when I explain that we offer an analysis of capitalism and economic injustice, they almost always say that they are looking for something different, a workshop on classism that addresses class differences and how people of different classes can understand one another better. Always I say that we don't know how to do that workshop – that perhaps they should contact someone who does work on human relations. Why, I always wonder, do people not want to talk about economic injustice and the systems that produce it?

And then in the workshops – after we have spent an hour or more discussing how capitalism requires for its existence a large supply of low-paid and unpaid labor and a lopsided distribution of resources, how women and people of color provide that labor and do not control the resources, and how therefore sexism and racism are essential to the maintenance of capitalism – invariably a hand goes up in the audience and someone asks, "But what about class? How does classism figure in?" I simply scratch my head and wonder just what it was we had been talking about. It seems in every instance that people are concerned about dismantling attitudes rather than dismantling a system of oppression.

And then I remember this country's carefully orchestrated repression of any discussion of the U.S. economic system. I am flooded with memories of the life-destroying red-baiting of the 1950s, the assassinations of leaders who put forth an economic analysis as part of their dream of justice, and more recently, the virulent pro-capitalism program of Reagan/Bush, which is sometimes mistakenly called pro-democracy when it extends beyond the borders of the U.S. to Eastern Europe, the Persian Gulf, or Central America. Is it any wonder that people are afraid to discuss anything beyond class relations on the individual level?

And then I think about the systematic suppression of social change movements through the infiltration of the FBI, through the criminal justice system's attacks on our leaders, through the undermining of unions, through persecution of social change organizations by the IRS, through control of our financial resources, through legal requirements that make us jump through hoops, and through media distortions that destroy popular support. Is it any surprise that by the 1980s people were ready to accept Reagan's emphasis on the individual rather than the collective and the personal rather than the group solution?

In this climate, people began to search for ways to improve individuals so that the country would subsequently improve. On the popular level, the market was flooded with self-help books, money-making programs for exercise, diet, and spiritual improvement mushroomed, entrepreneurism became the ideal in business, and the media focused on human interest stories of people who individually succeeded or who were "making a difference."

On the government level, entitlement programs, grants for services, educational support programs, etc., were cut back or eliminated, states and individuals were asked to pick up the slack in meeting human needs. The country's infrastructure began to deteriorate rapidly while the military grew in equipment and cost, and individuals, after the deregulation of almost everything, made obscene amounts of money, often through scams such as those of Housing and Urban Development (HUD) and Savings and Loans. White-collar crime hit an all-time high, and taxpayers – already burdened with the responsibility of providing individual charity to meet community needs – were left with enormous public debts to pay off on behalf of business and government's unchecked greed and unpunished white-collar criminals.

There are many telling examples of how the Reagan/Bush years moved us from the development of a responsible social policy to individual responsibility for major societal problems. For instance, in the 1970s, federal housing subsidies to poor families reached 800,000 families; by 1990, this number had shrunk to less than 30,000 families nationwide. These cutbacks struck every area of human need. Another example is that during the same period, Belleview Hospital in New York had funds for 10,500 people; now, in 1991, it is funded for 1,500. And where did those poor families and those psychologically challenged people go? To the streets to become the homeless of the 1980s and 1990s. They were left to beg on the streets from individuals.

To make up for the shortfall in money to address human needs, nonprofit organizations proliferated, trying to provide human services without the millions of dollars once provided by the government. In order to gain nonprofit, tax-exempt status, it is necessary to gain a government issued 501(c)(3) designation which requires governmental approval of the nature of the work. Given a conservative government, this work will, of course, be required to be conservative in nature. And then, when social change work came to be thought of as synonymous with nonprofit work, we began to be in trouble in the area of radical social change, for how can one dismantle an oppressive system while taking money from that system and abiding by its rules? Of course, very little government money goes to nonprofits. The majority comes from individuals and a small amount from private foundations. Of this total, over 80% goes to churches and universities which commonly do not do the work of social change.

What were once considered social change movements became more conservative in the face of cutbacks and the national push for individual solutions. We responded in the battered women's movement, for instance, with an emphasis on empowerment of battered women and a reluctance to involve battered women in strategies for systems change. (Did we ever really think that one person could empower another? Or did we think that the best we could do was to support others taking power through making sure all the doors were open?) For many, even empowerment took a back row seat to the delivery of services. And then came the move from community or group solutions to individual solutions. In many cases, the work stopped there. It was in the mid-80s that the call began for workshops on classism in terms of class relations rather than economic injustice, on "unlearning" racism or homophobia rather than anti-racism or "dismantling" racism, homophobia or sexism workshops.

It is my understanding that the "unlearning" approach assumes that since we were not born oppressors and therefore had to learn the oppression, then if we can go back to the roots of it in our lives, we can unlearn it, free ourselves from it. That seems to me to be a valid point of view, but one that does not go far enough if it stops with just individual improvement, because what remains are these ever-so-powerful systems and institutions that control our lives. And these must be changed as well. Now, you might say there's a chicken or the egg argument here. Which comes first? Don't individuals make up institutions and if we don't change, then the institutions don't change? One could argue on the other hand that institutions are now so solidly in place and so powerful that it is almost impossible for individuals – unless they are acting collectively – to change them. I say that the chicken and the egg now coexist in the same nest, and solutions have to embrace both arguments.

For instance, if eliminating class, race, gender, or sexual identity injustices were simply a matter of human relations – figuring out how to have "diversity" and get along with each other – then we would have these oppressions licked by now (like those groups that have someone come in to do a "diversity" workshop, then feel they have done the right thing, and their organizational conscience is salved). A couple of times each year, we would simply line everyone up (all nicely mixed, of course), hold hands across America, and sing some sweet song such as "We Are the World." Then we would hug each other, wipe our eyes, and get back to the workplace and our daily lives. Behavioral change is not necessarily synonymous with institutional change.

But what would we find back at the workplace and in our daily lives? Institutional systems that keep us locked into place. And these systems seem so overwhelming, so enormous, that they send us searching for individual solutions because at least there, on the individual level, we feel like we have some control. But the systems remain, and their enormity requires collective, community strategies for change.

Discussions of economic injustice, racism, sexism, and homophobia have to be conducted in the context of these systems. We need some basic skills before we take on these systems, so that they don't seem so enormous and unapproachable to us.

For example: We are living in a time of backlash that is orchestrated to condemn those of us who speak up for our right to live without oppression. In a targeted shift of blame, we get called the "politically correct" or the "thought police," and we are led to think, once again, that racism and sexism are simply individual points of view which everyone, under the First Amendment, has a right to voice. Implicit in this approach is that institutions are neutral places where everyone has a fair chance, and the institution's role is to provide "equal rights for everyone," as though a reality of our lives is that women have the same rights as men and people of color have the same rights as white people. Hence, it helps to assess institutions for their systemic oppression content. That is, in plain language: is this organization or business racist, sexist, or homophobic? Here's a handy-dandy three-minute assessment tool that can be used to check out any organization (including those we have created):

Check for visual integration, the "diversity" or "cosmetic" test: if you hold up a picture of all the people working for the organization/business, are there enough (and what is enough, anyway?) women, people of color, people with disabilities, openly lesbians and gay men, etc.? If it is all-white or all-male, or these people are grossly in the majority, stop right there. You don't have to go any further with the test. You know the results. Once you have the numbers, check to see what positions they are in. For instance, are most of the women and people of color in "support" positions, are they primarily on the low end of the pay scale? Are they in community relations, marketing departments, or in the non-profit sector, in outreach positions? What you are looking for is who is in decision-making positions because you want to know the answer to these key questions about the sharing of power that get at the heart of racism and sexism:

- Who sets the agenda, the goals, the plan, etc.? Is it the people whose lives are affected? All the workers, the constituency, etc.? A few people?

- Who controls the distribution of resources (financial

and otherwise) and how they are shared?

- Who controls the information – and access to educational opportunities?

Example: If you hold up a picture of the medical profession, you see that the "diversity" is good: over 80% are women and people of color. However, when you move to step two, you find that only 10% of administrators and doctors are women and people of color. End of test. We know the answer as to whether racism and sexism are present.

Example: By the year 2000, some 80% of the workforce is expected to be women and people of color. Corporations are currently scurrying to hire "diversity managers," and I believe that title is apt, for they are looking for people to manage this diversity so that the 20% of white men can still remain in control. The future poses a real problem to them. With these kinds of numbers, how will they be able to continue tokenizing women and people of color and placing only the most assimilated, pro-establishment people in decision-making positions? With this test, we don't have to spend precious hours arguing about whether a certain individual in the institution is sexist or racist. We can go to the heart of the institution and the heart of oppression and determine who exerts power and control over whom – or who has found just ways to share power, information, and resources.

Let me be direct here and say that I think we must apply this test *first* to the institutions we have created and work in, for we are responsible for them, and if they cannot be changed, what hope is there for change in the larger society? Our institutions must reflect the world we are trying to create or else our words and actions lack integrity. The first question for that internal examination is this: does the organizational structure of my institution look like a pyramid with a few people at the top making the most money, having the most decision-making power, and controlling the agenda and resources? Are people of color and women mostly on the bottom half of the pyramid, experiencing a glass ceiling as they move up the pyramid? If the answer to these questions is *yes*, then we have some very hard work to do at home before we can have the integrity to go forth in the community to organize for social change.

Clearly, in my politics I lean strongly toward *systems change*, toward *group solutions* rather than *individual solutions*. However, I also believe that institutions cannot be changed until the hearts and minds of people are changed as well. The question to be resolved is how to do both *simultaneously*.

For instance, I know I get frightened by the individual approach because of some of the inherent problems in it. Blaming the victim, for instance. "If Clarence Thomas can come from poverty and make something of himself, then anyone else who wants to can as well." Oh, yeah? Where is the abundance of opportunities? Or another blame that does so much damage: the attack on single, low-income mothers for subverting "traditional family values." How can one maintain family strength when all societal, institutional support for the family has been eliminated? And then there's the sentimental side of the individual approach: "fortunate" people staffing soup kitchens and distributing toys for tots at holiday time or rallying to provide funds for an enormously expensive operation for one attractive young person – when no one is talking about what must be changed so that *all people* have food *all the time*, and so that the medical system provides life-saving operations for *everyone*, attractive or not, young or old.

Once again, I'll say that I think we have to have both approaches – the individual and the systemic – but for me, I think the great danger lies in doing either outside the context of comprehensive societal change. I think of my dad and his ideas of individual goodness. During the 1950s, I often heard him say, "I'd never do anything to harm any 'colored' person I know." And I believe that was true: he never was anything but generous and good to the African Americans he knew personally, but he fought the changes of the Civil Rights Movement, feeling that it was an infringement upon his personal and his people's rights. And then I think of the systems change that came from the Civil Rights Movement – new laws for inclusion, voting, affirmative action – and how Black children were integrated into schools where white teachers, unchanged, treated them as lesser beings, and how because the hearts and minds of people were not fully changed along with those laws, they are now being dismantled and racism is on the increase.

Somehow, we must find ways to have both approaches, where we are not seduced into stopping at individual solutions and we are not overwhelmed at the idea of joining together to take on major systemic change. I remember with great appreciation the way that I and thousands of other women came to their political awareness in the 1960s and 1970s, and I still believe these three simple steps can work today:

1. **Gather together out of our isolation to talk about our personal experiences – that is, tell our stories.** This personal storytelling is at the heart of liberation education. At this initial step, we have to be sure to look around the table and see if all the voices are there to be heard – are we playing the role of the oppressor by excluding people who are not like us?

2. **Together, analyze those stories, and from them, recognize our common, systemic oppression. Recognize our connectedness.** (This step is currently tough for some people because our educational system does not encourage critical thinking, does not teach it, nor does the massive onslaught of the electronic media which attempts to numb us into a homogenous, monolithic glob – oh, what fertile ground for the seeds of fascism).

3. **Collectively, take action, speak out, work together to bring about change in the systems that oppress us.** (The group work gives a supportive context for individual voice and action. Without it, individuals become minimized, isolated, treated as outsiders and oddities).

These same steps can be followed by our own institutions for bringing about internal change. The central question is how to bring all of the people of the organization to the table to present their experiences, to analyze them together, and then collectively figure out the best way to get the work of the institution done in a way that is just and liberating for all involved.

And finally, we must come together to create a social change movement that has vision. When people discuss the left these days, they usually say it has three problems: it is fractured, it lacks leadership, and it lacks vision. And the Right is seen as having vision. I believe this analysis is accurate, for the most part. Certainly, the Right has a strong, unified vision: it wants to maintain a world that is dominated by one race, one gender, one sexual identity, and one religion. It has no problem finding models for its vision. It has a strategy: to link rightwing Christians with the organized Far Right in an approach that includes the racial politics of electoral initiatives (Bush, Duke, and anti-abortion, anti-gay initiatives, anti-affirmative action, etc.), the gender politics of the anti-abortion movement (Operation Rescue), and the intermingling of the anti-Semitic and racist preachings of the Christian Identity churches with the terrorism of neo-Nazis who appear in one form as skinheads and in another form as the suit-and-tied public speakers such as Thom Robb and David Duke.

The left, on the other hand, has few models for the world it wants to create. We seek a world where there are shared resources and opportunities and justice for all, a world where race, religion, sex, and sexual identity truly are not barriers. Our work is immensely harder than that of the Right with its backward vision. At the present time, we are fractured because we keep tripping over our own -isms. In the search for racial justice and equality, we trip over sexism and homophobia and anti-Semitism. Or, in our effort to eliminate sexism, we find ourselves right up against issues of racism and homophobia and economic injustice. The vision of inclusiveness and equality takes extraordinarily hard work to achieve. However, we are at a critical time in history when it is clear to almost everyone that we must decide what kind of society we want to live in. Our work is to figure out the knotty problem of how to have a participatory democracy that brings all of us to the decision-making table while allowing genuine, representative leadership to develop. We must figure out how people gain self-determination and control of their communities and also join together in linkages that create a larger society where we recognize our collective responsibility. Our work of social change is to figure out how to change the hearts and minds of people: to address their fears but also their hopes and dreams, their best selves. Then our work is to bring all of us together to create the institutions that will sustain quality of life for all of us, leaving out no one, on this very small planet we share together.

21.

The Next Step: Moving from Personal Growth to Building A Movement

1990

This week a reporter from the *Arkansas Democrat-Gazette* interviewed me for an article she was writing on the consciousness-raising groups of the early 1970s.[1] Our conversation helped me to recall what a life-changing experience my consciousness-raising group was for me, and then to analyze some of the things that happened to change and destroy these groups. They were the backbone of the wildly exciting activism that built the women's movement, but by the 1980s almost all consciousness-raising groups had disappeared, along with much of the political activism, and in their place was a concentration on self-growth through personal therapy and support groups that focused on single issues of victimization or addiction. It seems to me that these changes were not accidental.

First, the successes of consciousness-raising groups. These small groups of 8-12 women demonstrated the equality we sought in their very structures: they were grassroots and could be organized by anyone at any level of education or sophistication; they required no formal leader; the simple rules were empowering – safety, confidentiality, equal time and respectful attention for each speaker – and their form and content were controlled by the participants. These groups initiated the basic organizing that changed the world for women:

---

1. Originally published in the March 1990 issue of *Transformation* (Vol. 5, No. 2), the Women's Project newsletter.

- Bringing women out of isolation and breaking silence

- Telling our stories in a safe, respectful place

- Recognizing and analyzing the common experience, the universality of women's oppression that came out of our stories

- Giving a name and a face to the oppression we faced and working together to take action against it.

At each meeting a single topic was discussed: our experience of going through puberty; love relationships; sexual abuse; our economic histories, etc. For me, the group I attended for three years beginning in 1970 is at the very heart of my journey toward liberation and my work as an activist because it was there for the first time, at age 30, that I ever felt safe enough to tell anyone that I was a lesbian. I felt at that moment as though I were Atlas and the weight of the world had been taken from my shoulders, that for the first time I was able to stand upright and contemplate liberation for myself and others. What I learned in that group made me know that the world must be changed and that we were the ones to do it.

Given that these groups were so intensely meaningful to so many women and spawned such great political activity, why did they cease? Here are some of the reasons I saw:

- The groups were made up primarily of white middle-class women. Our failure to be inclusive of all kinds of women and to address directly issues of class, race, sexual identity, disability, etc., limited not only our analysis but our ability to make real and lasting social change.

- Repression began to affect the women's liberation movement, as it had been systematically destroying the civil rights movement. FBI infiltrators began appearing in our organizations and communities. They set forth to create disruption, diversion, and chaos. Trust and safety were affected.

- Having had their consciousness raised, women "graduated" from the groups and took on various forms of activism. What we did not do well was to develop the ways to bring new or younger women into the groups on a continuous basis so that there would always be a personal/political place of entry into the women's liberation movement. As a result, there is now a generation of unpoliticized women who have no understanding of what this movement gave them and who would, in fact, dissociate themselves from feminists or the label "feminist." Also, there are many new feminists who have not had such opportunities to develop analysis and action from sharing their personal experience with other women.

- Through having the safety to talk about our victimization at the hands of our oppressors, women began to feel the need to find ways to heal from their injuries. Support groups were developed around specific issues: rape, battering, incest, alcohol, drug abuse, etc. Many sought out private therapists. At first, with shared leadership of members of the group, women discussed issues in the context of sexism and looked at the systems that foster it. Healing was sought through understanding and activism. Soon, however, most of these groups became controlled by organizations or therapists, and the political context and analysis and activism were removed; both the experience and the healing were individualized and privatized; and there became a common understanding that professionals were required to lead most groups. Indeed, instead of the free groups that were controlled by the participants, suddenly it cost women to attend groups. Capitalism took over. An exception was Alcoholics Anonymous and the various groups that developed from its philosophy.

The decade of the 1980s brought us a pervasive self-centeredness with Ronald Reagan setting the standard. The watchwords became "personal growth" and "financial gain," with an emphasis upon the individual. People – primarily of the white middle and upper classes – who would not consider making even a $10 a month pledge to a social change organization, spent thousands on health clubs, personal gurus, and therapists. In this context, support groups that specialized in meeting specific needs proliferated, with some people attending several each week. The concern for individual healing and recovery spread to all sections of U.S. society. There was a slowing down of political activism, and racism and class differences increased. People began to think in terms of addictive individuals and even addictive societies; most change was on the personal level, and therapists, counselors and recovery centers made great financial gain.

One would have to be the Scrooge of psychological understanding to go so far as to say one did not believe in personal growth and individual healing, so I will not go that far. Indeed, I think that sexist and racist systems have fostered and supported individuals and institutions that have caused us terrible damage, and we need support to develop our strength in the face of that onslaught. However, I think we need much more because we live in a world that continues to maim, kill, and perpetuate horror. We once again must learn to talk about our experience in its political context so that we can understand the commonality of our experience and take action together to change society.

I've just returned from a Minnesota conference that looked at social change in the light of the teachings of Paulo Freire, and one of the concepts there was that we must do social change work that is *liberating*, not *domesticating*. That is, we must do the liberating work that enables us to develop our individual and group power so that we may change the world, not the domesticating work that enables us to adapt to or endure an oppressive world. I fear that support groups which encourage stories of victimization without the discussion of the political context and acts of resistance are doing little to change the face of oppression. The wounded and killed keep appearing in increasing numbers at the edge of the battlefield.

Personal growth and healing are good, no doubt about it, but we must use our regained power to build a movement that transforms the world. This movement will not be built from individual work within groups that do not address the context of our history and that charge for the opportunity to change and grow. Activism is antithetical to such groups. This movement must be built by ordinary women and men who take power into their own hands and work together to make change. A first step toward such a movement could be organizing free, non-specific discussion groups that examine life experiences within a political context and take actions, large and small, to change the systems that prevent our freedom.

22.

Power Analysis: Youth and Oppression

1997

Thoughts on Youth

I have always had a lot of empathy with teenagers, especially queer and questioning youth. Maybe it is because I remember so well my own youth.[1] My teenage years were the 1950s when I played basketball with utter devotion, identified with James Dean in "Rebel without a Cause," drove fast cars, went to church too many times each week, worked in the fields of our Georgia dirt farm, was sexual with both girls and boys, slouched rebelliously through school and read library books at home by the dozens, and did not even know the words "homosexual," "queer," "lesbian," or "dyke." I had survived childhood battles with my family who wanted desperately to tame me and somehow make me into a gender-appropriate girl with a ticket to acceptance and conformity. I, however, was that butch kid who wanted most of all to have a horse and a holster, to wear the neighbor boy's hand-me-down clothes, to communicate with animals, and to travel. By the time I was a teenager with raging sexuality, I was in love with basketball, danger, a boy and a girl. I was a leader of sorts and was constantly organizing gangs of youth to commit acts of rebellion. I was ignorant as sin and had more courage than good sense. My survival came from a combination of luck, happenstance, and the miracle

1. This previously unpublished essay expands on themes outlined in Pharr's workshop, "Youth, Sex, Power" presented at the Gay, Lesbian & Straight Education Network (GLSEN) in Seattle, WA in 1997.

217

that my huge family and small community somehow did not cast me out.

Surviving bad schools and my own often bad behavior, I was then saved by living in a time when young white people were offered great opportunity: low-cost education with loans and scholarships available, the new Peace Corps, unionized jobs, a stable economy with rising salaries, and a great wave of social change led by young people.

As I face the millennium and my seventh decade (that is, my 60s), I find myself increasingly concerned about young people. While I feel privileged to have lived through and participated in some of the major movements of this country (Civil Rights, Anti-Vietnam War, Women's, Queer) and to have been respected at each stage of my life and work, I see young people today as lacking both the context of a movement and respect from society. And when I look at our social change organizations, for the most part I see people with graying hair, particularly those in leadership roles. I am alarmed both for young people and for social change movements.

Why is it that we in the progressive queer community (and progressives in general) – who have been so capable in our analysis of the oppression of queers, women, people of color, and, sometimes, poor people-have been so slow in developing a power analysis of youth (people 13 to 21) in this culture? And in acknowledging them as an oppressed group?

This country's major progressive movements have been fueled by youth and direct action. One need look no further than the Civil Rights Movement and the thousands of young people who took part in sit-ins, boycotts, and who were at the front of the police barricades. The same is true for the Anti-War Movement. Young people and adults worked both in separate, autonomous organizations and side by side. Yet, in today's graying queer movement, young people are in large part unacknowledged, disrespected, and locked out of leadership roles. We not only mirror society's contradictory attitudes toward young people, but we are also limited by our fear of association with them because we are held in terror by words such as "predator," "recruiter," "abuser." Our hope for a major movement is hamstrung by our attitudes and held hostage by our fear.

Contradictory Attitudes

First, let's take a look at society's contradictory attitudes toward youth. There is now a greater separation between youth and adults that has occurred over the past 20 years or so. Youth are considered a separate group that is either to be protected and mentored to ensure the future – or they are to be vilified and criminalized as enemies of society today.

Here are some examples of the contradictions:

- Americans romanticize the young. Youth is considered the time of innocence, of simplicity, of good bodies and good times. As baby boomers grow older, many long to be associated with youth, to be young themselves.

- Romanticizing youth and longing to be young supports a commodified youth culture. The idea of innocence, good bodies, and rebelliousness is used to sell goods, targeted both to youth and to older people. Though characterized as innocent, youth are constantly eroticized and sexualized by advertising and the media. Youth culture is essential to today's consumerism.

- While extolling the innocence of youth that needs protection, our society has taken away the services and entitlements that support families. The majority of people on welfare are children. Physical and sexual violence against children within families of all classes are rampart. An observer could easily assume that our culture hates children.

- Youth are also seen as predators, members of gangs, mass murderers, thieves, out of control – as enemies of society who should be restrained, controlled, tried as adults in criminal courts, and locked up. Though there has always been adult control of the lives of youth and along with it, oppression, there is now a dramatic change in the attitudes of adults toward young people. This change centers around the idea of young people as sexualized marketing targets and simultaneously – for poor youth especially – as violent predators. Youth are now faced with prejudice against them.

Youth Oppression

If one defines oppression (such as racism or sexism) as institutional power plus prejudice, one would have to argue that, today, youth are oppressed. They have no institutional power, and prejudice against them as a group permeates the culture. If one looks at the common elements of oppression, they all apply to the treatment of youth: they lack social and economic equality; they are stereotyped, demonized, and dehumanized; they experience isolation and tokenization, self-blame, societal blame, and internalized oppression; and their sense of powerlessness leads to horizontal hostility, as evidenced in youth viciously bullying and even killing other youth. Overall, they are controlled by violence (often from birth onward) and by lack of economic access and independence.

In a power analysis, we usually examine the idea of power over, looking at how one group of people has power over another and attempts to control them. Adults maintain consistent power over youth, limiting their access to money, mobility, association, information, and the uses of their bodies for sexual pleasure or medication or reproductive choice. Information in the classroom, on the internet, or in libraries is restricted, for example, and youth are left to gain from hearsay some of the most important information they need. And, as we all know, people without power seek power and survival where they can. The one place where youth can seek personal power is through sexual expression, whether or not condoned by adults, or safe, positive or destructive. It is not surprising that youth sometimes find themselves in sexual trouble – unwanted pregnancies, STDs, etc. – since they are not allowed access to the complete information they need.

Youth and Progressive Organizations

How does all of this translate into the work of progressive organizations? While many people would assert a belief in children's rights, when it comes to incorporating youth into programmatic work either as employees or board members, it rarely happens. While we would stand strong on a belief that people should not be violent toward youth and that they should have access to good schools and health care, we do not see them in general as part of the immediate social change we are trying to bring about. If there are youth programs, they are service provision, educational, or recreational, and in most cases, led by people over 21 years old. For the most part, youth are not in positions of institutional leadership.

Our attitudes and politics tend to fall into two positions:

1. Youth are our future. From this position, we believe that they must be protected, mentored, taught, and "brought along" to take our places someday. It probably comes as no surprise that youth find this point of view patronizing. For the most part, they are left out of leadership opportunities. Sometimes adults say, "We can't hire you because you haven't paid your dues yet." It's a version of the old, "you can't get a job until you have experience," and "you can't get experience until you get a job." As adult activists, we have to ask ourselves, "In what currency are these dues?" "To whom does one pay them?" "And who assesses their value and hands over a card saying they have finally been paid?"

2. Youth are the present. From this position, we believe that they are leaders today, that what they have to contribute is important to the work we do this moment

for people of all ages, not just youth. It requires that organizations find ways to hire youth and place them on boards in groups of two or more, i.e., not tokenized, with power and authority to act on behalf of the organization. And it requires that we do not offer leadership only to the culture's most accepted youth: white or college educated or middle class. Believing and acting upon the idea that youth are the present requires struggle and change and growth.

I believe the only truly progressive position is the second one. However, I do think it is possible to combine elements of the two. For example, what is "mentoring" other than what we customarily call "leadership development" for older people? And we all need political education, consciousness raising, and more experience in different kinds of organizing. We should provide these opportunities to everyone, regardless of age.

Without the presence of young people in progressive organizations, our efforts for social change are always incomplete. Not only do we lose major sources of inspiration, energy, and fresh ideas for social change – just as we do when we exclude any group – but we fail to understand and respond to the lived experiences of a large segment of the population. Those experiences make up a portion of the political realities of our time. To exclude youth means that we work always with partial truths and incomplete answers.

The Queer Movement

Queers have another impediment to our work with youth that goes beyond the general societal attitudes we hold. Because rightwingers, conservatives, and homophobes cleverly link queer sexuality with the abuse of children and because many people do not have enough knowledge of queer life to reject this argument – much of the queer response has been to avoid employment, volunteerism, or settings that require contact with children. This core argument against the rights of queers to live peacefully in the world with equality and justice suggests we are not fit to be in decent society because we are predators and we recruit and sexually use and/ or abuse children. Of all the arguments that comprise homophobic attitudes and policies, this one is the most emotionally charged and damaging. Because the general population tends to accept this argument to be true, and because there are some among us who do have cross-generational sex, a wedge has been driven between queers and youth and children. Many queers live in terror of association with queer youth or with heterosexual youth because they are afraid they will be accused of sexual misconduct. Consequently, we are one of the few oppressed groups that is separated across all other divisions from the young, both queer and heterosexual. Not only does this keep us from being able to combat homophobia among the young who are surrounded daily by homophobic messages, or to provide, by our presence, examples of queer life, or to support queer youth – this separation keeps us from involving queer youth in the work of queer liberation.

To overcome this separation, we have to dismantle the homophobic construction of our sexuality, both for ourselves and non-queer people. To do this, we will have to know more about ourselves and about each other. It will require telling the truth of our experiences as youth, and with youth. Sexual stereotyping will not be stopped simply by presenting a positive stereotype to replace the negative. For example, it is not helpful to assert that queers do not have sexual relationships with youth, when some do in the present, and when some of us have had youth/ adult relationships when we were young. Instead, we will have to hear the many stories that represent the realities of our queer lives those from people who were harmed through their relationships with older queers and from those who relished them as healthy ways to live sexually.

There are many points of view to be heard about adult/youth relationships, but the most critical discussions to be held are those which analyze power, its use and misuse. An analysis of power is the core of all political meaning, all political work, and our corning to understand the uses of power and developing ways that power can be justly and fairly shared is the political gift we can offer each other and the progressive movement. It is also the work that will lead us to be able to include youth fully in the struggle for queer liberation and to support the leadership they provide.

Finally...

As someone who came into my 20s during a time when many of us believed that no one over 30 could be trusted, I always thought that after I reached 30, there would be masses of younger people rising up to take my place in the leadership of whatever movement I was active in. To my disappointment, that replacement corps has not appeared. However, during the past year or so, I have begun to witness the small bubbling up of a youth-driven movement. Increasingly, I have met queer youth (and particularly youth of color) who have taught me new analyses of race and gender and different ways of approaching organizing. I feel privileged to have been offered their leadership.

In general, this activity of youth has not been recognized, but I suspect that is because too many adults are either standing in the wrong place or looking in the wrong direction to be able to see it. We are out of touch with what is happening with youth, especially those who are not attached to our organizations in some way. And that is most of them.

It seems to me that there is great possibility contained within youth leadership and this bubbling, often underground and unresourced, movement. There is new possibility for change, not as the people of the 1960s or 1970s or even 1980s may have envisioned it but with the vision and strategies called for today. A question for older leaders such as myself is whether to join in this new day, embracing change, or to move out of the way.

IV

Making Connections

23.

Speech for Mother's Day Political Gathering

1980

We are here today to talk about survival.[1] There was a time when we had the luxury of discussing the quality of life, not just its existence, but now we are moving into a time when we must discuss if and how we are to exist. This is true for all low-income, oppressed, and exploited peoples, and it is compellingly true for lesbians.

In my work as a women's political organizer, I travel the state each month and encounter a large variety of people, representing diverse lifestyles and philosophies. I am here today to report that the mood of the land is one of fear and despair on one hand, especially among the poor, and of smugness and power-grabbing blindness mixed with violence on the other. Squashed in between the two is the current high energy of a few activists who see this as a vital time to get moving, to pull people together, and to get something done.

All of us gathered together today know that we are number one on the attack list of the "New Right," that we have been chosen as focal points or scapegoats in the build-up of moral fervor in the program to elevate family and church to a position of fascistic power. We know also that we are an easy target because we – alone among oppressed peoples, I think – have no constituency, no broad base of support – in most cases, in fact, not even the support of our families. Worse still, great numbers of us, because of our closeted fears, are cut off from each other. We are isolated, easy prey in too many cases.

1. From a speech given at a women's political gathering in Fayetteville, AR in May 1980.

We know also that a political climate is being created – and sanctioned by the White House – that permits mistreatment of powerless peoples. We know that a series of oppressive events doesn't suddenly begin occurring by chance. For instance, we know that all these events are connected:

- The acquittal of the Klan in North Carolina;

- The killing of gay men in major cities;

- The inflated publicity of Billie Jean King's relationship;

- The killings of the Atlanta children;[2]

- The racially motivated erection of the street barricade in Memphis and the Supreme Court's approval;[3]

- The Supreme Court's approval of the loss of child custody by a lesbian mother if she takes a lover into her home;

- The Arkansas Legislature's resolution against the teaching of a course about homosexuality in a "free" university;

- The Creationism bill;

- The anti-abortion amendment;

- The "New Right's" success in getting rid of University of Arkansas personnel who are "feminist and lesbian sympathizers";

- The "New Right" money that is being put into the anti-gay campaign in San Francisco.

2. https://www.ajc.com/news/wayne-williams-atlanta-child-murders/
3. City of Memphis vs. Greene, 1981

These events are connected in their representation of a conservative, repressive swing of mood in the country, and they indicate a climate where such discriminatory practices are permitted and often sanctioned. I point these out not to strike fear in our hearts but to establish a general awareness so we can begin to work. After all, the question before us today is what can we do to ensure our survival. This is no time for us to cower, closet, and be mute from fear. Instead, it is time for us to get on the offensive.

As long as we are isolated from one another, alone with our anxieties and fears, I think we have very little chance for survival. Remember when it was unacceptable to talk about being a rape or incest victim, a battered woman, a lesbian – remember how isolated and cut off from each other we were and how powerless? After all, it is not by chance either that the general movement of life in 20th Century America has been toward alienation, isolation, the destruction of community, of meaningful work where one feels part of a whole. And it is not by chance that it is now easy to section off and pit groups against each other: white against black; men against women; heterosexuals against homosexuals; working class against the poor; Arkansans against Cubans, etc., etc. And it is not by chance that the primary opportunities for social engagement are getting increasingly institutionalized through purchasable therapeutic groups or consultants who offer training in human relations.

In the face of our disconnection, I am here today to recommend some ways for lesbians to organize to survive:

- We must join together to support each other and to develop a community. To do this, we will have to seek ways to open ourselves and our lives to each other and to dialogue with open hearts and tolerance about our differences. We will have to find ways to bond together, to establish deep friendships, to develop loyalties that will transcend temporary difficulties. We will have to develop ways and places to get together, to meet openly and freely – lovely, clean, well-lighted places, not like the grimy bars of the past. We will have to find ways to offer one another, singly and collectively, protection and security. We'll have to make a commitment to stand up and be committed when things turn bad and we are needed.

- We must form networks and coalitions in the larger community; we must integrate ourselves in a positive, strong way. We must seek a way to talk with heterosexual feminists and get support for ourselves in return for the support we've given all these years to the movement. (We must make sure that lesbian rights are seen as a women's issue, equal in importance to abortion rights, the ERA, and that we all must work equally together for each.) We must dialogue with and join human rights groups and support them in their battles against racism, imperialism, nuclear arms, and we must ask their support in return. We must not fail to see the interconnectedness of all these issues and the forces that oppose them. And importantly, we lesbians must fight with all our power homophobia, sexism, racism, and classism, recognizing that they are part of a whole which oppresses us all. We defeat ourselves in seeing only a piece of the whole.

- And finally, to do all these things, we must not necessarily be shouting that we are lesbians but showing proudly that we are lesbians, that we are saying to those who oppress that we are not adding to the climate of violence and despair by our silence. Our lives are endangered by fear. Because of fear, we fail to form communities, to support one another, to be loyal and true, and ultimately, we fail to love.

There is now urgency in our need to be a part of a greater whole, to give ourselves to mutual good and survival. There has not been in our lifetimes a more important time to be strong and courageous and proud.

24.

The Third Wave of the Women's Movement: Making the Connections

1987

There has been a women's movement in this country for over one hundred years, beginning with those women who worked for abolition of slavery and then crested in the effort for the vote, continuing in a strong ebb with those women who created settlement houses, organized trade associations for working women, formed temperance unions, worked for birth control, and moved into the second wave with the publication of *The Second Sex*[1] and *The Feminine* Mystique,[2] and the creation of the National Organization for Women.[3] The media has recognized only the major waves of this movement with their crests and has ignored the ongoing work women have done on their own behalf. Since the late seventies, the word from the media has been that the women's movement has crested; the word feminist has been discredited; and women have won just enough gains to be satisfied and are slipping back into complacency.

During the first and second wave of the women's movement, the media (and many women) kept focused only on the white middle and upper class women who were activists, not on women of color, poor women, and lesbians. And each wave of the movement suffered from its lack of inclusiveness, from its willingness to defer the needs and dreams of all women for short-

1. Beauvoir, Simone de. *The Second Sex*. United Kingdom, Knopf, 1974.
2. Friedan, Betty. *The Feminine Mystique*. United Kingdom, W. W. Norton, 1964.
3. Originally published in the April 1987 issue of *Transformation* (Vol. 2, No. 1), the Women's Project newsletter.

term gains for the more acceptable few. The white women of the first wave have been criticized for their willingness to sacrifice the inclusion of black women in order to gain the inclusion of more white women and the support of white men in the struggle for the vote.

The second wave, which covers the period from the late sixties until about 1980, has been criticized for its white dominance and its concentration upon the Equal Rights Amendment (ERA) and abortion rights and for its middle-class goals of reform rather than radical change. Many people have felt it was characterized by a desire for making white women equal to white men instead of bringing about liberation and equality for all women. It sought to place more women in positions traditionally held by men within a system that still continues to oppress women of color, poor women, lesbians, the differently abled, older women, etc., leaving the traditionally voiceless and under-represented still at the bottom of an economic system that thrives on their labor.

What has gone unnoticed by the media – and by many mainstream feminists – is that there is a growing swell of a third wave of the women's movement that is making connections among all women and therefore among all oppressions, nationally and internationally, and is looking at liberation in a much more all-encompassing way than before. This movement is made up of battered women, lesbians, poor women, old women, sex workers, women with disabilities who see that the majority of the world's women suffer from more than one oppression and that all of these oppressions are connected. This movement sees that oppression is about power and control and coercion and intimidation. It works against racism, classism, sexism, homophobia, ableism, ageism, anti-Semitism. It sees no single issues.

The work of this current women's movement is not easy. It requires going against all the old familiar forms of power that people have come to accept as what is and must be. That power is deeply entrenched and not willingly shared. Those who go against it take great risks and often suffer large personal losses, but we have learned that to make change that does not include all women, that does not challenge the source that holds power and control over us is change that has little long-term meaning and is hollow at its core. We are learning that our success comes from hearing the truth of our stories, from working together in all our diversity and powerful differences, and from visioning our movement as a choir of many voices, not as a few solo artists.

This movement sees no one group or type of woman as being more acceptable than others. It works for the empowerment of individuals, for the development of real coalitions, for a new distribution of resources, for shared ownership and decision-making, for peace in the home and in the world. It is a movement of high energy, of great struggle, and of extraordinary commitment and hope. It works not for integration of women into an oppressive system but for the deep lasting change that will bring social justice and equality for all women.

25.

Why the Women's Project Would Support a New Trial for a Convicted Rapist – And an Introduction to the Women's Watchcare Network

1989

Last week, a friend of ours dropped by our office to give us a flyer she had found being put on legislators' cars outside the Arkansas state capitol.[1] On one side was a picture of Black man hanging from a tree with a dog snapping at his heels and a crowd of men with guns in the background. At the top was "Death to Rapists!" and beneath was "It's time for old-fashioned American Justice," and the credit line was to the Blue Cross Mothers of America, London, Arkansas. On the back of the flyer was a caricature of a black man with a bloody hand, a knife dripping blood, and a white woman lying on the ground, her skirt pulled up and her neck bleeding. The heading in large caps is "THE BLACK PLAGUE" and underneath is written, "Every 30 minutes … a woman is raped somewhere in the U.S.A." Beneath the picture of the man are the initials "BLF," the initials of Barry Lee Fairchild, a Black man and a convicted rapist on Arkansas' death row facing execution this month, the first execution in twenty-four years in this state.

A follow-up article in the *Arkansas Gazette* (3/1/89) indicated that Ralph Forbes (the same Forbes who directed former

1. Originally published in the March 1989 issue of *Transformation* (Vol. 4, No. 1), the Women's Project newsletter.

KKK Grand Wizard David Duke's campaign), the executive director of the Sword of Christ Good News Ministries, had designed the flyer because "the number of rapes committed would decrease if Fairchild were hanged in front of the state Capitol." He also said that the name, Blue Cross Mothers, "represents loyalty, the cross of Christ and traditional women's rights – that women shouldn't be forced to work."

The circumstances of Barry Lee Fairchild's case and the responses to it touch on many issues of deep concern to us. Our mission is to eliminate sexism and racism, and here is an instance in which a Black man is convicted of raping a white woman and being an accessory to her murder. We have spent the lifetime of this project working to end violence against women and we have worked in the same way against racial injustice, and here is a case in which the two merge. We abhor the fact that this innocent woman was raped and killed, and we grieve for her family. However, all we have read about the Fairchild case indicates that there are many unanswered questions, especially about the issue of police coercion and brutality and about whether this man had the mental capacity (IQ in the low 60s) to understand his rights or the Miranda statement. A police dog was sicced on him, and the pictures of Fairchild on videotape show him wearing a large bandage on his head, where the dog bit him.

It is common knowledge in this country that a grossly disproportionate number of people on death row are people of color. In fact, the two main characteristics of the majority of people incarcerated are that they are poor and people of color. For instance, the daughter of a member of the Women's Project – a young black teacher who was a leader for others – was raped and killed by three white men several years ago. Those men received minor sentences and are not on death row; neither is anyone calling for "old fashioned American justice" (lynching) for them. We have serious questions about the equality of justice for those who are poor and are people of color.

The implication of the Blue Cross Mothers' flyer and numerous letters to the editor is that rapists are Black and their victims are white. However, those working in the criminal justice system with perpetrators or in organizations that support victims know that the vast majority of rapes are within the rapist's own identity group. It is both false and inflammatory to suggest that those responsible for raping white women are Black. Such suggestions are designed to promote and increase racial hatred. We do not know whether Barry Lee Fairchild is guilty or innocent. What we do know is that there are serious unanswered questions. And we think that every person deserves justice in the courts. As much as we abhor rape, we also find injustice an abomination. Hence, our staff has been joining the weekly vigils to demand justice for Fairchild.

This information came just as we were helping to put in place our new project, the Women's Watchcare Network, which will monitor racial, religious, sexual, and anti-gay violence, and the activities of hate groups in Arkansas. We are establishing a network of 150 women over age fifty-five, plus volunteers from gay and lesbian communities to do the monitoring. Two women in each county will clip articles from newspapers, listen to the radio, and be our eyes and ears in the community. They will send us information each month which we will compile, analyze and report back to our monitors and other interested persons, as well as to churches, social change groups, community organizations, etc. The volunteers will receive training from the Center for Democratic Renewal and North Carolinians Against Racial and Religious Violence, two organizations that monitor hate groups, and once a year all of the volunteers will meet to share their work.

Our primary goal is create a network of people who have a high awareness of bigoted violence in the state so that we, working together, can develop strategies to bring an end to that violence. This is the project that brings all our issues together as we work for social and economic justice for all women and against the interconnected oppressions of sexism, racism, and homophobia.

Why do we need a project such as this? We have had increasing reports of racial incidents in schools – not only fights but racial slurs written on walls, name-calling, etc., the presence of skinheads and evidence of hate group recruitment. At the University of Arkansas at Fayetteville, there have been anti-gay flyers distributed by a group that calls itself the Gay and Lesbian Student Bashers. There are many hate groups in Arkansas: the KKK, the Christian Patriots, The Sword of Christ Good News Ministries, etc. The national hotline for the KKK is located in Harrison, AR, and the computer center for the Aryan Liberty Net is in North Little Rock. Thom Robb, recently elected Grand Wizard of the KKK, lives in Harrison, and there are indications that his leadership will result in more white supremacist meetings being held there in the survivalist country of the Ozarks. The politics of Gerald K. Smith are at work in and around the Passion Play in Eureka Springs, and A.J. Lowery lives in Clinton and edits the ironically named *Justice Times*, the publication of the Christian Patriots.

For four and a half months, we read two of the three statewide newspapers for acts of violence, and the violence perpetuated against women and children was startling. It clearly paints a picture of women's lives being expendable. From shopping malls to the workplace to their own homes, women are vulnerable to being killed, raped, or beaten. There were nine women killed. In two cases, young women and their mothers were both killed by the ex-boyfriends of the young women. An increasing number of violent acts have left evidence of devil worship or satanic rituals. We documented twenty-two rapes of women and girls, ranging in age from an infant to a sixty-seven-year-old victim. Twelve women were assaulted or abducted, including one who was left paralyzed from the neck down after being shot by her boyfriend. This documentation does not cover the entire state because our newspapers do not pick up all small town news.

We also began this project in order to involve churchwomen in the work against violence. There are many conservative churches and religious groups (such as Christian Identity) that support the politics of bigotry and hatred. We feel that church people who believe in peace and justice need to be offered productive ways to support their beliefs. This project will enable over 150 women from both white and black churches and Native American, Asian, and Latina groups to be actively involved in social change. To be offered a meaningful and productive role in society is of real benefit to older women and it is also of major benefit to social change organizations. Not only will we increase the numbers of active, socially educated and aware people in the state, but they will provide the important information that will be the basis and impetus for organizing to take action against bigoted violence.

Of all our projects, this one ties together all of our issues, provides an opportunity for diverse people and groups to work together, involves our constituency in important social change work, and provides the information necessary to make informed decisions and develop strategies to end bigoted violence.

26.

Hate Violence Against Women

1990

Women and men in Canada, the U.S., and worldwide were stunned and appalled by the massacre of fourteen women in the University of Montreal engineering school.[1] There has been outrage, grief, and intense questioning in the aftermath of this murder.[2] People have wanted to know what could be the motivation for such an outrageous act, and there has been some relief drawn from the suicide note that many read as a statement of a deranged mind, suggesting that these killings were an isolated incident.

However, those of us who are longtime workers in the women's anti-violence movement know that these killings, while seeming to contain elements of madness, are simply one more piece of the more routine, less sensational hate murders of women that we deal with every day. According to the FBI, there are several thousand women killed by their husbands and boyfriends each year. This number does not include the great numbers of women killed by rapists on the street and in their homes. Almost all are women who die horrible deaths of brutality and terror with no public outcry and outrage for the waste of their lives.

1. Originally published in the January 1990 issue of *Transformation* (Vol. 5, No. 1), the Women's Project newsletter, and reprinted in the National Network of Women's Funds and Women in Foundation Corporate Philanthropy's "Violence Against Women Supplement," spring 1991.
2. https://www.cbc.ca/archives/entry/1989-gunman-massacres-14-women-at-montreals-cole-polytechnique

There is media and public response when the murder is sensational either in numbers, in the esteemed worth of the victim, or when it is cross-race and the perpetrator is a man of color. Hence, we have the extensive coverage of the white female investment banker in Central Park, and the Republicans' use of Willie Horton as the rapist most to be feared. Otherwise, when murders and rapes of women are briefly reported daily in our papers and on television, the public, accustomed to the ordinariness of rape and murder of women and desensitized to it, simply sees it as one more trivial incident in the expected way of life for women. It's just one more woman violated or dead; turn the page; flip the channel.

To see how staggering these numbers are, let's look just at one state, the small (pop. 2.3 million), mostly rural state of Arkansas. At the Women's Project, for almost a year now we've been monitoring hate violence in Arkansas, and unlike other monitoring groups, we include sexist violence along with racist, anti-Semitic, and homophobic violence. During the first six months of the year, we were putting the project in place and quite possibly missed some of the murders of women; nevertheless, our records show thirty-seven women and girls murdered in 1989. Their killers were husbands, boyfriends, acquaintances, strangers.

Most of the women were killed in their homes and all were murders in which robbery was not the motive. Their ages ranged from 5 years old to 88. Some were raped and killed; all were brutal murders. Some were urban, some rural; some rich, some poor; some white, some women of color.

A few examples will be enough to show the level of hatred and violence that was present in all the murders. A 67-year-old woman was shot twice with a crossbow and dumped into a farm pond, her head covered with plastic and her body weighted down with six concrete blocks; a 22-year-old woman was abducted from her home by three armed men while her small children watched, brought to an abandoned house, raped, sodomized, and killed; a 30-year-old teacher was slashed and stabbed dozens of times; a 19-year-old woman was beaten to death and buried in a shallow grave; a 5-year-old girl was raped, strangled and stuffed into a tree;

a 32-year-old paraplegic was killed, a 35 lb. weight tied to her, and dropped into the Ouachita River; an 86-year-old woman was suffocated in her home.

Added to these brutal murders are the statistics from Arkansas Children and Family Services that indicate 1,353 girls were sexually assaulted in 1988, and from the Arkansas Crime Information Center that 656 rapes were reported in 1988. In November the *Arkansas Gazette* reported that in the first six months of 1989, Little Rock had more rapes – 119 – than Washington, D.C. – 90 – a city three times its size. When we understand that only about 10% of all rapes are reported, these numbers become significantly larger. All in all, when the numbers of murders, rapes, and sexual assaults of girls are put together there emerges a grim picture of the brutal hate violence launched against women and girls.

I don't believe Arkansas is an exception in this violence. From battered women's programs, from rape crisis programs, from crime statistics, we know that women are beaten, raped and killed in every state of this country, every day. Because so many women are viciously beaten and their lives placed in jeopardy, this country has over 1,100 battered women's programs, all filled to overflowing, and more being developed every day.

Wherever we live in the U.S., women live in a war zone where we may be attacked, terrorized, or abducted at any moment. Women are not safe in the home, on the street, or at the workplace. Or, as in Montreal, in a school setting on the eve of final exams for fourteen women about to enter engineering jobs that only recently became accessible to them in a world that considers engineering "men's work." There is no safe place, no "proper" kind of woman whose behavior exempts her, no fully protected woman.

While we recognize the absence of safety in all women's lives, no matter what class or race, we also are aware that women of color have even less safety than white women. Women of color are the targets of the combined hatred of racism and sexism, and as such, they experience both racist and sexist violence against their lives from white people as well as sexist violence from men of color, and often racist responses and services when they seek help.

Recently, the writers of a hate crime bill that went before Congress could not agree to put women alongside people of color, Jews, gay men, and lesbians as targets of hate crimes. This seems to me a critical error in moral and political judgment, one reminiscent of the immoral decision the white women of the 19th Century women's movement made when they decided to turn their backs on Black women in order to secure the participation of white Southern women. There is never a "more politically appropriate" time to bring in a group of people – in this case, 52% of the population – that is this country's largest target of hate crimes. When hate crimes are limited to anti-Semitic, racist, and homophobic violence, there is inherent confusion: when Jewish women are killed, when women of color are killed, when lesbians are raped or killed, it is often impossible to determine if they were attacked because of their religion, race, sexual identity, or their gender.

The U.S. Justice Department's guidelines to determine bias motivation for a crime include common sense (i.e., cross burning or offensive graffiti), language used by the assailant, the severity of the attack, a lack of provocation, previous history of similar incidents in the same area, and an absence of any other apparent motive. Under this definition, rape would be an apparent hate crime, often severe – including armed assault, beating and killing – often repeated in the same neighborhood or area, no other apparent motive, and almost always abusive woman-hating language.

The same would be true with our monitored cases of battering that ends in murder. In the majority of the cases, the woman was beaten (sometimes there was a long history of battering) and then killed. Rather than cross burnings or offensive graffiti, the hate material is pornography. Most telling is the absence of any other apparent motive. And then there are the countless beatings and acts of terrorism that don't end in murder but do lasting physical and psychological damage to women. An example from Arkansas:

[A woman] reported battery and terroristic threatening. She said her neighbor/ex-boyfriend threatened her with a handgun, and beat her, knocking her down a flight of stairs where she landed on a rock terrace. [She] sustained permanent damage to her eardrum, two black eyes and extensive bruises and lacerations. She stated her assailant was not intoxicated; that he bragged of having been a Golden Gloves boxer; and he allegedly told her he could not be arrested for beating her with his hands open.[3]

Men beat, rape, and kill women because they *can*; that is, because they live in a society that gives permission to the hatred of women.

This country minimizes hate violence against women because women's lives are not valued, because the violence is so commonplace that people become numb to it, because people do not want to look at the institutions and systems that support it, and because people do not want to recognize how widespread the hatred is and how many perpetrators there are among us on every level of society.

It is only when women's lives are valued that this violence will be ended. If thirty-seven African Americans were killed by whites in Arkansas, our organization would be leading the organizing to investigate and end the murders; or if thirty-seven Jews were killed by gentiles; or if thirty-seven gay men or lesbians were murdered by heterosexuals – for all of these other groups we monitor violence against, we would be in the forefront of organizing on their behalf. But why not on behalf of women? We talk about violence against women and help develop organizations that provide safety and support for victims, but even we sometimes get numbed to its immensity, to its everydayness, to the loss of freedom it brings with it.

All of us must stop minimizing this violence against women. We must bring it to the forefront of our social consciousness and name it for what it is: not the gentler, less descriptive words such as family violence, or domestic violence, or wife or spouse abuse, or sexual assault, but *hate violence against women.* It does not erupt naturally or by chance from the domesticity of our lives; *it comes from a climate of woman hating.*

3. *Washington County Observer.* August 17, 1989

For too long when women have named this violence as what it is, we have been called man-haters by people who want the truth kept quiet. "Man-hater" is a common expression but "woman-hater" is not, despite the brutal evidence of woman-hating that surrounds us: murder, rape, battering, incest. The common use of the word "man-hater" is a diversionary tactic that keeps us from looking at the hard reality of the source of violence in our lives. The label "man-hater" threatens women with loss of privilege and controls our behavior, but more importantly, it keeps us from working honestly and forcefully on our own behalf to end the violence that destroys us.

Social change occurs when those who experience injustice organize to improve or save their lives. Women must overcome the fear of organizing on behalf of women, no matter what the threat. We must organize together to eliminate the root causes of violence against us.

We must make sure that hate violence against women is monitored and documented separate from general homicides so that we can be clear about the extent of it, the tactics, the institutions and systems that allow it to continue. We must hold our institutions accountable. In December 1989, the *Arkansas Gazette* ran a series of articles about local hospitals "dumping" rape victims, that is, refusing to give rape examinations because they did not want to get involved in legal cases. Such inhumane practices are dehumanizing to women and lead to public indifference to rape and its terrible consequences.

We must create a society that does not give men permission to rape and kill women. We all must believe that women's lives are as important as the lives of men. If we created a memorial to the women dead from just this war against them – just over the past decade – our memorial would rest next to the Vietnam Memorial in Washington in numbers and human loss to this nation. The massacre must end.

27.

Framing the Issues

1991

Almost three years ago when we at the Women's Project in Arkansas began monitoring racist, religious, anti-gay & lesbian, and sexist violence, we found ourselves almost immediately in the middle of a national debate about whether violence against women should be considered a biased crime.[1] We had modeled our Women's Watchcare Network after North Carolinians Against Racial & Religious Violence and also the Center for Democratic Renewal whose work monitoring hate groups we much admired. Ours differed from theirs in three ways: we also monitored individual acts of biased violence, we used a community organizing approach to monitor and to respond to the violence (educating and working with over 200 volunteers), and we included women as a targeted group.

It was the inclusion of the latter that brought us into a national dialogue because at the time – and perhaps still today – we were the only group that included women. Because we also maintain an anecdotal record of the rape, battering, abduction, terrorization, sexual assault, murder of women, we have a large pool of evidence for creating the argument for why this violence is indeed biased. And we can lay out the evidence side by side with our record of racist, religious, and anti-gay and anti-lesbian violence. We have newspaper accounts of all four forms of violence and we maintain a log that details each incident.

---

1. A talk presented as part of a panel for the National Network of Women's Funds in April 1991.

This debate has arisen at this particular time for several reasons, I believe, which have to do with women feeling pushed over the edge of their tolerance and patience:

- Violence against women is escalating: the Department of Justice reported this month that over 100,000 rapes had been reported this year; before the Biden committee they reported that crimes against young women have increased 48% since 1974 while crimes against young men have decreased by 12%; in Arkansas alone sixty-eight women were killed by men in 1990.

- The Montreal massacre and the public's response to it became symbolic of the intensity of crimes against women and the acceptance of them.

- We have an increased sense that through our battered women's and anti-rape movements we have saved lives by providing support services but we have not decreased violence against women: we have not succeeded in making lasting social change.

- We were intentionally excluded from the national Hate Crimes Statistics Act which was designed for criminal justice personnel to maintain records of biased crimes.

The exclusion of women from the Hate Crimes Statistics Act has been a source of great anger for many women – not because we thought that inclusion would end violence against women but because it was one more example of the minimization of the violence against us. And we were particularly angered by the very telling reasons given for the exclusion:

- *Including women would insure the defeat of the Act.* What clearer statement do we need about an almost all-male Congress who could not recognize that violence against women is a biased crime because that would necessitate having to examine their participation in the perpetration of it?

- *There are too many acts of violence to document.* Excuse me? This is a reason to exclude rather than a dramatic reason to include? Some people suggested that the battered women's movement and rape crisis centers are already monitoring violence against women. First of all, this is a very narrow view of violence against women – rape and battering – but secondly, there is no organized effort to do this monitoring, and even if there was, it would be placed in a different category from the national effort made by the Department of Justice.

- *If women are included, it will dilute the issue, and people will not focus clearly on racist, religious, anti-gay and anti-lesbian violence.* This is an old turf argument where protectionists believe that more makes less rather than more makes more – that is, the more one brings in, the greater the possibility for making strong coalitions and building a movement.

- *Violence against women, unlike the other three, is cultural violence.* That is, it has been such a historical given, such a fact of our culture, that it cannot be separated from our mores. I would argue that the same has been true for racism, for example. As a Southerner, I grew up understanding that racism was a culturally unexamined way of life – until a Civil Rights movement forced the nation to examine its culture and institutions in the light of a moral conscience.

- *Violence against women cannot be a biased crime because in the majority of the cases we know the perpetrator and are often in some kind of relationship with him; hence, we have some responsibility in the interaction that leads to the crime.* I argue that this knowledge makes this particular biased crime all the more horrendous because there is societal permission to hate women so much as a class that men can feel entitled to destroy even those closest to them. There are no boundaries.

One might ask what is the goal in working to get violence against women named as a biased crime? Certainly I do not believe that getting women included in the Hate Crimes Statistics Act will end violence against women or even bring an immediate reduction in the violence against us. To have the Department of Justice keep track of the crimes against us is analogous to having the foxes monitor the attacks against the hens in the henhouse. We will have to do that documenting ourselves. However, I do believe that the inclusion of women will serve as an educational piece sending a signal that the violence against us is of equal importance to the violence against other groups who are attacked for who they are and not for what they do. Also, naming it as a biased crime gives us one more way to talk about the sources of that bias and to name the ways it is institutionally supported and sanctioned. The clearer naming of causes makes it easier to create strategies that strike at the heart of the problem rather than its symptoms.

There is no doubt in my mind – and for most women I talk with – that violence against women is a biased crime for many reasons. Some of them:

- We are the most consistently attacked, maimed, and murdered worldwide. The violence is so widespread that few among us have not experienced direct violence in our lives, and all of our lives and behavior are shaped by the constant threat of violence.

- The attacks against us are so commonplace as to be accepted as simply a way of life for women, yet the content of these attacks are so horrendous that they defy any concept of a civilized society. We see them in our news media but also as a familiar theme in the entertainment media of television and movies. The lives of over half our population are considered expendable, and the destruction of them is a source of titillation for many. Because of the devaluation of our lives, women do not have to do anything to bring violence against us: we are destroyed simply for who we are.

The violence against women has strong commonalities with violence against gay men and people of color. In murders, for example:

- The strongest similarity is in the brutality, the overkill, where the victim is not killed simply with a gunshot to the head or heart or one or two stab wounds, but is beaten to a bloody mass or stabbed over 100 times. In Arkansas in 1990, a young woman was found the day after her first anniversary stabbed by her husband over 130 times in the eyes, breast, vagina; another had a rope tied around her neck and was dragged facedown behind a car for a quarter mile; the torso of an older woman, with a history of being battered, was found in a cooler floating in a lake – her husband had cut off her head and limbs with a fine precision instrument. There is an attempt to annihilate the victim's humanity. When a woman is shot in Arkansas, it is often with a shotgun directly in the face, wiping out that part of the body most exposed to the world, the part that talks, that shows our sorrow and happiness and anger and love: all that we count as human.

- There is almost always a sexual aspect to the violence: being stripped of all or part of the victim's clothes, raped, cut or beaten around the genitals. The promise of a sexual encounter is often used to get the victim alone.

- There is some kind of terrorization: abduction, gang attacks, torture, mutilation. The terrorization is often framed as some kind of punishment.

Finally, violence against women meets any definition given for biased crimes whether from the Department of Justice or state or local groups working on hate crime legislation. Here is ours:

> *The Women's Project believes that violence by white people against people of color, by gentiles against Jews or Protestants against Catholics, by men against women, by heterosexuals against gay men and lesbians, etc., is institutionally supported violence because the perpetrating groups have power over the institutions of our society and control their policies, while the targeted groups do not have access to full institutional support for their lives. We use the terms of the California Attorney General's Commission on Racial, Ethnic, Religious, and Minority Violence. This violence is any act of intimidation, harassment, physical force or threat of physical force against any person, or family, or their property or advocate, motivated either in whole or in part by hostility to their real or perceived race, ethnic background, national origin, religious belief, sex, age, disability, or sexual identity, with the intention of causing fear or intimidation, or to deter the free exercise or enjoyment of any rights or privileges secured by the Constitution of the United States.*

I believe that I and others have been debating this issue of violence against women as a biased crime from the wrong place. Somehow we have felt that we needed to convince people – specifically men – that it is a biased crime. We need to start from a different place, much farther down the line, because there is no debate about whether or not it is. It is. What we need to be discussing with other people is what is preventing them from including violence against women as targets of biased crime, what is the barrier to their confronting and working to end the violence. We do not need any more evidence for our case: we are overloaded, and it takes major, active, intentional denial not to recognize that evidence. The question we need to be asking men is what is the matter with them that they cannot take this information in and then move to make change concerning it? We need to name their resistance for what it is instead of working continually to create better use of evidence, new and better arguments about the realities of this violence.

I believe the major work before us in this decade is to develop an integrated analysis of violence against women that includes sexism, racism, and economic oppression. Then we must use this analysis to develop the strategies that confront the sources of violence against women in all women's lives. We can no longer do single issue work that does not include the other oppressions women experience. This expanded vision gives me hope for a movement where all women can bring their whole selves, their particular realities that are based on their class, race, sexual identity, disability, age, or combinations thereof. Once we have expanded our vision, then I believe there will be hope for putting violence against women on the agenda of every progressive movement – whereas now it is simply on the agenda of the women's liberation movement – and then there will be some real hope for changing the world.

28.

The Blue Mountain Dialogue on Violence Against Women

1992

Twenty-six women gathered at Blue Mountain Center for a long weekend in October of 1991 to discuss why violence against women continues to escalate and what can be done about it.[1] Recognizing the inseparable mix of racial and sexual oppression to be the dominating politic of our times, the planning committee invited six women from each of five racial groups: African, Asian, European, Indigenous, and Latina. For many of us it would be the first time we had participated in a racially-balanced group. We hoped this particular combination of people and experiences would help us get closer to our goal of understanding how racism, sexism, and economic injustice combine to produce violence against women.

As a member of the planning committee, I went into the meeting wondering what we could truly expect to accomplish with thirty women and so little time. We were not looking for a definitive analysis, for consensus, or a position paper. We hoped for a shift in our various analyses, a renewed commitment, a deeper understanding, and fresh strategies to take back to our work. While we found the time together much too brief, we did meet most of our goals. Developing fresh strategies was the most difficult goal and the one we most longed for, but we did not

1. Originally published in the January/February 1992 issue of *Transformation* (Vol. 7, No. 1), the Women's Project newsletter. Critically read by seven participants: Karen Artichoker, Debbie Lee, Kelly Mitchell-Clark, Beth Richie, Beth Rosales, Maria Zavala, and Helen Zia.

succeed in creating specific concrete strategies. Perhaps we needed more time and a better sense of knowing one another in order to develop them. However, I felt we were successful in a most important area of change: the four days of discussion, candid and passionate, led us to a deepening of our analysis that will have far-reaching effect in our work with our constituencies.

The Context

We invited women who had long experience in the movements to end violence against women, and also women who work on a wide range of other community issues. There were a few women who do not identify as feminist but who work on behalf of women. Some were urban, some rural, and all regions of the country were represented. Despite differences of history, belief, and approach, we found common cause and a way to talk with one another instead of at one another. And through this process, we gained a rarely achieved cross-fertilization of ideas.

Because of our many differences, we came to the meeting with varied expectations. There were women who felt isolated in their work and missed kindred communities, and women who felt they were just beginning their work and wanted a broader perspective. Others wanted to look at the bigger picture, to make connections, to discuss goals and strategies for the long haul. During the weekend, almost everyone said she was longing to be part of a movement that had a vision. Some women simply said they were seeking hope.

What gave us common ground was our shared sense of the context for our discussion. Each of us had witnessed a worsening of violence against women and of violence against people of color. Because of the deepening recession, some people in all of our communities are facing the basic survival issues of food, shelter, and jobs, and these of necessity are clear priorities, often relegating work on violence to a secondary place. We discussed the increase in racism as evidenced in the increase in hate crimes, the attack on affirmative action, the blame for economic problems placed on welfare recipients and new immigrants, the support for the gubernatorial campaign of David Duke. The increased organization of the rightwing has touched all our communities and impacted our work negatively. On the other hand, we expressed a disappointment in the U.S.-based left for being fragmented, often leaderless and without vision.

The Assault on Communities

From this common understanding we began to consider an analysis of violence against women within our individual communities. Women of color reported a masterplan of genocide against their communities: an assault so ferocious that communities face imminent destruction through poverty, disempowerment, violence, and cultural extinction.

Latinas reported that the assault on their community includes lack of access to employment, education, and health care – the latter is particularly critical when AIDS is the number one killer – loss of control of land and water in the Southwest, and negative policies and attitudes toward immigrants. Immigration has now become a code word for the racist perspective that people of color are "taking over." Poverty is extreme. Destruction of the culture has led to self-hatred and a low sense of self and place. As a consequence, there is a high incidence of drug and alcohol use. Cultural survival in the face of rapid cultural extinction has become the primary issue.

For African Americans, there has been the withholding of resources, resulting in widespread poverty, and the simultaneous blaming of them for the country's economic problems. What women referred to as genocide has been felt through a complex interconnection of what seem to be conspiracies: the coded language of anti-affirmative action and welfare abuse and subsequent unemployment; the reduction of school loans and educational opportunities; the unavailability of health care and rise in teenage pregnancy, infant mortality, and chronic disease; the introduction of crack cocaine into communities and the subsequent rise in violence within the African American community; the discriminatory injustice of the criminal justice system.

Asian women reported that invisibility, erasure, and anti-Asian violence are major issues in their communities. On the one hand, there is a perception that Asians are all immigrants and foreigners and do not belong here, yet on the other hand they are considered the model minority: both perceptions lead to erasure and silence about their poverty as well as the startling number of hate crimes they experience. Additionally, these stereotypes lead to both a lack of recognition by society in general and the progressive community in particular, which tends to see racism in only Black/White terms. Because many are a recent immigrant population, language barriers bring increased discrimination and isolation from services for survival, as well as the targeting of Asians in English-only and anti-immigrant movements.

Indigenous women said that racism in this country is based on Indian-hating. From the beginning of U.S. history and the invasion of white men, they have faced colonization, cultural extinction, and mass destruction of their people. Wards of the Department of the Interior, their self-determination is blocked politically by the U.S. government and culturally by the Christian church. Poverty is enforced by U.S. policies. The central issue for cultural/spiritual survival is regaining their land (decolonizing the Western hemisphere), gaining acknowledgement of treaties, saving the environment, and becoming self-sufficient.

White women reported a lack of solidarity and difficulty with the definition of white community: dominance carries privileges and assumptions that forbid categorization. People of color communities are assaulted as a whole and have to defend themselves against white domination and annihilation. However, while women in white communities are assaulted by white men's domination, as white women we still participate in the overall domination by white culture. Consequently, feminist white women have difficulty in identifying with "community," and often fall into the trap of acting as though racism doesn't exist (thereby naming sexism as the central issue) or as though racism is done only by white men. A critical issue is to decide where they stand in the line of oppression/oppressed: white bonding suggests collusion with racial dominance, and rejection of whiteness creates isolation and inability to work for change among white people.

Working on Violence Against Women in Our Communities

For women of color and white women the question is this: how can we incorporate our work on violence against women with our work on racism and economic injustice.

Some women of color reported that their lives and work are inextricably tied to the entirety of their communities – women, men and children – because they share the common enemy of racism which threatens their lives every day. It is necessary to work across all issues affecting the community and to work with men. White women working against violence, however, are not usually so connected to the community as a whole because the primary perpetrators of all the oppressions are their white male counterparts. It becomes more difficult to decide how to work across issues and to work with men. While some women of color feel a responsibility toward issues that affect men of color, white feminists often do not feel such toward white men.

In all communities, however, the issue of violence against women is seen as an "add-on" to the supposedly more important issues facing the entire community. Violence against women gets subsumed within the work of daily survival and often does not get worked on directly.

African American women reported that they had not challenged the Black leadership enough regarding violence against women, created forums for discussion, or discussed what a healthy relationship or Black sexuality is. The current focus has been on the destruction of men and boys, and discussion of violence against Black women has been viewed as the politically charged criticism of the Black family which needs support.

Latinas said that there was a generalized silence about sexuality in their communities; a woman's identification as sexual means being a prostitute or a lesbian and thereby deserving of what happens to her. The ownership of women goes unchallenged by the community and condones excesses of violence. To leave an abusive relationship means leaving the community as well and living in isolation. To leave the community means leaving support for all the other aspects of day to day survival. The woman is therefore caught in a double bind of loss.

And for Indigenous women, violence against women is not traced to patriarchy but to genocide, to the violation of mother earth and the extinction of a people. Currently, violence is not dealt with community wide because all resources are controlled by the federal government and the Christian church. Tribal governments and institutions were created by the federal government to mimic them and consequently they have become gatekeepers.

In the Asian community, with the exception of a few shelters for battered Asian women, the subject of violence against women has not been dealt with. Instead, the focus has been on anti-Asian violence in general. It was noted that people could name fifty men who have been victims of anti-Asian violence but not the name of one woman. Within the community, women have no status and no voice. The *New York Times* recently reported that 100,000 women are missing, mostly in Asia: from census figures, analysts deduced that this many females are lost from infanticide and abortion of female fetuses.

Among white people, violence permeates every aspect of life because of the culture of dominance. To focus on violence against women means addressing all parts of that dominance. The culture gives it a low priority because successful work on ending violence against all women would mark the end of dominance: success would mean the dismantling of all "-isms" that serve white male domination and collude to create violence against women.

Women Activists Within Communities

Everyone reported difficulty in working against violence against women in the context of community and within a broad range of compelling social change issues. Perhaps the greatest block to this work is the systematic discrediting of the women who work on behalf of women and specifically to end violence against women. All over the world, when women's voices are raised, women are seen as divisive to community.

A chilling testimony came from African American women. Prior to the 1960s, Black women were seen as having a strong role within the family and community as both single heads of households and community leaders. Their strength was seen as positive. In the late 1960s and 1970s, they were viewed as a problem in the community, taking the jobs of Black men, being too strong, robbing men of their power and pride. By the late 1980s, they had come to be seen as destroyers of the family and enemies of the community. A journey from being recognized as a strong leader to being a problem to the enemy has brought many women to begin to internalize the message that by securing employment and availing themselves of educational opportunities they have betrayed their race. To focus attention and work on violence against women is interpreted as accentuating that betrayal.

This theme of betrayal was carried further by Latinas who talked about what it means to work in their community as out lesbians. Being a lesbian means erasure, constant self-betrayal and self-abuse because they are caught in an impossible conundrum. To be out as a lesbian means they cannot work in community and therefore must feel as though they are betraying their race. To keep their lesbianism invisible and work in community means they must constantly betray themselves. Whether out, visible, or invisible, lesbians working on women's issues will be seen as betrayers of the race and hence must betray themselves as women.

Responding to the report of the African American women, Asian women said that they had always admired the leadership of Black women, despite the attack against them, because Asian women have been rendered so invisible that there has been no recognized leadership. It would be a statement of *presence* to be so singled out for such an attack. In all of China's history there have been only three recognized female leaders, and each of them has been reviled. From both within and without the community, there is the view among East Asians that Asian women's role is to be passive, sexual commodities who take anything; this perception, combined with lack of status and lack of voice, makes women's leadership difficult.

Before colonization, Indigenous women did have power in a society that was based on shared power and respect for the earth and the rightful place of all things on it. But now there is the discussion of the disempowerment of Indian men because women are seen as taking their jobs, and the community understands this as a strategy to maintain oppression. However, women activists are viewed as aggressive, not as the enemy, and because of internalized oppression, that leadership may be seen as negative. There is not such a sense of betrayal and separation. Violence against women did not exist in Indigenous cultures before colonization, so there is now a place for men and women to dialogue about this violence in the context of discussions about colonization.

When white women work on women's issues and violence against women, they are not seen so much as betrayers of the race as betrayers of men. It was among white people that this attempt at discrediting women's work originated: feminist = man-hater = lesbian. Heterosexual white women, in particular, struggle with issues of betrayal concerning their intimate relationships with men. If they have intimate relationships with men, are they sleeping with the enemy, compromising politics, and reinforcing compulsory heterosexuality? If they do not have intimate relationships with men, are they then to deny their lives as sexual beings? To work on ending violence against women in the white community is to threaten all relationships with the men whom violence serves.

Difficulties in the Movement

Not only have we faced the discrediting of women who work on behalf of women, but there have been major problem areas internal to the movement to end violence against women.

One of those areas has been the professionalization of the movement which caused a division between those providing social services and those working for social change. Along with service providers came an emphasis upon the need for degreed workers.

There was a call for therapists rather than organizers, and the application of twelve-step programs to victims of violence which caused women to be seen as culpable, co-dependents, or enablers. Part of the movement began to rely on a medical model for the treatment of battered women and survivors of rape.

Little more than lip service was paid to children's programs, and a small underground movement evolved to save children from the fathers who incested them, but this effort received very little support from shelters and rape crisis programs. In contrast, more concern and funding dollars were given to programs for batterers, and increasing numbers of men were elected to boards of shelters and rape crisis centers. Lesbian baiting has been an ongoing issue in the women's anti-violence movement. Virtually all women who work on ending violence are exposed to efforts to control us by naming us as man-haters or lesbians for the work we do. Social change work is perceived as lesbian led, funding is threatened, and in many instances, programs demand that there be no lesbian presence.

The movement has failed to reach out to many battered and raped women: drug addicted, prostituted, homeless, immigrant/refugee women, lesbians, and women with disabilities. Sometimes we have followed a fad to reach these populations, and then the efforts have faded.

Each racial group reported the impact of sex trafficking and prostitution on women in their communities, yet prostituted women have been shunned by the women's anti-violence movement as a whole as programs pushed for professionalism and credibility. Core issues of violence against women – prostitution, pornography, and sadomasochism – are obscured by euphemisms of supposed freedom: prostitution equals "career choice;" pornography equals "free speech;" sadomasochism equals "sexual expression." Women have lost in the effort to end violence against women through our refusal to deal with this violent center of women's oppression whose goal is to provide males with unconditional sexual access to women and children based solely on the ability to pay.

One of the most difficult issues has been working with the criminal justice system, an institution that has not ended violence against women yet has brought about the increased criminalization of women. In the movement, the initial goals for working with the criminal justice system were to help individual women; to force public recognition of the problem; to deter violence; and to have men take responsibility for the violence. But now we have to ask these critical questions: Are women safer now? Are men battering and raping less? Do men take responsibility for violence? Have we gotten justice? Any of us? All of us? Have the levels of danger decreased? Unfortunately, the answers to these questions is for the most part a resounding *no*. Through trying to reform the system, we often became advocates of the system instead of advocates for women.

And yet there have been some successes. While racism still continues to be alive within the movement, a tremendous struggle about racism and leadership by women of color has emerged – more than in any other part of the women's movement. The same is true for the struggle and education about homophobia and the leadership of lesbians. There are over 2000 battered women's programs and rape crisis programs throughout the country. Thousands of women's lives have been saved. Through education, millions of people now understand that violence against women exists and is an openly talked about societal problem. Those very successes brought twenty-six strong women together at Blue Mountain Center to talk about how to intensify the work to end violence against women.

Strategies

It was very difficult for us to focus on strategies, I think perhaps because we still needed more discussion before undertaking them, but time pressed us onward.

Some people in the group distrusted contemporary national organizations because they felt they have failed to respond adequately to the needs of grassroots people. Hence, they did not want to develop new national organizations but instead wanted to begin the long, steady work of building from the ground up, developing ways to connect issues in a practical way and to link grassroots groups together in a national network that features decentralized networking. Others felt a need for national organizations that can help link grassroots efforts, keep communications going between them, and organize forums for dialogue – because it is through these links and dialogues that we build a national movement.

We agreed that violence against women affects every aspect of the community, and that effective social change includes the entire community. We must get people together to push the limits of what is possible. To do the work we must develop the tools that save the entire community from destruction, but we must make sure these tools, these actions and strategies, do not reinforce dominance and repression. To make these linkages and to develop these tools, we want to find ways for activists to share training with each other. A women's school based on the Highlander folk school model, bringing together women and sometimes men, that would address women's issues would be one approach; another would be to develop an activist-exchange program among grassroots organizations. Because of the overwhelming influence of the media, we thought a media institute would be helpful to assist us in setting our own agenda and naming our own leaders instead of just responding to the media's choices. In every community we need to return to consciousness-raising cells or small groups, so that women together can create analysis, develop politics, and take action.

The major emphasis was working on the community level: saving our communities, developing a cultural critique to use in the further development of culture, establishing self-determination, and bringing violence against women onto center stage with all the other compelling issues facing the community. To accomplish these goals, we want to figure out how to do community engagement instead of community invasion. We have a history of talking well among ourselves about social change but frequently talking at those who are not yet part of our work. We need to find new ways to discuss and categorize violence against women in the U.S. There is a movement internationally to make it a human rights issue, and perhaps it would be useful for us in the U.S. to use this human rights paradigm to broaden understanding of violence against women. An attempt has been made to categorize this violence as a biased hate crime but while it is equal to a hate crime, it is not the same. A strategy is to figure out where the violence against us fits among biased crimes, civil rights, and human rights.

A central goal was to put violence against women on the agenda of grassroots groups, civil rights groups, human rights organizations, hate crime coalitions, and other organizations of the left, including women's organizations that do not specifically address violence against women. And in return, we expect women's anti-violence groups to bring issues of racism and economic injustice into equal partnership with our work against sexism. We felt that the 1992 recognition of the invasion of this country by Columbus is a powerful vehicle for bringing all of these issues together, providing opportunities for discussing the beginning of colonization and genocide that has continued through these 500 years and provides the context for everything we discussed during our four days at Blue Mountain.

Most participants spoke of longing for a national movement that would bring people together in a mood of resistance to the destruction we face and provide a place where we can process and belong and create a vision for the world we want to live in. This movement would be based on women's needs, on human needs. Grounded in people and place, it would have a spiritual and cultural content. Through our work together, we would work on not only our basic physical survival, but also our resistance to the forces of extinction while developing a vision for creation of a society where everyone can be whole.

Finally, our being together made us realize what few opportunities there are these days for activists to gather together and think collectively about our work. Part of our working time was spent getting used to the notion of having the time and a process for working together. A critical part of repression is the prevention of such meetings that intensify the work and sharpen the tools for doing it. *To come together and make connections is an act of resistance.*

Providing the funding for this time for us was a powerful statement of the politics of the Funding Exchange, the Phoebus Fund, and Blue Mountain Center. We left desiring other opportunities to talk about our experiences, our work, our hopes and dreams that we call vision.

29.

The Connection Between Violence Against Gay Men and Lesbians and Violence Against Women

1991

In the fall of 1990, Larry Kramer called for gay men and lesbians in NYC to carry arms against the increasing violent attacks against them.[1] His voice was met by a number of people who were alarmed that the attacks were escalating both in number and seemingly in severity and who felt that nonviolent solutions would not work.

This dramatic call for arms came after the release of the National Gay and Lesbian Task Force (NGLTF) report of their documentation of violence against lesbians/gay men nationally and after the successful campaign to get lesbians / gay men included in the Hate Crimes Statistics Act along with people of color and religious minorities. The 1989 National Gay and Lesbian Taskforce Report documented over 7,000 attacks. Then in 1990 their report indicated that violence against gay men/lesbians was the fastest growing violent crime (in percentages) in New York City. The gay/lesbian community was put on alert.

Though there has been little evidence that many people in our communities have taken up the call to arms, the ensuing controversy over violent/nonviolent solutions has helped focus our communities' attention on the violence directed toward us. According to NGLTF:

---

1. A speech given at Columbia University in April 1991.

In 1990 there was an unprecedented level of organizing against anti-gay violence. Outraged by rising attacks, lesbians and gay men in communities across the U.S. launched street patrols and public safety awareness campaigns, conducted violence surveys, initiated or expanded anti-violence projects, built coalitions with non-gay groups to oppose hate violence, lobbied for hate crime legislation, and participated in direct action – including public forums, rallies, demonstrations and civil disobedience.[2]

Certainly the rise in violence on all fronts brought me this year to sharpen my awareness and focus more intensely on the causes and the strategies for eliminating it. For a very long time I've been concerned about violence in our gay and lesbian communities. *From without*: the violence inflicted upon us by our families, our neighbors, by strangers who seek us out in the very places where we seek safety. *From within*: lesbian and gay battering and rape within intimate relationships, bar fights, sadomasochism, suicides – all seem to me to be responses to gay and lesbian hating and restrictions on any sexual behavior that goes beyond the missionary position within heterosexual marriage. As a people we live with the constant threat of violence in a gay and lesbian hating world.

However, my focus has never been just on the gay and lesbian community. I cannot think about gay men and lesbians without thinking about women and people of color and the connection between gay and lesbian hating and sexism and racism. Because of this concern about the connections, we at the Women's Project monitor racist, religious, anti-gay/lesbian, and sexist violence. Because we include sexist violence we have been in the center of some national controversy. We are constantly questioned about how violence against women can be considered a hate crime and stand among the other three targeted groups that were included in the Hate Crimes Statistics Act. We are asked to prove how it is similar to racist, religious, and anti-gay/lesbian violence.

It would take more space than I have to draw the connections among all three, and what I want to focus on here

---

2. "The 1990 National Gay and Lesbian Taskforce Report."

is the connection to anti-gay/lesbian violence. In fact, I believe the question is framed the wrong way: what we should be asking is how can anti-gay/lesbian violence be included and violence against women omitted, for violence against gay men and lesbians is directly related to our connection to women? Briefly, I want to outline that connection and offer some strategies for working against violence.

Violence against women

Violence against women issues directly from male power and control. To maintain power, men must employ the dual weapons of economic control and violence over women. Men do not assault, rape, torture, and kill women because they are sick; they do it to keep a system of power in place. They do it because there is societal permission to do so. This system of power in the U.S. is white, male, and heterosexual, and all institutions are dominated and controlled by this group. The subjugation of women is vital to the continuation of their power and control.

Violence and the threat of violence is a primary means of keeping women controlled and subjugated. In 1990, there were over 100,000 reported rapes in the U.S.; our 1100+ battered women's shelters were filled to overflowing; and in Arkansas alone 76 women were murdered by men. Violent crimes against women are on the increase. According to Senator Joseph Biden in an article in the *Atlanta Constitution* on March 10th, 1991; The evidence of this epidemic is overwhelming. One out of every five American women will be raped during their lives. More women will be beaten by their husbands this year than will get married; flight from domestic violence is the No. 1 reason why women are homeless.

Women are abducted, tortured, maimed, and killed every day, by the thousands, on the streets and in the home. A massive pornography industry thrives on violence against women. Women are taught that violence is our lot in life; it comes with our gender at birth. Because such large numbers of us experience violence in brutal forms, it seems obvious that what is going on is not just about individual women but widespread, institutionally supported attacks against us as a class.

Violence against lesbians

First, violence is directed toward lesbians because we are women. Our gender alone brings extraordinary possibilities of violence into our lives, and when we experience it, we find it hard to sort out whether it comes because of our gender or our sexual identity. Unless there are names such as dyke or queer or lesbian used, then most lesbians no doubt assume that we are being attacked simply because of our gender.

Along with that assumption goes another: the age-old message that violence is what we as women should expect in life. The belief that violence is our due because of gender, combined with a history of women being blamed for the violence acted against us, leads many of us not to report the violence. For instance, only an estimated ten percent of all rapes are reported. This reluctance to report has direct implications for our lesbian/ gay anti-violence projects because lesbians carry the pressure of potentially being blamed for the violence as well potentially being outed in our lesbian lives which causes us fear of even greater loss. At the New York Anti-Violence Project three gay men report for every one lesbian reporting. There are other reasons for lesbians not reporting, but large among them is this reluctance that comes from a sense that women are not entitled to safety and that reporting creates greater danger. I do not believe the difference in the greater numbers of reported incidences of violence against gay men reflects that there is more violence against men: instead, it reflects differences between men and women in a sexist society in which men feel entitled to a life without biased violence and therefore more readily report.

The second reason for violence against lesbians is that we threaten male power and control. Lesbians are perceived as women who have stepped outside of sexual/economic dependence on men. We have broken from male ownership of women, from the privilege (however tenuous) gained from association with men through intimate relationships. If there are women who can live independently from men, and if any woman potentially can be a lesbian, then how can the stronghold of male power and control be maintained? The very existence of lesbians strikes a blow at the heart of sexism. Violence, then, must be used against us to keep us afraid and subdued, to keep us invisible so that women as a whole are not offered an alternative to living under male dominance.

Violence against gay men

In our project to monitor racist, religious, sexist, and anti-gay/lesbian violence, we get an opportunity to look at all the forms of violence side by side and observe trends, similarities and differences. It is from this work that we have come to be even more convinced that gay men are hated not just because of their breaking ranks with male dominance but because they are seen as being like women or being women.

We have compared our anecdotal records of the murders of women with those of gay men compiled by NGLTF, and we have found the way the violence is inflicted to be very much the same. Here are the major similarities:

- The strongest similarity is in the brutality, the overkill, where the woman or gay man is not killed simply with a gunshot to the head or heart or one or two stab wounds, but is beaten to a bloody mass or stabbed over a hundred times, as in one documented case. There is an attempt to annihilate their humanity. When a woman is shot in Arkansas, it is often with a shotgun directly in the face, wiping out that part of the body most exposed to the world, the part that talks, that shows our sorrow and happiness and anger and love: all that we count as human.

- There is almost always a sexual aspect to the violence for both women and gay men: being stripped of all or part of the victim's clothes, raped or, with gay men, raped anally, cut or beaten around the breasts or genitals. With both women and gay men, males often use the promise of a sexual encounter as a way to get the victim alone.

• And finally, there is some kind of terrorization: abduction, gang attacks, torture, mutilation. The terrorization is often framed as a punishment for sexuality or a means of gaining sexual access prior to the violence.

Police are beginning to tell members of lesbian/gay anti-violence projects that they can often tell if a homicide victim is gay simply by looking at the circumstances of the killing. I believe that knowledge comes from recognizing those characteristics I just listed. I would like to note here that racist violence also often follows these same characteristics. This is not the way white heterosexual men are killed; it is the way women and gay men and people of color are killed through biased violence.

Hatred of women permeates our society – indeed the world – and gay men, through being identified with women, receive a large portion of this hatred. As long as women are hated, and as long as men subjugate women in order to maintain power and control, gay men will be hated. Additionally, gay men are hated for threatening male power and control through their refusal to cooperate. Through choosing intimate relationships with men, they are perceived as breaking ranks, as putting a rent in the fabric of male dominance, because they are stepping outside male ownership of women. How can male dominance survive if there are large numbers of men who do not participate in the ownership of women?

How gay men and lesbians contribute to violence against women

It is only visible, anti-sexist gay men who truly threaten male power and control. When white gay men choose invisibility, they still maintain solidarity and privilege with heterosexual white men who control our institutions and ultimately our lives. When gay men of color choose invisibility, they have personal power over women, but they are not directly connected to the white ruling class; they still maintain a connection, through race, to an oppressed class. In both cases, though, male domination is supported. The invisibility of white gay men feeds both male domination and white domination which combine to make a ruling class.

Similarly, lesbians who choose invisibility keep a connection to heterosexual women who gain privilege from men, and this invisibility feeds male domination. Nevertheless, we are connected to an oppressed group and can develop politics around gender, but the risk in this focus is for white lesbians to exclude the politics of race, thus contributing to the twin sources of white male power: sex and race. As long as heterosexuality with its connection to male dominance is supported as the dominant norm, then violence against women will continue.

The history of our progressive movements – Civil Rights, Women's Liberation, Gay and Lesbian Liberation – is that we have asked people to bring only one piece of their selves, of their oppression, into the movement: only race and not gender or sexual identity, or only gender and not race, or only sexual identity and not race or gender. I believe this single oppression approach has been at the core of our failure to make lasting social change. When gay men do not see the connection between the hatred of themselves to the hatred of women and act against sexism, then there is still support for the violence that sexism produces. When white gay men and lesbians fail to see the connection between racism, sexism, and gay and lesbian hating – all from the same system of oppression – and act against racism, then racist violence is supported. The same is true for those who fight for racial equality and turn their backs on gay men and lesbians. In the end, we all lose.

Strategies

I believe that as long as sexism exists, gay and lesbian hating will exist and that sexism and racism are so intertwined that both will have to be eliminated simultaneously. Their continuation assures the perpetuation of violence against women, against people of color, against gay men and lesbians. If this is true, how do we as lesbians and gay men work for our liberation?

I believe we have to spend our privilege by putting ourselves at risk in the fight against other oppressions. That is, gay men of all colors must put themselves on the line against sexism – openly, vehemently, with no regard to their reputations as "men." White lesbians and gay men must go full force against racism, taking risks, avoiding white assumptions of privilege and solidarity. We don't get to choose the privilege that comes to us because of the gender or the race we were born into, but we do have choice about how we use it – to further oppression or to work against it.

The more privilege we have – because of race or gender or class – the more we can afford to be out, to be visible. We need to use our portion of privilege to be queerer than queer, where there's no mistaking that we are the alternative to male domination. In this way, we will stand in the face of white heterosexual male power and control.

I want to end by speaking specifically to gay men about ways to address this enormous issue of sexism that works to control not just my life but yours.

You call on me to work with you, to be your sister, and more and more often, I feel I have to say to you and to other progressive groups that don't have my life concerns on their agenda, "I'm tired of giving my strength, my talents and energy to people who add to my oppression. It's time for you to give." Here are a few suggestions:

- **Truly identify with women.** Recognize our oppression in your oppression. Don't identify with us in negative ways. When you choose the language and ways that so symbolize our oppression, we experience you as being in collusion with our oppressor. It is never funny when you call each other "cunt" and "bitch" and speak of female ways in one another as weakness. As a lesbian, it is hard for me to separate out your hatred of women and your self-hatred – or are the two so intermingled?

- **Begin your work on sexism right in our lesbian/gay organizations.** We have alliances to build with each other. Lesbian issues are women's issues; don't let them get subsumed under gay, with a focus so narrow that only our oppressed-lesbian or sexual selves can be brought into the organization. (Just as no one should expect lesbians and gay men of color to leave their racial politics outside the door – please.) We have to work together on not just what is of concern to us as lesbians but to us as women. Again, there is a parallel to racial politics.

- **Don't expect lesbians to be in the service of gay men – in our organizations, in the HIV/AlDS movement, in personal lives.** We live in a sexist world with striking power imbalances: in our organizations, we need to figure out true ways to share power. We need as much evidence of gay men supporting lesbian lives and concerns as there is of lesbians supporting gay men.

- **Understand that the work against sexism in our organizations will help create new models for how men and women can live and work together.** Already, we offer a different model for sexual and emotional intimacy – daring to have same sex relationships – and now we need to round out that risk-taking in a way that changes the world through offering life-supporting alternatives to oppressive behavior.

- **Seek non-violent ways to end violence against women, gay men, and lesbians.**

To return to the notion that carrying guns is the way to end violence against us, I couldn't disagree more. Is this a solution that we would hold out to all oppressed groups? As I said to Barbara Smith at the National Gay and Lesbian Taskforce (NGLTF) conference, does this mean as a Black lesbian woman, she would have to carry three guns? One against men, one against heterosexuals, and one against white people? I think so. And one of those guns would have to be against me.

No doubt gay men are horrified that they are now being threatened and attacked in some of the ways that women have forever experienced in major ways, and their sense of male entitlement could lead them to think that they should strike out, using violence against violence. But in the two decades of the women's anti-violence movement, using violence against violence has never had a serious place on the agenda. We have always known that violence begets violence, and have looked to community organizing, to the empowerment of women, to civil disobedience, to support of victims and strengthening lives. However, our success has been slow, partly because of the immensity of the oppression and its effect on the hearts and minds of women, and partly because there have been so few men to join us. This is the time for a rare first: for women and gay men to work together to end violence.

We are now at a historical moment for making real change. If members of oppressed groups can learn that the violence against them issues from a common source and work in ways that do not support any forms of that violence, then we can make alliances that can demand and create change. In this time of escalating violence, we must work not only for our survival but our *liberation* that brings with it a free and healthy place for us in the world.

30.

Multi-Issue Politics

1994

At the National Gay and Lesbian Task Force's Creating Change Conference, I was asked to give a luncheon speech to the participants of the People of Color Institute and the Diversity Institute.[1] Right off, I told them that I thought I was an odd choice for these groups because I don't really believe in either diversity or identity politics as they are currently practiced. Fortunately, people respectfully stayed to hear me explain myself.

First, diversity politics, as popularly practiced, seem to focus on the necessity for having everyone (across gender, race, class, age, religion, physical ability, etc.) present and treated well in any given setting or organization. An assumption is that everyone is oppressed, and all oppressions are equal. Since the publication of the report "Workforce 2000" that predicted the U.S. workforce would be made up of 80% women and people of color by 2000, a veritable growth industry of "diversity consultants" has arisen to teach corporations how to "manage" diversity.[2] With integration and productivity as goals, they focus on issues of sensitivity and inclusion – a human relations approach – with acceptance and comfort as high priorities. Popular images of diversity politics present people holding hands around America, singing "We Are the World."

---

1. Originally published in the January / February 1994 issue of *Transformation* (Vol. 9, No. 1), the Women's Project newsletter.
2. Packer, Arnold E., et al. *Workforce 2000: Work and Workers for the 21st Century.* United States, Hudson Institute, 1987.

I have a lot of appreciation for the part of diversity work that concentrates on making sure everyone is included because the history of oppression is one of excluding, of silencing, of rendering people invisible. However, for me, our diversity work fails if it does not deal with the power dynamics of difference and go straight to the heart of shifting the balance of power among individuals and within institutions. *A danger of diversity politics is becoming a tool of oppression by creating the illusion of participation when in fact there is no shared power.* Having a presence within an organization or institution means very little if one does not have the power of decision-making, an adequate share of the resources, and participation in the development of the work plan or agenda. We, as oppressed people must demand much more than acceptance. Tolerance, sympathy, and understanding are not enough, though they soften the impact of oppression by making people feel better in the face of it. Our job is not just to soften blows but to make change, fundamental and far-reaching.

Identity politics, on the other hand, rather than trying to include everyone brings together people who share a single common identity such as sexual orientation, gender, or race. Generally it focuses on the elimination of a single oppression, the one that is based on the common identity, i.e., homophobia/ heterosexism, sexism, racism. However, this can be a limited, hierarchical approach, reducing people of multiple identities to a single identity. Which identity should a lesbian of color choose as a priority – gender, race, or sexual orientation? And does choosing one necessitate leaving the other two at home? What do we say to bisexual or biracial people? Choose, damnit, choose??? Our multiple identities allow us to develop a politic that is broad in scope because it is grounded in a wide range of experiences.

There are positive aspects of organizing along identity lines: clarity of single focus in tactics and strategies, self-examination, and education apart from the dominant culture, development of solidarity and group bonding, etc. Creating organizations based on identity allows us to have visibility and collective power, to advance concerns that otherwise would never be recognized because of our marginalization within the dominant society.

However, identity politics often suffers from failing to acknowledge that the same *multiplicity of oppressions*, a similar imbalance of power, exists within identity groups as within the larger society. People who group together on the basis of their sexual orientation still find within their groups sexism and racism that have to be dealt with – or if gathering on the basis of race, there is still sexism and homophobia to be confronted. Whole, not partial, people come to identity groups, carrying several identities. Some of the major barriers of our liberation movements to being able to mount a unified or cohesive strategy, I believe, come from our refusal to work directly on the oppressions – the fundamental issues of power – within our own groups. A successful liberation movement cannot be built on the effort to liberate only a few and only a piece of who we are.

Diversity and identity politics are responses to oppression. In confronting oppressions, we must remember that they are more than people just not being nice to one another: they are systemic, based in institutions and in general society, where one group of people is allowed to exert power and control over members of another group, denying them fundamental rights. Also, we must remember that oppressions are interconnected, operating in similar ways, and that many people experience more than one oppression.

I believe that all oppressions in this country turn on an economic wheel; they all, in the long run, serve to consolidate and keep wealth in the hands of the few, with the many fighting over crumbs. Oppressions are built in particular on the dynamic intersection of race and class. Without work against economic injustice, against the excesses of capitalism, there can be no deep and lasting work on oppression. Why? Because it is always in the best interest of the dominators, the greedy, to maintain and expand oppression – the feeding of economic and social injustice.

Unless we understand the interconnections of oppressions and the economic exploitation of oppressed groups, we have little hope of succeeding in a liberation movement. The religious Right has been successful in driving wedges between oppressed groups, because there is little common understanding of the linkages of oppressions. Progressives, including lesbians and gay men, have contributed to these divisions, because generally we have dealt with only single pieces of the fabric of injustice. We stand ready to be divided. If, for example, an organization has worked only on sexual identity issues and has not worked internally on issues of race and gender, then it is ripe for being divided on those issues.

The Right has had extraordinary success in using homosexuality as a wedge issue, dividing people on the issues clustered around the Right's two central organizing points: traditional family values and economics. An example is their success in using homosexuality as a way to organize people to oppose multicultural curricula, which particularly affects people of color and women; while acting to "save the family from homosexuals," women and people of color find themselves working against their own inclusion. If women's groups, people of color, and lesbian and gay groups worked on gender, race, and sexuality issues internally, then perhaps we would recognize the need for a coalition and a common agenda for multicultural education.

An even more striking example is how the Right, in its "No Special Rights" campaign in Oregon, successfully plays upon the social and economic fears of people, using homosexuality as the wedge issue, and as the coup de grace, pits the lesbian and gay community against the African-American community. Ingeniously, they blend race, class, gender, and sexual identity issues into one campaign whose success has profound implications for the destruction of democracy. In summary, the goal of the "No Special Rights" campaign is to change the way this nation thinks about civil rights so that the groundwork is laid for the gradual elimination of civil rights. This is not an easy idea to present to the general public in a straightforward manner. Therefore, the religious Right has chosen homosexuality and homophobia to open the door to thinking that is influenced by racial hatred and its correlatives, gender and class prejudice. Depending upon the persuasion of racism, sexism and homophobia, the religious Right seeks these basic twisted and distorted changes in our thinking about civil rights:

- They suggest that civil rights do not already exist in our Constitution and Bill of Rights; they are a special category for "minorities" such as people of color and women. The religious Right refers to these people as having "minority status," a term they have invented to keep us focused on the word minority. Most people think of minorities as people of color. Recently in Oregon, signs appeared that read, "End Minority Status." They did not specify gay and lesbian: the message was about minorities and what that so-called "status" brings them.

- Then they say that basic civil rights are themselves "Special Rights" that can be given or taken away by the majority who have ordinary rights, not "Special Rights."

- They argue that "Special Rights" should be given to people based on deserving behavior and hardship conditions (especially economic) that require special treatment. In their words, people who "qualify" for "minority status."

- Then they introduce the popular belief that "Special Rights" given to people of color and women and people with disabilities have resulted in the loss of jobs for deserving, "qualified" people through affirmative action and quotas. This introduces the notion that rights for some has an economic cost for others; therefore, the enhancement of civil rights for everyone is not a good thing.

- They argue that lesbians and gay men have no hardship conditions that would require extending "Special Rights" to them. Further, homosexuals disqualify themselves from basic civil rights because, by the nature of who they are, they exhibit bad behavior. They do not, according to the Right's formula, "qualify" for "minority status."

- Then there is the pernicious connection: There are other people who already have "Special Rights" who exhibit bad behavior and prove themselves undeserving as they use and deal drugs and commit crimes of violence and welfare fraud. The popular perception is that these are minorities. However, the Right also extends its description of the undeserving to those who bear children outside of two-parent married families, women who choose abortion, and even those who receive public assistance.

- And finally, their logical and dangerous conclusion: because giving "Special Rights" to undeserving groups is destroying our families, communities, and jobs for good people, who deserves and does not deserve to be granted "Special Rights" should be put to the popular vote, and good, ordinary citizens allowed to decide who gets them and who gets to keep them.

Clearly, the religious Right understands the interconnection among oppressions, and in this campaign plays directly to that interweaving of racism, sexism, classism, and homophobia that is virtually impossible to tease apart. To see this campaign as single issue, i.e., simply about lesbians and gay men, is to ensure defeat of our efforts in opposing it. It has to be responded to as the multi-issue campaign that it is. If the "No Special Rights" campaign is successful, everyone stands to lose.

The question, as ever, is what to do? I do not believe that either a diversity or identity politics approach will work unless they are changed to incorporate a multi-issue analysis and strategy that combine the politics of inclusion with shared power. But, you say, it will spread us too thin if we try to work on everyone's issue, and ours will fall by the wayside. In our external women's anti-violence work (working against police brutality in people of color communities, seeking government funding for AIDS research, etc.) we do not have to work on "everybody's issue," but how can we do true social change work unless we look at all within our constituency who are affected by our particular issue? People who are infected with HIV are of every race, class, age, gender, and geographic location, yet when research and services are sought, it is women, people of color, and poor people who are usually overlooked. Yet today, the AIDS virus rages on because those in power think that the people who contract it are dispensable. Are we to be like those currently in power? To understand why police brutality is so much more extreme in people-of-color communities, we have to understand why, even within that community, it is so much greater against poor people of color, prostituted women, and gay men and lesbians of color. To leave any group out leaves a hole for everyone's freedoms and rights to fall through. It becomes an issue of "acceptable" and "unacceptable" people, deserving and undeserving of rights.

Identity politics offers a strong, vital place for bonding, for developing political analysis, for understanding our relationship to a world that says on the one hand that we are no more than our identity, and on the other that there is no real oppression based on the identity of race or gender or sexual identity. Our challenge is to learn how to use the experiences of our many identities to forge an inclusive social change politic and practice. The question that faces us is how to do multi-issue coalition building from an identity base? The hope for a multi-racial, multi-issue movement rests in large part on the answer to this question.

Our linkages can create a movement, and our divisions can destroy us.

Internally, if our organizations are not committed to the inclusion and shared power of all those who share our issue, how can we with any integrity demand inclusion and shared power in society at large? If women, lesbians, and gay men are treated as people undeserving of equality within civil rights organizations, how can those organizations demand equality? If women of color and poor women are marginalized in women's rights organizations, how can those organizations argue that women as a class should be moved into full participation in the mainstream? If lesbian and gay organizations are not anti-racist and feminist in all their practices, what hope is there for the elimination of homophobia and heterosexism in a racist, sexist society?

When we grasp the value and interconnectedness of our liberation issues, then we will at last be able to create true coalitions and begin building a common agenda that eliminates oppression and brings forth a vision of diversity that shares power and resources. In particular, I think there is great hope for this work among lesbians and gay men. First, we must reconceptualize who we are and see ourselves not as the wedge, not as the divisive, diversionary issue of the religious Right, but as the bridge that links the issues and people together.

If we indeed represent everyone – cutting across all sectors of society, race, gender, age, ability, geographic location, religion – and if we develop a liberation politic that is transformational – that is, that eliminates the power and dominance of one group over another within our own organizations – we, as old and young, people of color and white, rich and poor, rural and urban, lesbians and gay men, can provide the forum for bringing people and groups together to form a progressive, multi-issue, truly diverse liberation movement. Our success will be decided by the depth of our work on race, class, and gender issues.

Instead of the flashpoint for division, we can be the flashpoint for developing common ground, a common agenda, a common humanity. We can be at the heart of hope for creating true inclusive, participatory democracy in this country.

31.

The Struggle for Democracy

1993

I'm going to begin and end by talking about why I think we're going to be victorious in this struggle for democracy.[1] Let's just start with this recent issue of how many lesbians and gay men are there anyway? This week, three studies were quoted as saying that gay men are only one percent of the population. Everyone is in a flap about it. Well, here's what I think. You know how the religious Right thinks that to talk about homosexuality promotes it? That is, talking about it makes people become homosexual? Remember when Louis Sullivan suppressed the Health & Human Services study on teen suicide because it found that over thirty percent were struggling with sexual orientation. He didn't want this in the hands of teachers, counselors and administrators because their talking about it would promote homosexuality. Well, sisters and brothers, I'm here to tell you that if talking about homosexuality promotes it, I would say heterosexuality is done for this year. The religious Right has put our issues on the lips of everyone in America. Everybody is talking about it.

And why is this going to make us victorious? Because they have given us the greatest opportunity to do public education about who we are that we could have ever dreamed of. I want to talk a few minutes about four of their central organizing issues – the linchpin issues of their crusade.

1. A speech given in Cincinnati, OH in April 1993 at an LGBTQ event.

Civil Rights

There should be no qualifying exam for civil rights. Everyone should have the tools to fight discrimination in employment, housing, public accommodations, and to protection from biased violence – no matter what race, religion, sex, age, physical ability or sexual orientation. We have watched group after group – people of color, women, people with disabilities – be discriminated against and have to fight tooth and toenail to gain equal access to protection.

Some groups of people are singled out for discrimination because they are seen as *lesser than*; for these people we have to have laws that insure they are included in democracy and that they are protected from discrimination. Lesbians and gay men are discriminated against as a class; the religious Right is working to convince people that not only lesbians and gay men are lesser than heterosexuals but that it is justified and moral to discriminate.

As long as some groups of people – because of who they are – are singled out for discrimination, there can be no equality or justice. The development of civil rights protections in this country is the simple pursuit of justice and equality. The goal is for no one to get more or less than anyone else: it is Jesse Jackson's dream of the level playing field.

Child Abuse

There are some people who work for community solutions; others spend their time creating community problems. The religious Right, in singling out one group for scapegoating, is developing community problems – setting up systems of exclusion instead of inclusion.

Communities can work together to solve problems. If child abuse is the problem, then the community must come together to find ways to prevent it and to control those who commit it. We have to tell the truth about it: that the vast majority of the abusers are heterosexual males that children trust, most commonly in the home but often in the church or school. Since we don't want to punish all heterosexual males by creating laws to control them, we must work together to find successful ways to deal with anyone – heterosexual or homosexual, male or female – who abuses children, individual case by individual case, all treated equally. And we absolutely have to tell our children the truth so that they can protect themselves. Otherwise, they will be misled into being on guard only around strangers rather than in the home where the risk is greatest.

If the religious Right is truly concerned about children, why is it not advocating for laws and programs that support their lives? We have not heard them speaking in favor of tougher child support enforcement, battered women's shelters which are filled with children whose lives are marked by violence, parental leave, pay equity for women so that mothers can support their children, publicly funded childcare centers, universal health care for pregnant mothers and for children.

We have to make responsible community and individual decisions about the well-being of our children. If, for instance, one of the problems is that we don't like negative influences on the education of our children, we as parents have total authority over a major influence on our children's education: the television. If we don't want them to see women degraded, then we can turn it off. If we don't want them to see hours of violence each day, then we can turn it off and provide better educational alternatives.

What scares me is someone else deciding to cut it off for me. When there is legal censorship, then the control goes out of our hands and most often into the hands of zealots. One of this country's great gifts is freedom of speech and expression. That means we are free to explore all of the world's possibilities, not just a few that are chosen for us. I don't want anyone telling me what I can read or watch or listen to.

Racism

The religious Right is trying to convince the public that lesbians and gay men are perverted people doing bad things. They think if they can convince us that lesbians and gay men are evil, then discrimination will become a moral issue. That is, you will actually become a good citizen if you discriminate. For this strategy to work, the targeted group must be dehumanized so that people can feel justified in their violence or discrimination against them. The lies of negative stereotypes are used for scapegoating.

This is an age-old tactic. When Native Americans tried to protect their homelands, they were depicted as godless savages who preyed upon women and children. It was seen as heroic to kill them. African Americans were seen as godless and sex-crazed, worthy of only hard physical labor. Slavery was seen as a socially good institution for using people who were not considered fully human. It was applauded morally when owners whipped their slaves and killed those who tried too often to escape.

The religious Right borrows and extends the tactics of racism in its attack against the lesbian and gay community.

The "No Special Rights" of the Right's current campaigns comes from race discrimination. The religious Right (and many other Americans) see affirmative action as giving people of color jobs and educational opportunities they haven't earned rather than simply a program that attempts to redress past discrimination. It tries to level the playing field for people who were systematically denied equality.

Economics

The primary tactic the religious Right uses is to seek out people's fears and then to build on them. Of course, most of us are frightened about the economy, so the religious Right uses the argument of "special rights" to suggest that lesbians and gay men are going to take our job through gaining minority status.

Why, we must ask, does the religious Right avoid talking about real economic issues? When have they ever said *one word* about...

- The Savings & Loan (S&L) bailout which benefited the rich and was paid for by us?

- The Housing and Urban Development (HUD) housing scandal which made a few well-positioned rich people richer?

- The trickle-down Reagonomics that permitted unregulated massive buyouts that made a few people rich and cost millions of us our jobs?

- The way the government attacked and almost destroyed the unions, the only collective voice working people have to protect our rights – the unions that brought us the 8 hour work day, health standards in the workplace, worker's compensation, etc.?

- The unrestrained greed of major corporations that move to less developed countries and manufacture goods there and then bring them back to this country to sell to people who have now lost their jobs because of this practice?

We all agree there is a serious economic problem in this country, but it is not caused by lesbians and gay men seeking anti-discrimination laws. The Right would have us think that our economic problems are caused by people of color, women, people with disabilities – and now lesbians and gay men – having access to the workplace and protection from discrimination. Any thinking person knows that just isn't so. The more fully supported workers we have in the workplace, the better off this country is: what we need are decent paying jobs, good working conditions, and equality of treatment. What we must examine is who is really *causing* the economic crisis and who is *benefiting* from it.

I want to end by talking a few minutes about why I believe we are going to be victorious in the face of this attack of the Killer Lies. As I said in the beginning, I believe we will be able to use this moment to do mass education. We know from national polls that the more people know someone of an oppressed group, the less likely they are to hold bigoted or discriminatory attitudes. We will use this moment to put a human face on the oppression. In individual and community acts of courage, we will talk with our families, our neighbors, our fellow workers.

The second reason is that the lesbian and gay community and our allies are beginning to get it: the broad attack of the religious Right against people of color, against women, against poor people and against lesbians and gay men has helped us to realize how interlinked oppressions are. We understand what and who the targets are when the Right attacks affirmative action, multiculturalism, secular humanism, reproductive rights, sex education, parental leave, welfare, etc. We as targets in all our differences can see how essential we are to the well-being of democracy and its need for diversity and inclusivity. We're beginning to realize that if all oppressions are linked, then it only makes sense that all oppressed groups could be linked. The next step is simply to work together to link our solutions so that all of us can live whole lives filled with equality and justice.

This is my fervent hope. This year, this shining moment in time, we are going to cross the barriers of race, class, gender, and sexual orientation – as well as age, religion and physical ability – to build deep and true relationships and coalitions to bring about a powerful, comprehensive movement for justice and liberation for all of us. We will have victory on our terms of freedom.

V

Crossing Divides, Finding Ways Forward

32.

Building a Lesbian and Gay Liberation Movement

1990

Two weeks ago, I attended a conference that changed my life and my political work – which is my life.[1] The conference, held in Minnesota, was "Social Change for the 90s" and was based on the teachings of Paulo Freire and two of his students, Peter Park, a Korean American teacher, and Pat Roselle, an African American teacher.

For those of you unfamiliar with Freire, let me tell you briefly that his work on literacy with peasants in Brazil has created a liberation education movement that is worldwide in its reach. It is based on the notion that our lives within our particular historical context hold the material we need to know and understand in order to become free, and that an understanding of our repression and resistance to it lead to a transformation of the world.

The concepts are simple but profound. My temptation is to tell you everything I learned there with the 360 social activists who attended the three days, but I am going to try instead to hold myself to talking about several questions that are on my mind concerning lesbian and gay liberation. The major Freirean concept that I will be using to think about this movement we are creating is the difference between liberating and domesticating work. *Liberating* work is that which resists oppression, gives it a face, and, from a place of group power, transforms the world. *Domesticating* work

---

1. A speech given at the Wisconsin Community Fund in Madison, WI in 1990.

is that which enables us to adapt to an oppressive world, to endure it.

The first question I ask is about the nature of this oppression and whether we put a face on it or allow others, as Peter Park says, to obscure its face so that it recedes from us. Its face is obscured when gay men and lesbians are blamed for society's hatred and mistreatment of us. It is blaming when we are told that it is wrong to be gay or lesbian, that we are sick or sinful. It is not wrong to be gay or lesbian; it is simply a way of being in the world, a sexual identity. What is wrong is homophobia and heterosexism and the people and institutions who limit wholeness and freedom. We will name and define ourselves, and we will not allow our oppressors to do it. We must look this oppression in the face, in its many faces, if we are to resist it rather than adapt to it. We must take power over our lives, our communities, if we are to be free.

My second question is who does it serve for us to be controlled and intimidated by accusations of immorality and sickness? And along with that question is another: How do we resist this control and intimidation? To understand the controlling systems of homophobia and heterosexism, we have to understand the oppressions of other people, especially women. As some of you know, I believe that homophobia is directly related to sexism and is used to keep sexism in place. It is an interactive relationship.

On the one hand, gender roles are maintained through a threat of loss of privilege, safety, life. The ability to be invisible as gay men and lesbians – and the fact that one cannot prove, certify sexual identity – makes it possible for the sanctions of homophobia to be used against everyone. And what greater sanctions could there be than threatened loss of job, of family, of children, of community, of safety and life – to name a few? And who benefits when gender roles are enforced through intimidation? Men, particularly white heterosexual men, who also gain from the enforcement of racism. What do they gain? Control over both resources and behavior.

It is an interactive relationship because on the other hand gay men and lesbians are hated because we are seen as the nightmare extremes of the hated female. Lesbians are seen as women gone wrong, the ultimate threat of life without dependence upon a man, and gay men are seen as betrayers of male control who imitate this despised half of humanity. We then receive the extremes of woman-hatred, fed by the fear of loss of power and control.

What does it mean to receive the hatred that is directed toward women? In case you are one of the many who minimize that hatred and the violence that accompanies it, let me tell you about the kind of violence we're seeing just in Arkansas. As women are hated and raped and maimed and killed, so are lesbians and gay men to be brutalized. We must cast our lot together and resist. That is to say, the Women's Liberation movement must take on homophobia and heterosexism as a major primary issue and the Gay and Lesbian Liberation Movement must do the same with sexism – just as we must work against racism that is rooted in the same economic source as sexism.

How can we resist in ways that transform the world? Just our very visibility is a major act of resistance, but I want to talk about another means of resistance. One of the ways we can resist is to expand the limits of both gender definition and restriction, and family and relationship definition. We can be serious about doing what is jokingly called gender bending. For instance, I think we need a greater appreciation of men in drag, butch women, cross-dressers, transgender people, etc. Expansion of the idea of gender is resistance to *control*. However, we need to ensure that our resistance is clearly on target and not also repressive.

For instance, I believe that butch/femme dressing among both lesbian and gay men can joyously expand our notions of gender, or they can imitate the most oppressed or oppressive qualities of the opposite sex. For men in dresses to call each other cunt and bitch is not an act of liberation; it is adapting to oppression through women-hating end self-hating. The same is true when women take on tough, non-verbal, violent male roles. I would like to see cross-dressing and role reversals taken on as conscious political acts. I would like to see an effort to remove gender roles from our society by highlighting them as both ludicrous and destructive methods of social control.

One final comment on who it serves for us to be controlled and intimidated. As I've stated, I believe that homophobia is connected to sexism, and sexism is connected to racism (the leg bone's connected to the thighbone…), and economic domination/subordination is the link that ties them all together. However, when I think about these connections, I have some worries about how some of us view liberation. I worry about women who see the solution to inequality as having white women get the same power and privileges as white men, and I worry even more when I see white gay men wanting to maintain the same power and privileges as white heterosexual men with the only difference being who they sleep with. The road to liberation cannot be built on the backs of women and people of color. No white gay male can claim to be working for liberation if he does not do anti-sexist and anti-racist work.

That's the larger movement picture but also within the context of our own movement, we recognize that gay and lesbian liberation is not about just white and male: it is about white and people of color; male and female; old and young; able-bodied and people with disabilities − all the differences society has to offer fall within what we know as gay and lesbian. The intertwining of oppressions involves us all, and we'll all get to freedomland or none at all.

My final question is, how do we negotiate, organize, and build coalitions from a place of power? On the most basic level we must return to small group work and build the framework for a movement. Talking together, we must reconceptualize what it has been to live in a homophobic world; we will recognize the ways we resisted, the ways we adapted for survival. Through telling our stories, we will experience grief and rage but move through these emotions to an analysis of the oppression into the creation of healthy social action groups that are hungry for change.

As we develop ways to resist and begin the transforming change, we need to develop those long, careful methods that hold within their very steps the seeds of freedom. That means we have to find a way for all our voices to be heard and respected. That means we will not see overnight "victories." That means that the process will be as important as the goal. That means organizing will be local and not top-down.

Let me use as an example some of the controversy surrounding AC- UP (AIDS Coalition to Unleash Power). Many of us have great appreciation of ACT-UP's high spirits and creative approaches to direct action. On the other hand, still others of us are not happy with their hit-and-run techniques away from their home towns. A case in point is the sodomy protest in Atlanta on January 6 when ACT-UP members from around the country outnumbered local activists at an estimated 4 to 1. The visitors had fun, made some strong political statements, dropped their pants in a local bar, but local people are asking what they accomplished. Our important questions here are: Who was liberated, changed, transformed? Was the process liberating? What was achieved?

Local people must be in control of their lives and consequently their organizing, for that is where empowerment comes from. The Black Panthers said in 1968 to their people, "We will not be colonized. We will be in control of our lives, of our own communities."[2] The message, the analysis, is still true.

Finally, this is how we negotiate from a place of power. To return to this theme again – as a people, we talk together about our historical context, both personal and collective. Through telling our stories of how we resisted the control of a homophobic world and how we sometimes adapted to it in order to survive, we will develop a picture of the nature of the oppression we all have experienced. We won't call this process "dealing with internalized homophobia," we will call it "the ways we dealt with oppression" – and then together we will seek ways to change that oppression we have analyzed and understood. Our work together, our understanding, our action, will make us strong.

From this place of strength we will enter into coalitions and alliances with other groups of people who are bringing their issues to the organizing/negotiating table. We won't come saying, "You must understand us, you must develop tolerance, you must accept

2. DeVinney, James A, Julian Bond, and Henry Hampton. *Eyes on the Prize: America's Civil Rights Years, 1954-1965*. Alexandria, VA: PBS Home Video, 2010.

us." Instead, we will come, in our great diversity, and say, "There will be no liberation for anyone unless we are included, for as long as you keep us out, the oppressors will use your fear of us as terrorism against you, and you will be held hostage by it. You will remain stuck in the first non-inclusive step toward freedom. And we will be the dumping ground of your fear and the violence it spawns. No one, including you, will be safe."

For a liberation movement to happen, all the players have to be at the organizing table, and we as lesbians and gay men are indispensable players. So we come to our liberation work with the full power of our humanity demanding no more and no less than the full benefits of freedom. We will work side by side with other oppressed peoples for freedom for us all – as equals in this movement – and we will resist oppression with the force of our collective strength.

33.

Lesbian Battering: Social Change Urged

1987

Despite its long existence, lesbian battering has only recently become a public concern of the battered women's movement and of lesbian communities.[1] A 1983 National Coalition Against Domestic Violence conference on lesbian battering and the subsequent publication of an anthology of writings on the issue has begun to break the silence on this painful subject.[2] Women both within the battered women's movement and lesbian communities are beginning to tell stories of lesbian battering and to develop strategies for providing services and ending the violence. But we are at the very beginning.

We are as much at the beginning as the battered women's movement was in the early 1970s: analysis and theory and strategies are still tentative; the need is great; there is fear and hesitancy; there is little popular support or understanding; and yet a few courageous women are struggling along to do something to save lives, even if it isn't the perfect thing. Despite the difficulties, there is reason for great hope in this beginning of our work, for we have the possibility of learning from the successes and errors of the past fifteen years of the battered women's movement.

It seems a second chance. It is for this reason that I want to strike a note of alarm here, a warning about some of the things I see

---

1. Originally published in a 1987 issue of *NCADV Voice*, the National Coalition Against Domestic Violence newsletter.
2. Lobel, Kerry. *Naming the Violence: Speaking Out About Lesbian Battering.* Seattle: Seal Press, 1986. Print.

beginning to happen across the country among people who work with battered lesbians.

I feel the greatest thing the battered women's movement has done is to provide support for the empowerment of battered women and consequently for all women. The way it provided this support has been simple: the first was to bring women together in shelters where they could talk together in groups and realize for the first time that they were not alone, that the violence was not their fault, and that their batterers had much in common. It was radicalizing for women to learn that there is a system of belief in our society that supports battering. From this recognition, battered women came to understand that battering was about power and control, and not about sickness, stress, alcoholism, co-dependency, or the failures of women.

The second thing the movement did was to recognize that battered women are the primary source of all we can ever know about battering. Their stories are the truth of the movement. We recognized that not only do battered women hold the truth of their lives but they also hold the answers to what they want and need. The movement, at its best, took a clear position that it was not shelter workers' role (or that of anyone else) to give battered women answers or to tell them what they should do. The result, of course, was deeply empowering.

And finally, the movement came to understand that the way to end violence was to create a world that did not permit it. It recognized all the ways that violence is fostered through systems of sexism, racism, homophobia, anti-Semitism, classism, etc., how those systems support a batterer's sense of privilege, and how those systems converge in a battered woman's life. We saw immediately that we could not work on battering as an isolated phenomenon between two people. To bring about an end to violence against women, we had to seek a societal solution.

But now we see the movement divided in its pursuit of these goals. Many people have allowed battered women's programs to be defined by funders and consequently have moved away from individual empowerment through group participation and organizing and have turned instead toward the delivery of services that assume battering is an individual problem (or a family system problem) and offer "treatment" for the victim and counseling for the abuser. It is a mental health approach that views battering as a disease that can be cured by professional counselors.

It is here that I want to strike my note of alarm. As we now begin providing services to battered lesbians and seeking ways to end lesbian battering, we are finding that the first people to move in to meet the needs of lesbians are mental health professionals. (Let us be clear here that the issue is not that someone is a mental health professional but that she uses a mental health approach to dealing with lesbian battering – an individualized approach that does not lead to group analysis and action about the larger issues of violence that keep battering supported in our society).

The majority of services we hear about are one-on-one therapy or support groups led by therapists, and both services require that the victims pay, which of course prevents many women from getting help.

There are several reasons that mental health professionals are moving first to fill the need for dealing with lesbian battering. A major reason is that battered women's shelters, because of homophobia and fear, are not willing to take on the issue. If shelters are unwilling to consider battered lesbians as battered women, then the most appropriate place for battered lesbians to receive services is within the lesbian community. It is here that battered lesbians should form support groups (for free, facilitated by themselves); it is here that all lesbians should take on the issue of lesbian battering and develop analysis, do public education, and develop strategies to eliminate battering in our community. However, due to the strong denial within the lesbian community, we have been slow to take this issue on and consequently it has not felt safe for battered lesbians to be public.

Therefore the need is being met by therapists who have private practices and enough safety to provide individual services in the privacy of their offices. They are the people most readily available to meet the needs of women experiencing violence at the hands of their loved ones. But because the violence is seen as a disease, in many instances the batterers are receiving more attention and services than the victims. We are facing here what we are facing in the battered women's movement as a whole: we can offer counseling to individuals forever (and probably sustain a good income from it) but we will do little to change the system of belief and behavior that continues to provide us abusers and victims.

But with lesbian battering we are at the beginning and have a second chance. We don't have to repeat the mistakes of the battered women's movement. Our plea is for lesbian communities to end denial about lesbian battering, to learn about it directly from battered lesbians, to begin offering safe places for battered lesbians to meet in support groups, and to organize to end this violence among us. As part of this, we ask those therapists now involved with lesbian battering to become political, to organize with the community, to seek group and societal solutions, to take a social change as well as individual approach. And finally, we call on battered women's programs to work to eliminate homophobia and to make shelters safe places for battered lesbians, places where lesbians can be both safe from their abusers and safe from the abuse of homophobia.

It is not popular or easy to do organizing for social change. In fact, there seems an organized effort to discredit it. Instead of lasting social change, our society seeks efforts of charity to help individuals that suffer. We appease our consciences by paying $10 and holding hands for thirty minutes across America to raise money to feed the hungry – and we do not eliminate one single cause of hunger or poverty. We pay $15 and go to a concert for farmers or the homeless – and we do not change anything except a few individual circumstances. And we can then go back to our comfortable homes and feel righteous in our effort to help those who experience hardship. These efforts are on the level of Christmas baskets for the poor. They make a few people feel better for a day or two, but they do not change the conditions that produce the poverty or discrimination or violence.

When we give woman after woman individual counseling, we help her learn to cope with or improve her own circumstances, but we do not change the causes of violence in our society.

In this battered women's movement that includes heterosexuals, lesbians, poor and rich women, women of color, old and young women, we must renew our commitment to change the society that creates and supports violence in our lives.

34.

Future Directions of the Battered Women's Movement – Or Being a Dreamer of Dreams

1983

To talk about the future of the battered women's movement, one has to talk about dreams, about visions, or at least educated guesses.[1] Thanks to the many new books written about the battered women's movement, we know quite a lot about its origins, its history, its theory and practice: we know what we have to build on. We know for instance that it began as a grassroots movement, with women taking women into their own homes for safekeeping, with women creating shelters for other women, with leadership coming from battered women, low income women, lesbians, and women without "proper" credentials. It began with no money, no public credibility, no licensing, no certification, no permissions and sanctions from higher authority. It began because women were being beaten, and because women were becoming strong. It began because it had to be.

Some parts of the movement are still tied in very closely with these beginnings, working through safe homes, shelters with two staff members and minimal budgets, programs run by formerly battered women. Other programs have gained public sanction through state funding, federal funding, have large staffs, serve hundreds of women, and have budgets that provide competitive salaries. This battered women's movement is not easily described

1. Original Author's Note: A gift for Donna Medley, Director of the National Coalition Against Domestic Violence (NCADV) – from Suzanne Pharr, who for a moment in time forgot she hated to write. May 1983

as one whole that falls into simple categories. It has great diversity and therefore enough differences to create a fertile atmosphere for growth and sometimes for disagreement and conflict because there is no single party line or an absolute politically correct position. It is a movement that has dealt with all of the most vital women's issues at one time or one place or another: battering, rape, marital rape, incest, employment and economics, housing, transportation, reproductive rights, lesbian rights, racism, the rights of the differently abled, the care of children, equal education opportunities, etc. And out of our dialogue and argument and creativity about these issues, we have begun to change the way women are viewed and the way we view ourselves, and this is no small achievement. It is in this way that we transform the world.

But the question now is where do we go from these beginnings, from this history? Clearly, we want to continue through our work to transform the world, for we work to create a world where violence against women and children has ended, where women, children, and men use other means to resolve conflict, where there is equality, and freedom, and growth, and respect, and dignity, and self-worth, and all those many, many other things that we all honor and dream of. The question is what direction to take, what methods to use, what politics and philosophies to embrace?

Perhaps we should look at lesser visions first, those possibilities that might occur if we have little or no sense of direction, if we do not analyze our work and develop strategies to achieve what we believe in, what we want most.

Imagine this:

- That all battered women's programs were funded by the State (capital S on that one) and in return, as is its wont, the State requires its pound of flesh;

- All shelters must be licensed in order to operate – any unlicensed upstarts will be closed down;

- All shelter staff must have a Master's in Social Work or above – formerly battered women who are non-degreed can work only as closely supervised volunteers;

- Every program must have an administrator whose job is to complete the reams of paperwork required by the State;

- Periodic inspection by the State insures that the battered women all follow strict rules (which are posted), and that no one stays longer than fourteen days – each shelter has an enforced limit to the number of residents it admits and all others are turned away;

- All battered women are called "clients," are professionally counseled, and their records are open to inspection and subpoena;

- Each battered women's program must state that saving the family is its main goal, and funds must be spent equally on services to battered women and to batterers;

- All staff must dress professionally, of course – up with heels and hose, down with Nikes;

- The personnel is organized hierarchically, with top down decision-making and authority.

But what a different vision we could have:

- Battered women's programs would be funded by women throughout the country who tithe a portion of their paychecks to the movement because they know that it is through violence and the threat of violence that all women are controlled and kept from being our best selves, strong and free and safe;

- Each program would be autonomous and would answer only to the women in its community, women who would collectively care for it, nurture and guide it;

- Staff would be made up primarily of women who have experienced violence, and they would be diverse, representing all ethnic groups, classes, sexual orientations, ages; it would be difficult to tell the difference between staff, volunteers, and resident battered women; traditional education and degrees would be honored no higher than self-education and life experience;

- There would be no racism, classism, anti-Semitism, or homophobia in the shelters; every battered woman, staff person, and volunteer would feel free to be and act out who she was; cultural and personal differences would be cherished, honored, celebrated;

- The guidelines of the shelter would be formed by the staff and volunteers and residents working collectively together; when people asked, "Who owns (runs) the shelter?" the answer would be, "All women do;" there would be no hierarchy of power and authority because women would work together to make the shelter a home for those who have been driven by violence from their homes;

- No battered woman would ever be turned away from a shelter due to limitation of space; every woman would receive safety and support;

- Paperwork would be minimal and all records would be confidential; this confidentiality would be defended with all the program's collective woman-strength;

- A top priority in each program would be problem solving and support groups for women; and battered women would continue in similar groups after leaving the shelter;

- Each program would have a strong group of children-loving-women to work and play with the children in shelter; these children would be honored as people, respected for their ideas and wishes;

- The primary purpose of each battered women's program

would always be twofold: to provide safety for battered women, and to work to end violence against women and children; battered women, staff, volunteers and community women would all join together as part of an organized effort to say no to violence, to transform the world into a place where all people live in safety and freedom and equality.

In this battered women's movement, as in many areas of our lives, the choice of direction is ours as long as we're willing to do the hard work of introspection, analysis, and strategy, and as long as we let ourselves be dreamers of dreams and creators of visions.

35.

The Marriage Issue as a Distraction: Watching for Canaries in the Coal Mine

2005

Many people these days use the metaphor of "canaries in the coal mine" when talking about people or the environment under attack.[1] It is a common reference to how canaries were placed in the coal mines because if the oxygen supply decreased, they were the first to die. Their death was the warning signal for everyone else to know what was moving toward them.

Using this metaphor, I believe queers, immigrants, and prisoners are the proverbial canaries in the coal mine for the destruction of civil liberties and human rights in this country.

How these three groups of people are treated raises essential questions about human rights:

- How much can people be restrained, denied human dignity, treated as inhuman?

- How much will society allow?

- How much can be placed under the name of so-called safety and morality and stability in a society that is inching towards totalitarianism?

Immigrants, prisoners, and lesbian/gay/bi/trans people are struggling to breathe the air of freedom in a climate of increasing

1. Original Author's Note: This article first appeared in the September 2005 issue of *La Voz de Esperanza* (Vol. 18. No. 6), the newsletter for the Esperanza Peace and Justice Center based in San Antonio, Texas.

restriction. Watch these canaries closely for what they tell us about changes in our country. While these three groups share commonalities to be explored, for now I want to focus on LGBT people and how vital we are to a vision of a free and equal society.

We cannot underestimate the importance of our daily struggle to make change and its effect on society at large. LGBT opposition to rightwing authoritarianism and our efforts to envision greater freedom offers breathing space – lifesaving and creative – to all sexual beings who desire a relationship with another. Within us, there is the possibility of the potential integration and freedom of mind, body, and spirit. In our work for liberation, we are trying to carve out and expand the space for all people to live as full human beings.

We are vital to struggles for freedom. In our very bodies and aspirations we call the question: What does it mean to be fully human? Where does sexuality fit? Do we have the right to a sexual relationship? Do we have the right to our own bodies? We as LGBT people struggle for self-determination and choice, the foundation of freedom for individuals and communities, the center of our belief in human rights.

We are critical to the Right's strength and also to the fulfillment of a progressive vision for change. Homosexuality and gay marriage are used by the Right not just to divide people on the issue of sexuality but to build authoritarianism, sending the message that obedience, rigidity, and contraction of rights will save us and our crumbling society. The messages are cleverly crafted to play to people's very real fears about a changed world in which public institutions are gutted, distant corporations unsettle our work lives, and families are struggling to survive.

The marriage issue is only a very small part of the Right's much larger agenda to define family narrowly, to restrict relationships (benefits and social recognition tied to compulsory heterosexual marriage), to limit who is allowed to adopt or foster children, to increase control over our lives by closely defining who has a legitimate place in society.[2] It is part of an agenda that restricts our freedom to express our full humanity. The narrow definition of family affects not only LGBT people but also everyone whose family does not fit the definition of one man and one woman married with children.

Here is a place where we can play a critical role. *No one understands family better than we do.* We are the only oppressed group that, as a people, has to fight for inclusion in and support from our families. We have struggled with ours, sometimes lost them, sometimes gained them, and we have always *created* family. We can bring a new focus on families as they are now diversely configured in a constellation of social arrangements that has adapted to our changing culture. We can be a frontline defense against a rightwing movement that creates a hierarchy of acceptable and unacceptable, legitimate and illegitimate families.

We must make the expansion of family the ground we will constantly build and defend. There is a small moment of opportunity because, as we speak, family is being defined in the narrowest way: one man, one woman married with children. We all stand to lose: single parents, blended families, families that differ from the white U.S. cultural norm – and especially single low-income women who are parents because they will be in the first line of attack, along with LGBT folks.

In the midst of this marriage debate (or distraction), our work is to join others who are harmed by narrow definitions of family and to create definitions that include us all. Should the definition of family include only male/female relationships plus biological children sanctioned by both church and state? Or should family include those who are bound together by mutual responsibility and accountability, by common interest and by a commitment to one another's well-being? If family is the basic building block of society, then isn't it better to expand rather than limit it?

2. As outlined in greater detail in Adrienne Rich's "Compulsory Heterosexuality and Lesbian Existence"

In the discussion of marriage and family we must be careful. The Right depends on LGBT people wanting to be mainstream, to be "just like everyone else." *Mainstreaming* is important to the Right because it takes us back to central norms: white, able-bodied, middle-class – and they figure we will always default to the power of the norm. For example, in the rush to gain traditional marriage, we can easily position ourselves as "uncontroversial" couples who espouse the very same so-called norms that oppress poor people, people with disabilities, people of color, Trans people, immigrants, etc., etc.

Election season is upon us again, and anti-gay marriage amendments are on the ballot. It is time to beware: we've had too much experience with campaigns run by white, middle-class people who afterwards explain that people of color were not available to be hired. Our lesson from this: *expediency always defaults to power, not to liberation.* Campaigns often appeal to some middle ground of conservatism, promising a commitment to stay true to conservative institutions and mainstream values. We cannot let the issue of gay marriage serve to maintain or increase oppression.

The marriage issue provides a fine opportunity to work for liberation. For liberation, for the human right of relationship and full sexuality, for our desire for control of our bodies and choice, for our desire for freedom for all our identities, we must seek the leadership of those who help us expand our place in the world. For instance, we can look to Trans people and queer youth of color for new ways of thinking about the fluidity of gender, race, and sexuality. It is not conservative institutions that will save us, but those who have the courage to explore new paths to freedom. Our work is to expand possibility. Our task is to figure out in our lives, in our work, in our interactions how to broaden our definitions of family and community, of gender, of self, of choice and self-determination, how to expand our dream of democracy.

Remember: the canaries, most at risk, can not only warn us but also can lead us into the sunshine and fresh air of lives of equality, justice, and freedom.

36.

Rural Organizing: Building Community Across Difference

1994

In 1993, Wanda and Brenda Henson purchased land to create a women's education center and retreat in Ovett, Mississippi.[1] When the townspeople came upon a newsletter that, among other things, indicated that lesbians were involved, there was a highly emotional reaction to this perceived threat to the local community. After organizing by some preachers and local officials, two town meetings, relentless media coverage, intervention by Janet Reno, and supportive responses from lesbians and gay men nationally, the situation in Ovett can be described as an emotionally charged, potentially violent stand-off.

The complicated conflict that has unfolded between the women of Sister Spirit and the townspeople of Ovett, Mississippi has been much on my mind for some months now. I have been fearful that someone would be killed: a member of Sister Spirit, a townsperson, or a visitor arriving to observe the situation. With trepidation, I have watched the widespread media coverage help keep emotions intense and people stratified and polarized.

The conflict has been depicted as between diametrically opposed groups, with little middle ground: the dykes against the bigots. I've been wishing, however, that I could see more of the middle ground. I know it's there, because I'm standing on a little piece of it. As a lesbian, I have strong identification with the women of Sister Spirit, and as a woman from a low-income rural,

1. Originally published in the June 1994 issue of *Sojourner: The Women's Forum.*

Southern family, I identify with the working-class people who make up Ovett. They are both my people.

I have a vested interest in these groups learning how to make community together, for if they and others like them cannot, how then can lesbians such as myself live openly with and among our rural families and friends? If we cannot do rural organizing around lesbian and gay issues, then rural lesbians and gay men are left with limited options: leaving our roots to live in cities; living fearful invisible lives in our rural communities; or with visibility, becoming marginalized, isolated, and endangered. Not one of these options holds the promise of wholeness or freedom. We are propelled to do rural organizing because we cannot accept freedoms restricted by geography – or by race or gender or class or any other boundary our society uses for exclusion.

Ovett, then, becomes for us an opening to talk about rural issues, about how to create social change in all of our communities, without exception.

It's difficult for me to talk about rural life without first talking about the anti-rural attitudes that are prevalent in this country. Urban dwellers, particularly within the lesbian and gay movement, are pretty consistently disrespectful of rural people, especially Southerners. Our first clue is in the language that describes rural places as "hinterlands," "boondocks," "the sticks," "back side of nowhere;" and the people as "rednecks," "clods," "bubbas," and "bigots." For a movement that touts "difference" as positive, this level of prejudice and ignorance is appalling. Articles about Sister Spirit in the lesbian and gay press, as well as the mainstream press, have been filled with these anti-rural attitudes.

It is remarkable to me that someone writing from the chaos and deterioration of our major cities would assume a position of condescension toward rural people. We all have our troubles in this country, no matter where we live. I believe, however, that anti-rural attitudes are based in class prejudice. The rural United States, outside of resort and retirement communities, is mostly working class and often low income. Because of isolation and an inadequate tax base due to low population density and income, rural areas are often characterized by limited services. We must remember that lack of access and economic standing do not equal ignorance or stupidity or bigotry. Culture simply gets shaped along different lines, with different values. Both urban and rural life offer positive and negative values.

The first rule of rural organizing (as it is for all other groups) is that it needs to be done by the people affected, not others imposing their vision and will. Since resources in rural areas are often limited, this organizing should be supported, but not driven, by urban people. To achieve this partnership, we all have to get over our bad attitudes: urban disrespect and rural resentment of outsiders.

I believe that the basis of all of our organizing has to be building relationships. This belief runs counter to the notion that we are in a war, and a shoot-out is required as we line up along strictly marked and separated sides. In Ovett, community has to be built if Sister Spirit is to stay on its land and thrive; otherwise, there will have to be a shoot-out of one kind or another (guns, lawsuits, increasing harassment), and there will be death or flight or the restricted and tortuous life of two armed camps. It is through building relationships that we achieve transformation.

One day, when I was being particularly angry at the people of Ovett (having very little information about them and forgetting that they were my people), I began thinking about my own rural background. I remembered my first sixteen years of lesbian invisibility, how terrified I was of losing my family and community relationships, and how I lost their authenticity anyway because I cut so much of myself off from them. I thought about how everybody lost: I lost part of my humanity, and they lost a chance to develop theirs through knowing me. The road to coming out publicly was long and slow. Building relationships based on authenticity (our whole and true selves) is slow work. Now, 25 years later, I have deep, loving relationships with my large rural Georgia family, people very much like the townspeople of Ovett. Yet here I was in 1994, judging the people of Ovett harshly because they couldn't do overnight what it took me, as a lesbian, sixteen years to do: to overcome my fear, my misunderstanding, my lack of information and support, and my internalized homophobia. I had to stop myself and say, "Isn't it a bit much to ask the local people to do immediate change?" Yes, far more information is out there now to help them (and young lesbians and gay men), but who is delivering that information and how?

Relationships are not built on abstractions but on human interactions: they have to have a human face. Part of our work is to figure out how to put a human face on what, for most people, is the *idea* of homosexuality, to transform it through genuine relationships with lesbians and gay men.

In rural communities (and elsewhere), whether we are just becoming public about being lesbian or gay or are moving in from the outside, we are usually entering the community for the first time. It is, in a sense, someone else's community, because we have not had a presence there as who we are in this part of ourselves. Consequently, we have to be thoughtful about how we enter. We have to ask if immediate confrontation gives the best result, that is, does it open up the most space for living freely, for creating the most productive dialogue?

In the early 1970s, I spent four years on a women's farm in a thinly-populated rural farming area in the mountains of northwest Arkansas. Our household ranged from five to twelve women and children, plus dogs, cats, goats, and countless visitors who were part of the great lesbian migration back and forth across the country at that time. Our farm was both isolated and exposed, and we could not survive there without strong relationships with our neighbors.

We built those relationships slowly in numerous ways. The first was by introducing ourselves to our neighbors and to those who lived in the small town and by constantly asking for advice. We hung out where the local people did – at stores, the lumber mill, restaurants – and had long conversations about ourselves and about the area. We purchased goods and services from people who lived around us. When people drove by and stopped on the dirt road by our house to chat, we stopped whatever we were doing and talked. We went to community events such as basketball games and estate sales and church fundraisers. People became interested in our successes and disasters and our stubborn hard work. They thought we were strange but good hearted and often amusing.

Our sexual orientation was not directly announced to the community at large but lived openly and talked about to some privately. While trying to live as openly as possible, we also tried to respect the community's customs. For example, almost every urban lesbian who arrived at our door to visit wanted to 1) take off her shirt and "be free," and 2) let her dog off its leash to "be free." We did not permit either. This was not a simple nor an easy decision. We understood that bare breasts had become symbolic of women's freedom (if men can bare theirs…) and that urban women had dreams and fantasies of some isolated place where they and their dogs could run free. We lived among farming people, however, and the dogs, untrained in farm behavior, threatened both our animals and the animals of our neighbors. As for the bare breasts, we decided that this was not the issue we would choose as the focus for our struggle for freedom. There were many more compelling issues, and besides, we wanted to choose them for ourselves as long-term residents rather than having them pressed upon us by someone who was merely passing through.

This work was not always easy or successful. One of the local teachers at Kingston (town of 300) was fired for being a lesbian because she was seen hanging out with us. Generally, though, the community came to terms with us as we did with them. The greatest dissension and conflict came not from our being lesbians or part of the perceived back-to-the-land hippie lifestyle, but from our political work that threatened their economic lives. The major chemical companies were bringing back defoliants from Vietnam and selling them to local farmers to clear their mountain land of trees and brush. These defoliants (now called Agent Orange) contained dioxin and were already causing concern about their effect on the community's health. We were documenting stillbirths, deformities, cancer, and other ill effects and vigorously and publicly opposing the use of 24-D and 245-T, the chemicals used. It was this work that brought rage from the farmers because they felt hurt economically when they could not use this new technology to create previously impossible-to-reach pastureland.

The lessons we learned then remain true now in this time when lesbians and gay men are under the massive attack from the Right. All of the polls show that when people personally know lesbians and gay men, they often overcome their homophobia. It is the lack of knowledge that creates the climate for prejudice and bigotry.

I am struck by the fact that those who made trouble for my friends and me in northwest Arkansas for being a lesbian teacher or fighting Dow Chemical and the policies of the Vietnam era are the same ones making trouble in Ovett. They are rural people entrenched in the literal interpretation of the *Bible*, unfamiliar with lesbians and gay men, and, most importantly, struggling for economic survival in an economy that is discarding them. The difference is that they are now bolstered by national organizations that provide support and money and who pump out strategic misinformation so fast that people live in a state of heightened confusion. Another major difference is that twenty years ago we had time to deal with our differences and to do it on the community level. Today, a fast, ever-circling media shapes public opinion so rapidly that we are impeded in doing the slow, face-to-face work that must take place in community.

Putting a human face on homosexuality addresses one part of the issue. The Right's primary success, however, comes from being able to scapegoat effectively lesbians and gay men as contributing to economic ills, just as they have scapegoated African Americans and Jews. Their major success has come from linking civil rights to "minority status," which supposedly provides "special rights" such as affirmative action and quotas. In the historic rhetoric of anti-Semitism, the Right argues falsely that lesbians and gay men, though small in numbers, are wealthier than "average" citizens and control institutions such as the media secretly, from behind the scenes. Then, with a leap into rhetoric of racism, they argue that if lesbians and gay men achieve civil rights enforcement through "affirmative action and quotas," we will indeed take away jobs from deserving heterosexuals and destroy the small piece of the pie now allotted to low-income people. Clearly, building community will take more than getting people to recognize our humanity as lesbians and gay men; it is also necessary for all of us to learn how to make connections with people around issues of economic injustice. Those were the conversations we failed to hold in northwest Arkansas while we were busy breaking new ground around lesbian and gay issues.

The places where those economic justice connections can be made in rural areas are most obvious in the arena where direct services and community organizing meet: food banks, housing construction (such as Habitat for Humanity), battered women's organizations, youth organizing (especially through community sports), senior centers and meals-on-wheels, and environmental cleanup. These are some of the places where lesbians and gay men belong, a visible presence working for economic and social justice and talking about our lives.

What I have learned from rural organizing is virtually the same as what I have learned from urban organizing: we must build lasting authentic relationships across many boundaries – race, gender, class, sexual identity, physical disability, and so on – but of all of these, the most difficult for U.S. citizens as a whole is class. It is here that we do not make full connections, that we have not built alliances and coalitions. And it is this refusal to deal with economic injustice that will trip us up over and over again and prevent our dream of creating a multiracial multi-issue movement for justice. We cannot separate ourselves from rural communities or communities of color or working-class communities or any other community where economic injustice has had an extraordinary impact. To do so takes the heart out of our work for social justice, and without that center, it will not hold; we will always be working on the fringe of true and lasting social change.

37.

A Match Made in Heaven: Lesbian Leftie Chats with a Promise Keeper

1997

In February, as I boarded a plane to Portland, Oregon, I overheard a man say to a woman, "We're almost all Promise Keepers on this flight. We are returning from an Atlanta meeting of 43,000 pastors."[1] "Forty-three thousand pastors," I thought. "That's like 43,000 organizers because they have influence over their congregations." I entered the plane thinking, "We're sunk."

For the last couple of years I have been watching the growth of the Promise Keepers with fascination and fear. As a Southern lesbian feminist and anti-racist worker, I am keenly interested in any group of white men organizing around issues related to women and people of color.

As a long-time community organizer, I have to admire the brilliance of the Promise Keepers' organizing strategy. How smart it is to recognize not only the anger and confusion that men have about this changing society, but also their desire for connection and purpose.

How smart to bring them into sports stadiums around the country to sing, touch, do the wave, and bond through physical and emotional contact they rarely allow themselves.

I believe the Promise Keepers are the ground troops in an authoritarian movement that seeks to merge church and state. It does not matter that a rightwing agenda is not overt in the

---

1. Published in the June 1997 issue of *Quest: A Monthly for Religious Liberals.* Reprinted with permission from *The Progressive.*

formative stages of this movement; when the leaders are ready to move their men in response to their agenda, they will have thousands disciplined to obey and command.

The plane was full of men sporting new Promise Keepers shirts. The scene reminded me of the 1987 March on Washington, which I attended along with thousands of lesbians and gay men. For the first time in our lives, we were the majority in airplanes, subways, buses, restaurants, and the streets. The experience was exhilarating. The Promise Keepers on the plane seemed to be having a similar experience, as though they had found each other for the first time.

After trying to escape through reading, I finally gave up and began chatting with the man next to me, dressed in a blue work shirt and jeans and reading a Tom Clancy novel. He reminded me very much of my brothers from rural Georgia. I asked if he was returning from Atlanta. "Yes," he replied. "I've just been to the Promise Keepers meeting, and I'm returning to my small town in Oregon."

I told him that I was a feminist, a civil-rights worker, and a lesbian, that I have very mixed feelings about the Promise Keepers, and that I wanted him to tell me about them.

He told me that he was pastor at a Baptist church, married, father of a teenage son, and that he would enjoy talking about his experience. "You are the second homosexual I've ever met," he said, adding with a grin. "I think." With that introduction, we launched into an hour-and-a-half-long conversation.

The pastor told me that the first thing the Promise Keepers make clear is that men are responsible for all that's wrong with the family; they are not victims.

I told him that was going a little too far for this feminist – I think women might have some responsibility for the negative side of the ledger, too.

He said the Promise Keepers were not to dominate their wives but to lead them. When I asked what this meant, he said, "Man's role is laid out in the *Bible* – 'As God is to man, man is to the family' – and it is to take charge of his family. This means listening to their needs and wishes, then deciding what is best for them."

I said, "As a feminist, I am deeply concerned about shared decision-making, about equality."

"We share the conversations, but I make the decisions," he said. "My job is to lead."

This talk about leadership made me feel that I was in a time warp in which the women's movement had never occurred. I thought about the current status of women struggling with families, jobs, and intimate relationships. I thought about stories I have read that mention how pleased some Promise Keepers wives are to have their husbands taking a dominant role in the family. With some sadness I considered how damning this is of many male-female relationships: that men are often so absent emotionally that women would be willing to give up autonomy in order to gain their husbands' presence.

I suggested the Promise Keepers could make an enormous contribution to women if they added an additional promise to their credo: that they would not lift their hand against women, and that they would stop other men from committing violence against women and children.

The Promise Keepers are against harming women, he said. They want to protect them. But adding an eighth promise would have to be up to the leadership.

Of everything that happened to this pastor at the meeting, the most life-changing, he said, was racial reconciliation. He said he had never thought about himself as someone prejudiced or discriminatory, and he came to recognize it in himself: "I'm not an emotional man, but I cried along with the audience when the men of color were called to the stage and they could not get there because they were intercepted by white pastors hugging them, shaking their hands, pounding them on the back."

The pastors were sent home, he said, to work to bring about racial reconciliation in their churches.

Since my conversation with the pastor on the airplane, Ralph Reed has been calling for racial reconciliation in the wake of the recent rash of Black church burnings in the South. Calls from the Christian Coalition and the Promise Keepers for racial reconciliation do not include any effort to end institutional racism, or to stop coded attacks on "welfare mothers" or immigrants or affirmative action. Rather, moving into Black churches gives the religious right a foothold in the Black community. In this way, the call for racial reconciliation is one of the most insidious aspects of the Promise Keepers and their allies on the Christian right. Just as the Right is hungry for people of color who are willing to denounce affirmative action and the civil rights struggles that have traditionally benefited their communities, the Promise Keepers' recruitment of Black church leaders looks like a way to persuade the Black community to act against its own best interests.

I asked the pastor about the Promise Keepers' attitudes toward lesbians and gays.

The pastor said it was not for a Promise Keeper to judge homosexuals ("That is God's job") but that they believe homosexuality is immoral because the Bible says it is.

"This is not judging?" I thought.

He said that he was sure there were many of us who were fine people but that we suffered from being identified with our "fringe" people who marched in those San Francisco parades.

I asked him if Jesus today would not be thought of as gay – an unmarried thirty-three-year-old who spent almost all of his time with twelve close male friends, one of whom in particular was "beloved."

He said, "No doubt if Jesus returned today, he might not be accepted in many churches."

We then talked about how few were the references in the *Bible* to same-sex relationships and how many were the references to sharing wealth, caring for those who have less, and opening one's home and heart to others. Why, then, did fundamentalists not have a strong economic agenda for the redistribution of wealth?

It's true, he said. This is a contradiction.

In the end, I thought we had communicated honestly with each other and that on some points, we had moved toward one another in understanding. It seemed to me that a great difference between us was his belief in the literal truth of the *Bible,* and my belief that it is an historical document with great spiritual content. I told him I thought that almost all of Christendom falls somewhere between those two positions. He agreed.

I wondered, can people who have very different beliefs and cultural practices live in peace with one another?

My final question to him was: Can you and I live in homes side by side, borrow sugar from one another, and encourage our children to play together? He said *yes*.

This conversation led me to think more deeply about the difference between the Right's *leaders* (those engaged in an organizing strategy that threatens democracy) and its *followers* (those searching for solutions to social and economic instability, whose heartfelt beliefs make them easy targets for manipulation). Many progressives write off the latter, discarding them as ignorant or mean.

Our conversation stayed on my mind for weeks afterwards, and I thought of this one Promise Keeper with respect and continued interest. Then one day he phoned me long distance from his small town, saying he was just calling to keep in touch and to say what a profound effect our conversation had had on him. "It eliminated whole areas of ignorance for me," he said.

"Me too," I replied. My conversations with this Promise Keeper made me understand that progressive people must rethink their relation to the American Right. *How do we point out the differences between the generals of this army and their recruits?*

How do we talk to people who are different from ourselves?

How do we hold different beliefs and still live in harmony?

Is there any hope for preventing the merger of church and state if we do not hold authentic conversations with those who believe fervently in the inerrancy of the *Bible*?

How do we get closer to people's real needs and their values in our organizing for change?

Finally, how do we carry on this conversation and organize as progressives committed to equal rights for everyone – nothing more, nothing less?

38.

Farming Our Politics

1989

I define myself as an organizer and an activist and, when I'm at my best, a farmer and a revolutionary.[1] As the eighth child of Georgia dirt farmers I sometimes think that working in the fields during my first eighteen years prepared the ground for most of my subsequent political thinking.

Ours was a family farm, the kind that never made any money but kept ten people alive and growing and thriving. On eighty-five acres, we farmed with mules and plows and finally, in the fifties, with a tractor. We sold some of our harvest at the state farmer's market out of the back of a pickup truck. To survive, we bartered goods and services, and our highest value was placed on independence and cooperation.

We knew we had to have both independence and cooperation in order to survive. If we lost our independence, we would lose our freedom to be who we were, and if we did not have cooperation with others, we would not survive: the result of these losses would be spiritual and physical death.

These values have carried over into my political beliefs: that I must work to enable all of us to have the freedom to be who we are and this must be done in a context of cooperation so that all of us survive. The practice of these beliefs necessitates equality: non-hierarchal structures, consensus, shared power.

Among farmers and people who think and talk about farming there are two different positions about the best way to

---

1. Originally published under the title "Farming My Politics" in the September 1989 issue of *Transformation* (Vol. 4., No. 3), the Women's Project newsletter.

grow the food for the world. The first position is that bigger is better, that we must produce on a large scale, that we must be big business. These people believe that large farms, usually owned by corporations or conglomerates, using high technology, large machinery and the newest chemicals are the only way to feed the world. These farms use enormous amounts of gasoline, water, electricity, oil, and they produce enormous amounts of goods. There is a sense that the land can be taken care of chemically and will keep producing as long as new farming technology is created.

The second position is that smaller is better, that we need small farms that are small businesses providing income for small groups of people who live on the land. These people believe in low technology and small machinery, in as few chemicals as possible, in decentralization, where produce is sold at state or local farmers markets. They believe that our resources such as oil are not limitless, and that our water-tables are disappearing. They believe in replenishing the land and in working to keep the topsoil from disappearing. They believe that land can be abused and destroyed.

I take the second position.

It didn't take me long in my political experience to discover that there were two similar positions people take about political movements.

The first position is that the way to get bigger and better is to create institutional structures as fast as possible and to connect them to the mainstream of society. Those who hold this position work for social reform by lobbying for legislative change, working on systems, engaging in electoral politics, and seeking government funding for programs.

The second position chooses farming language to name itself: grassroots. Those who hold this position believe that our work should be local, beginning with small groups of people seeking answers to local and consequently societal questions. They believe that change comes slow, and from within. Autonomy and independence from external controls are highly valued. Once the small group becomes strong, then there is a need for networking, coalescing, cooperating.

Here, too, I hold the second position.

Working with the earth takes patience. After the pleasure of preparing the ground and planting the seeds, there is the waiting which can be prolonged by droughts, floods, high winds. All can be destroyed in one day of disastrous weather. But the joy of farming is the possibility of beginning anew, if not this season, then next. Renewal is always possible as long as one respects the land. There is that green and shining moment of rebirth in the spring, and all of the work that goes with it. Life is not finished with one season's effort.

The land loves diversity. Plant the same crops year after year, without variety, and the land loses its vitality and ability to produce fully. Left alone, the land gives us hundreds of different plants on any given acre. Many types and varieties have been diminished through the application of high technology to farming, but people are countering this potential loss by collecting and saving old seeds to make sure that we can have on this earth all our wonderful variety.

The land requires replenishment. We cannot just take from it year after year for our own needs without returning sustenance to it. When that replenishment happens in a consistent and thoughtful way, then the yield of the land is large and unending.

I have never understood government involvement in farming. I don't understand paying farmers in the 1950s to leave fields unplanted, those same fields that are filled with scrub pines and sagebrush today throughout the South. I don't understand buying up surplus milk and cheese and wheat and corn and letting it rot in warehouses while large portions of the world's population go without food. I don't understand the practice of paying dairy farmers to have their herds slaughtered.

I don't understand the combined forces of government and banks urging farmers to expand their holdings at high prices and then foreclosing on them now when farm prices are low.

I need evidence that the government's involvement is for the best interest of farmers and food for a hungry world and not for political coercion and control.

I don't understand the involvement of the government in social change movements, here or abroad. I don't understand a government who calls dissenters at home "terrorists" and terrorists abroad "freedom fighters." I don't understand a government that says it has to destroy a village in order to save it. I don't understand a government that dismantles piece by piece our civil rights and civil liberties and calls those who struggle to maintain our civil rights and human values "anti-American" and puts them in jail when they protest government sanctioned injury to our people. I need evidence that the government's involvement in social change movements is because it wants to help create a world where all of us can be who we are, living with justice and peace in our lives.

Movement work, like small farming, is slow. It requires thoughtful, careful steps, autonomy and independent thought, diversity and inclusiveness. It requires resistance to adversity and a commitment to begin again after losses and defeats. Movement work is people putting their acts of resistance and creation and growth together, people who refuse to let the seeds disappear and who save them for the future, people who refuse to destroy a village in order to save it, people who believe that change is made one person at a time, until our numbers are legion.

39.

Reflections on Liberation

Author's Note: This selection originally appeared as the final chapter of *In the Time of the Right: Reflections on Liberation* (1996).[1] When I published this piece 25 years ago, I had witnessed multiple means social change activists used to lift up our common humanity and move us away from hate and division. I am including it again in this collection because I still believe the inspiration is needed in face of the rapid growth of violence and division we face. As Dr. Vincent Harding said, the world we want is yet to be born and it is our work to create it.

— **Suzanne Pharr, 2021.**

—

1996

Liberation politics: seeking social and economic justice for all people; supporting inclusion, autonomy, choice, wholeness; building and honoring relationships; developing individual and institutional integrity, responsibility and accountability; redefining and sharing power.

These political times call for renewed dialogue about and commitment to the politics of liberation. Because a truly democratic society is always in the process of redefining itself, its evolution is fueled by struggles for liberation on the part of everyone wishing to participate in the development of the institutions and policies that govern our lives. Liberation requires a struggle against discrimination based on race, class, gender,

1. Pharr, S. (1996). *In the Time of the Right: Reflections on Liberation.* Berkley: Chardon Press, 1996.

sexual identity, ableism and age – those barriers which keep large portions of the population from having access to economic and social justice, from being able to participate fully in the decisions affecting our lives, from having a full share of both the rights and responsibilities of living in a free society.

The politics of domination idealizes and promotes the values of being separate, of being elite, of being responsible for and to only a small group of people. As the Right practices them, such politics bring about not only separation but deep social divisions, forced rivalry, and mean-spiritedness. *The politics of liberation* offer us the values of sharing power, of leading a humane life responsible to and for one's fellow human beings and the earth. The one offers oligarchy for the few; the other democracy for the many.

Perhaps the single greatest difference between the Right and progressive people is our belief in democracy. We are the pro-democracy forces facing an anti-democratic agenda. We must seize the language of democracy and use its principles in our lives and work. We are part of an honored tradition of justice-seeking people and stand proudly on the shoulders of those who have gone before us: such great freedom fighters as Sojourner Truth, Mahatma Gandhi, Nelson Mandela, Lillian Smith, Martin Luther King, Jr., Joe Hill, Fannie Lou Hamer, Mother Jones, Emma Goldman, John Brown. The list goes on and on.

Because the voices dominating this country's leadership speak only of the false "democracy" of the captalist marketplace, rather than the democracy of diverse people living in community, we have to find ways to raise new voices that speak to the transformational and educational political work of building a wider, more inclusive community. Henry A. Giroux, in his compelling article, "Educational Leadership and the Crisis of Democratic Government," states that

> ...the real challenge of leadership is... educating students to live in a multicultural world, to face the challenge of reconciling difference and community, and to address what it means to have a voice in shaping one's future as part of a broader task of enriching and

extending the imperatives of democracy and human rights on both a national and global level.[2]

This is the challenge for all of us. The work of liberation politics is to change hearts and minds, develop empathy with and sympathy for other people, and help each other discover how we are inextricably linked together for our common good and our survival on this planet.

Like power, liberation cannot be given; it must be created. Liberation politics requires

- Helping individuals to fulfill their greatest potential by providing truthful information along with the tools and skills for using it, supporting their autonomy and self-government, and connecting them to life in community with others;

- Fostering both individual freedom and mutual responsibility for others;

- Recognizing that freedom demands people always be able to make their own choices about their lives;

- Creating a politic of shared power rather than power-over;

- Learning the nonviolent skills of compromise and mediation in the sometimes difficult collective lives of family and community – in organizations, the workplace, and governing bodies;

- Developing integrity in relationships through understanding that the same communal values – generosity and fairness, responsibility and freedom, forgiveness and atonement – must be maintained not just in personal relationships but in the workplace, social groups, and governing bodies;

- Treating everyone as a valued whole person, not as

2. Giroux, Henry. "Educational Leadership and the Crisis of Democratic Government." *Educational Researcher* 21.4 (1992): 4-11.

someone to be used or controlled;

- Maintaining civility in our relationships and being accountable for our behavior;

- Seeing cultural differences as life-enhancing, as expanding possibilities;

- Placing a broad definition of human rights at the center of our values, ensuring that every person has food, shelter, clothing, safety, education, health care, and a livable income.

Most of us who seek liberation do not believe that the Right will be overcome by force or by mimicking its tactics. In fact, we must not take on its language and strategies. We do believe, however, that we have to organize to defend ourselves from its attacks as well as organize to put our own vision of liberation in place. We must establish a proactive agenda that has justice and equality at its core. We believe that this organizing will be slow work because we need to develop political organizations with constituencies who fully understand the choices facing them and who are committed to progressive social change for all of us. Otherwise, people will be swayed by whatever the most charismatic leader of the moment says, whatever the most expensive media ads convey, or whatever fear tactic is used against them. Political education, linked with action, is imperative. Our work is developing people, not just ideas – people who are strong, knowledgeable, and courageous enough to take on the work for economic and social justice.

We are seeking ways to bring people together to work on common causes across differences. If, indeed, all oppressions are connected, then it follows that the targets of this oppression are connected as well as their solutions. This interconnection leads us to the idea of collaborative efforts to create democratic values, discourse and institutions.

We believe that we will succeed when we collectively create a vision that in practice offers a way of life so attractive that people will not be able to resist it. As progressive people across this country we are working to create a multi-issue, multi-racial and multi-cultural liberation movement; we are trying to redefine our work and bring more integrity to it; we are engaged in developing a clearer, more compelling vision, building stronger relationships among justice-seeking people, and including more people in the process of creating a democracy that works for all of us.

In the Time of the Right: Liberating the Life of the Spirit

In recent years, the left in this country has been successful in articulating and debating ideas but not very strong in touching people's spiritual lives. We often talk about the need to change hearts and minds as a kind of gesture in the direction of the emotional and spiritual life that exists in people. However, I think that what is needed is not just changing hearts and minds but connecting hearts and minds to each other; overcoming the false divisions between mind and emotions, matter and spirit, the intellectual and the intuitive life.

In the mid-1990s, we are seeing a rapid rise of mean-spiritedness, fed by talk radio and television, the rhetoric of cynical politicians, and the embittered disillusionment of people whose hopes and dreams have been destroyed and whose lives feel threatened. It is a mean-spiritedness that seems to feed upon itself, seeking everywhere someone to blame, someone who is the cause of this pain, this disappointment, this failure to succeed. The airwaves are filled with rancor and anger, cynicism and accusation. Recently, I have been asking people to describe the mood of the country. They respond, "depressed, angry, overwhelmed, feeling isolated and cut off, mistrustful, mean, hurt, fearful." To succeed, our organizing must address these feelings.

As progressive and moderate voices are excluded or silenced or mimic this rage and cynicism, I worry about our better selves diminishing from lack of nurturance and support. I think of our better selves as that place where compassion, sympathy, empathy, tolerance, inclusiveness, and generosity reside. What one might call "soul" is the ability to experience empathy and express sympathy toward others, especially those different from or less fortunate than ourselves. It is our feeling intensely connected to, not separate from, humanity. It is a part of ourselves that has to be nurtured and developed.

If access to our better selves could be visualized as a door, I fear that door is gradually closing. All of our strategies for social change will mean very little if we do not have access to that place inside us where generosity, for example, lives. Much of our work has to be focused on nurturing the life of the spirit, on keeping the door to our better selves as open as possible.

Cultural work offers one of our best means of nurturing the individual spirit and our sense of connection to others. It is through the creation of art and culture that the spirit is fed and kept alive and our common humanity is expressed and exposed. Through art and culture we enter the lives and experiences of others, gaining the possibility of understanding, the foundation for empathy and sympathy. In a democracy one of the highest goals should be multi-culturalism – the presentation of the experiences and expressions of the many, bringing us together and opening the way for participation in all aspects of society. Multi-culturalism is present when everyone has a voice, and when we present our lives truthfully in a setting of equality.

During this current movement of the Right toward authoritarianism and theocracy, it is not surprising that conservatives are eliminating funding for the National Endowment for the Arts (NEA) and the National Endowment for the Humanities (NEH). Not only is freedom of expression at issue in this defunding strategy ("our tax dollars won't be spent on things that don't support our values") but also at issue is the value of art and cultural expression in this democratic society we are developing. The NEA and NEH are institutions designed to make art and culture more inclusive of everyone; they are owned by the public and attempt to represent its diversity, its many cultures and voices. They are critically needed for building and supporting our humanness in this time of dehumanization. Without these national sources of funding, we reserve most of art and culture for the moneyed elite.

In much of our social change work, we incorporate art and culture only as "add-ons" – the concert after a conference, the song or poem at the beginning of the meeting. We rarely see cultural organizing as social change work. One reason is that we are stuck in the same old methods of organizing and do not question how people learn, what moves us to change. Another reason is that we become too focused on a single goal or issue and do not consider the wholeness of ourselves and our constituency. For instance, in building a movement, eating and singing together may be as important as handing out leaflets. Being able to involve our families with us in our work may be as important as recruiting new members. The basis for successful organizing work is people who are connected, not separated, people who feel whole, not fragmented. To insist upon our wholeness is to insist upon our humanity.

In a recent cultural workshop led by civil rights singer and cultural worker Jane Sapp, I witnessed another way of delivering a message about our humanity. A group of my peers struggled with the issue of how, in this time of anti-immigrant sentiment, to help people understand that they were a part of multi-racial, multi-cultural America. The result was a decision to transform several of the most powerful American symbols: the flag, the pledge of allegiance, and the "Star Spangled Banner." In a day's time they created a very complex design of a large traditional U.S. flag that had movable parts. It formed the backdrop for their presentation. This multi-racial group of cultural workers marched in the room to the beat of Japanese and Native American drums. They read a re-worded pledge of allegiance and sang a national anthem that were both inclusive and welcoming, offering opportunity and justice. Then they walked up to the flag, and in the rhythmic movements of dance, took it apart, piece by piece, and reconstructed a new flag from the pieces. It became a sun of blended colors with multi-colored beams and sun spots radiating from it. This symbol, with its new design and many colors, now included and represented all of us. It touched places in us that we did not know were accessible. Almost every one of the 30 of us in the workshop burst into tears because of the power of this new image of this country where we had sought recognition and support for our human dignity. We had not fully realized what great power these symbols held for us, or the depth of our feeling for a country that had marginalized so many of us.

Storytelling is one of the strongest traditional cultural expressions that helps us feel whole and connected. Nothing is more critical than storytelling to defining our humanity. Those who control storytelling have power over that definition and our understanding of ourselves. It is essential that we not give over the control of our stories to corporate and rightwing media. When telling our stories, we assert both our individuality and our connection to others, and we make others aware of our identity and history. What better way to counter gross stereotyping, demonizing, and dehumanization than by presenting a multiplicity of voices and experiences, each individualized, each unique, and each connected to a common history.

There are many examples of storytelling – through traditional storytelling, music, art, dance, film, and books – as part of social change work.

Jane Sapp spends much of her time working with African American children. Sitting at her piano with children grouped around her, she encourages them to talk about their lives, the hard parts, the shining moments, their indignation over injustice, their hopes and dreams. Then she works with them to create songs out of their own histories and experiences. In a matter of a few hours, one can see change in these children's faces, hear pride and enthusiasm in their voices, sense a transformation of spirit. They are building themselves.

In the early days of the women's anti-violence movement, women met in groups to tell the story of the violence that had occurred in their lives. For many, it was the first time they had told anyone what happened – the rape, incest, battering, torture – and telling the story to others brought them out of isolation and gave them connection to a group. But what followed next was the foundation for a women's anti-violence movement: after women heard each other's stories, they came to recognize the great similarities among them. Through discussing these commonalities, they created an analysis of the relationship between the perpetrator of violence and its target, and they recognized that though the victim is frequently blamed for the violence, the fault lay with the perpetrator and the society that accepted the violence. Those desiring to end violence against themselves and other women then moved to take action: creating safe homes and battered women's shelters, hotlines and support groups, working with police, changing laws, confronting batterers and rapists, providing political education and changing public policy. Telling stories is still the very heart of the women's anti-violence movement.

Telling stories provides especially rich results when dissimilar people share stories with each other. This has been our experience with the Women's Watchcare Network at the Women's Project in Little Rock, Arkansas. It is a project to monitor and expose hate violence. When we hold meetings in small towns, we bring together people from all of the areas of biased violence that we monitor, and for many it is the first time they have sat in a mixture of Jews, people of color, white women, lesbians and gay men. We have witnessed transformation take place when, for example, an African American gay man tells the story of the violence he has experienced, and an older white churchwoman realizes that it is akin to the violence she has known in her own life. When she recognizes that gay men are hated because they are seen both as being like women and as betraying male dominance, and that their murders are similar in almost every way to the murders of women (overkill, sexual assault, disfigurement), it is an epiphany for her and usually for everyone in the room. By telling their stories, people in these Watchcare meetings become connected through understanding the similarities of the prejudice and violence against them. Once one connection is made, there is an opening for people to begin seeing each other as individualized and fully human.

One of the legitimate criticisms of the left, or of progressive people, is that we spend too much time talking with each other and not enough time with people who do not share our views. We must find language and access for these conversations; we must take our stories to people who have not heard them, and we must listen carefully and respectfully to theirs. Recently, I had the opportunity, on a plane, to sit next to a rural Oregon pastor who was returning from a large meeting of the Promise Keepers. He said I was the "second homosexual" he had ever met, and he was the first Promise Keeper I had ever encountered. For an hour and a half, we talked about politics and our lives, frankly and with open hearts – sex, dominance of women, pedophilia, economics, violence against women, exclusion of lesbians and gay men from churches, male responsibility, racial injustice. By the end of that conversation, we had inched toward one another in our political/ social understanding. Did we agree on core beliefs? No. But in answer to the final question of our conversation – could we live in houses side by side, borrow a cup of sugar over the fence, and let our children play together? – the answer from both of us was yes.

Cultural work keeps us constantly grappling with the issue of values. It is currently popular for politicians and preachers to create a loud din of condemnation on the subject of "traditional values." Much of their focus is on scapegoating particular groups of people as being responsible for the breakdown of these "traditional" values: liberals, feminists, lesbians and gay men. In fact, cultural work and art offer the opposite of scapegoating: the celebration of both the individual and the community, the connections between us all; the possibility of building relationships. When we begin with this foundation (rather than one of authoritarianism and dominance) for determining values, we allow the development of empathy and sympathy which lead us to value generosity, inclusion, kindness, fairness, responsibility for ourselves and others. And these bring us to our great democratic goals of justice, equality, and freedom – for all.

Transformational Organizing and Building Community

For whatever reasons, progressive people have not always talked a great deal about the strong moral convictions underlying why we do this work of social justice: *it is because we believe every person counts, has human dignity, and deserves respect, equality and justice.* This morality is the basis for our vision, and when we do our best vision-based organizing (as opposed to response-based or expediency-based), all our work flows from this basic belief.

Ours is a noble history. Because progressive people believe in the inclusion of everyone in the cause of justice and equality, we have struggled for civil rights for people of color, for women, for people with disabilities, and now for lesbians, gay men, bisexuals, and Transgender people. We have worked to save the environment, to provide women autonomy and choice concerning our bodies, to end unjust wars, to end homelessness, hunger, and poverty, to create safe workplaces, decent wages and fair labor practices, to honor treaty rights, to eliminate HIV/AIDS and improve healthcare, to eliminate biased crime and violence against women and children. We share broad principles of inclusion, fairness, and justice. We must not forget what provides the fire for our work, what connects us in the struggle for freedom and equality.

We are living in a time in which people are crying out for something to believe in, for a moral sense, for purpose, for answers that will bring some calm to the chaos they feel in their lives. As progressive people, we have not always offered up our vision of the world, our activities for justice, as a moral vision. When we have, as during the Civil Rights Movement, people working together for a common good have felt whole.

I believe it is our moral imperative to help each other make connections, to show how everyone is interrelated and belongs in community, or as it is currently expressed, "We all came on different ships but we're in the same boat now." It is at our peril if we do work that increases alienation and robs meaning from life. Today's expressions of violence, hatred, and bigotry are directly related to the level of alienation and disconnection felt by people. For our very survival, we must develop sense of common humanity.

It may be that our most important political work is figuring out how to make the full human connection, how to engage our hearts as well as our minds, how to heal the injuries we have suffered, how to do organizing that transforms people as well as institutions. With these as goals, we need to re-think our strategies and tactics.

We have to think about our vision of change. Are we involved in a struggle for power that requires forces and resources on each side and a confrontational show-down in which only one side wins? If we are in a shoot-out, then the progressive side has already lost, for certainly there are more resources on the Right at this moment. In other cases where we can organize the most resources, such as the No on 9 campaign in Oregon in 1992, what is the nature and permanency of the win? The anti-gay and lesbian constitutional amendment was defeated, but in general, people did not have a sense of ecstatic victory. I think there were two primary reasons: 1) the Right immediately announced its intention to take the fight to local rural communities and to build a string of victories in areas where it had developed support – indicating that this is indeed a long struggle for the hearts and souls of Oregonians; and 2) the campaign did not facilitate the building of lasting relationships, of communities, of progressive institutions – because it did not see itself as part of a movement. At the end, I believe people felt a war-like atmosphere had been created, but that the language and tactics of war had failed them. In the months that followed the election victory, people seemed fatigued, wary, often dispirited and in retreat. Rather than being transformed into new politics and relationships by their experience, they seemed battered by it.

Transformational Organizing

There is something to be learned when victory feels like defeat. Somehow, people did not emerge from the Oregon experience with a sense of vitality, of wholeness, of connection. Justice-seeking people must call into question our methods of organizing. Often we have thought that effective organizing is simply being able to move people as a group, sometimes through manipulation, to act in a particular way to achieve a goal. Too often the end has justified the means, and we have failed to follow Gandhi's belief that every step toward liberation must have liberation embedded within it. By concentrating on moving people to action, we have often failed to hear the voice of their spirit, their need for connection and wholeness – not for someday after the goal has been gained, but in the very process of gaining it.

I am not arguing that we should give up direct action, civil disobedience, issue campaigns, political education, confrontation, membership and voter drives, etc. We need to do these things and much more. I am suggesting that we re-think the meaning of social change and learn how to include the long-term work of transforming people as we work for social justice. We must redefine "winning." Our social change has to be more than amassing resources and shifting power from the hands of one group to another; we must seek a true shift in consciousness, one that forges vision, goals, and strategies from belief, not just from expediency, and allows us to become a strong political force.

The definition of *transformational politics* is fairly simple: it is political work that changes the hearts and minds of people, supports personal and group growth in ways that create healthy, whole people, organizations, and communities, and is based on a vision of a society where people – across lines of race, gender, class and sexuality – are supported by institutions and communities to live their best lives. Among many possibilities, I want to suggest one way to do transformational work: through building community that is based on our moral vision.

Building Community, Making Connections

Where do we build community? Should it be geographic, consisting of everyone who lives in the same neighborhood? Based on identity, such as one's racial identity, sexual identity? Organizational or work identity? Where are the places that community happens?

It seems to me that community can be created in a vast number of places and ways. What is more important is the how of building community. To get to the how, we first have to define what community is. Community is people in any configuration (geographic, identity, etc.) bonded together over time through common interest and concern, through responsibility and accountability to one another, and at its best, through commitment, friendship and love.

To live in authentic community requires a deeper level of caring and interaction than many of us currently exhibit in our drive for individualism and self-fulfillment. That is, it calls for living with communal values. And we face a daunting challenge here because we all live in a culture that glorifies individualism. For example, what the Right calls "traditional family values" actually works against the often-quoted African proverb, "It takes a village to raise a child," which speaks to the communal value of the importance of every child in the life of the community, present and future. Such values point to very different solutions than those currently suggested for the problems of youth alienation, crime, and violence. Rather than increasing police forces and building more jails, with these shared values we would look toward more ways for the community as a whole to be responsible for and accountable to children. We would seek ways to support and nurture their lives. All of us would be teachers, parents and friends for every child.

Creating community requires seeing the whole, not just the parts, and understanding how they interrelate. However, the difficult part is learning how to honor the needs of the individual as well as those of the group, without denying the importance of either. It requires a balance between identity and freedom on the one hand and the collective good and public responsibility on the other. It requires ritual and celebration and collective ways to grieve and show anger; it requires a commitment to resolve conflict.

Most of all, it requires authenticity in relationships between and among whole people. This means that each of us has to be able to bring all of who we are to the relationship, neighbor to neighbor, friend to friend, worker to worker. Bringing all of who we are to community requires working across great differences in culture, in lifestyle, in belief. It demands that we look beyond our own lives to understand the lives of others. It demands that we interact with the lives of others. It requires understanding the connections among people's lives and then seeking comprehensive solutions to multi-issue, multifaceted problems. If we allow only certain parts of people to surface, and if we silence, reject or exclude basic pieces of their essential selves, then we begin designing systems of oppression. Community becomes based on power over others and non-consensual authority: those who have the most power and privilege dictate the community norms and their enforcement.

One of the goals of every political activity we engage in should be to move beyond superficial interactions to the building of relationships and community. Much of this work is simple, not difficult or complex; it merely requires redefining our values and how we spend our political time. For example, far too often I go to meetings, frequently held in sterile hotel conference rooms, where introductions are limited to people giving their names or, at best, what work they do. Building relationships – whether those of neighbor, friend, lover, work partner – requires that we ask who are you? In rural communities in the South and on American Indian reservations, people spend a lot of time talking about who their people are, how they are connected to people and place. Women activists in the housing projects in New Orleans get to know each other by telling their lifelines, the major events that shaped them along the way. It is almost ritual for lesbians to get to know each other by telling their coming out stories – when and how they first experienced their lesbianism.

Building connection and relationship requires that we give it time, not just in meetings but in informal opportunities surrounding meetings, structured and unstructured. For instance, when I did political education on oppression issues within the battered women's movement, there was always a dramatic difference in the relationships that were built when we stayed in retreat centers or self-contained places away from distracting outside activities rather than in city hotels. So much of what happened in people's growth and understanding came from living, sleeping, and eating together in an atmosphere that encouraged interaction.

As a way to think about building community, we can ask ourselves these questions:

- In what settings with other people have I felt most whole? What is it that makes me feel known and accepted as who I am?

- What conditions make me most able to work well in partnership with other people? What makes me feel connected rather than alienated?

- What are communal values? What are the practices that support them?

- Where are the places where community is occurring? (For example, in care teams for people living with HIV/ AIDS, in youth gangs, in certain churches or neighborhoods, in AA groups?) What are the characteristics of these communities?

- Who is being excluded from community? What barriers are there to participation?

- What are the qualities of an inclusive community as opposed to an exclusive community?

- What makes a community democratic?

Our communities are where our moral values are expressed. It is here that we are called upon to share our connection to others, our interdependence, our deepest belief in what it means to be part of the human condition, where people's lives touch one another, for good or for bad. It is here where the rhetoric of belief is forced into the reality of living. It is from this collection of people, holding within it smaller units called families, that we build and live democracy. Or, without care and nurturance, where we detach from one another and destroy our hope for survival.

Political Integrity and Multi-Issue Politics

It is one thing for us to talk about liberation politics; it is of course another to live them. We lack political integrity when we demand liberation for one cause or one group of people and act out oppression or exploitation toward others. If we do not have an integrated analysis and a commitment to sharing power, it is easy to act out politics that simply reflect a hierarchy of domination.

In our social change organizations in particular we can find ourselves in this dangerous position: where we are demanding, for example, liberation from sexism but within the organization we act out racism, economic injustice, and homophobia. Each is reflected in who is allowed to lead, who makes the highest and lowest salaries, who is allowed to participate in the major decision-making, who decides how the resources are used. If the organization does not have a vision and a strategy that also includes the elimination of racism, sexism, economic injustice, and homophobia (as well as oppressions relating to age, physical ability, etc.), then internal conflict is inevitable. People cannot single out just one oppression from their lives to bring to their work for liberation: they bring their whole selves.

Creating a multi-racial, multi-cultural, multi-issue vision of liberation is no easy task. It is much easier to stay within the framework of oppression where our women's organizations' leadership is primarily white, middle-class women, heterosexual or closeted lesbians; our civil rights organizations are male-dominated; our gay/lesbian/bi/transgender organizations are controlled by white gay men and/or white lesbians. And where the agendas for change reflect the values of those who dominate the leadership.

It is easier to talk about "diversity" than about shared power. Or to use a belief in identity politics to justify not including others in a vision for change. I do not believe in either diversity politics or identity politics as they are currently practiced.

First, diversity politics seem to focus on the necessity for having everyone (across gender, race, class, age, religion, physical ability) present and treated well in any given setting or organization. A core premise is that everyone is oppressed and all oppressions are equal. Since the publication of the report, "Workforce 2000," that predicted the U.S. workforce would be made up of 80% women and people of color by the year 2000, a veritable growth industry of "diversity consultants" has arisen to teach corporations how to "manage" diversity[3]. With integration and productivity as goals, they focus on issues of sensitivity and inclusion – a human relations approach – with acceptance and comforts as high priorities. Popular images of diversity politics show people holding hands around America, singing "We Are the World." People are generally reassured that they do not have to give up anything when they diversify their workplace. They simply have to include other people and become more sensitive to differences.

Because the history of oppression is one of excluding, of silencing, of rendering people invisible, I have great appreciation for the part of diversity work that concentrates on making sure everyone is included. However, our diversity work fails if it does not deal with the power dynamics of difference and go straight to the heart of shifting the balance of power among individuals and within institutions. A danger of diversity politics lies in the possibility that it may become a tool of oppression by creating the illusion of participation when in fact there is no shared power. Having a presence within an organization or institution means very little if one does not have the power of decision-making, an adequate share of the resources, and participation in the development of the workplan or agenda. We as oppressed people must demand much more than acceptance. Tolerance, sympathy and understanding are not enough, though they soften the impact of oppression by making people feel better in the face of it. Our job is not just to soften blows but to make change, fundamental and far-reaching.

Identity politics, on the other hand, rather than trying to include everyone, brings together people who share a single common identity such as sexual orientation, gender, or race. Generally, it focuses on the elimination of a single oppression, the one that is based on the common identity; e.g., homophobia/heterosexism, sexism, racism. However, this can be a limited, hierarchical approach, reducing people of multiple identities to a

3. Packer, Arnold E., et al. *Workforce 2000: Work and Workers for the 21st Century.*
   United States, Hudson Institute, 1987

single identity. Which identity should a lesbian of color choose as a priority – gender, race or sexual identity? And does choosing one necessitate leaving the other two at home? What do we say to bisexual or biracial people? Do we tell them to choose? Our multiple identities allow us to develop a politic that is broad in scope because it is grounded in a wide range of experiences.

There are positive aspects of organizing along identity lines: clarity of single focus in tactics and strategies, self-examination and education apart from the dominant culture, development of solidarity and group bonding. Creating organizations based on identity allows us to have visibility and collective power and to advance concerns that otherwise would never be recognized because of our marginalization within the dominant society.

However, identity politics often suffers from the failure to acknowledge that the same multiplicity of oppressions, a similar imbalance of power, exists within identity groups as within the larger society. People who group together on the basis of their sexual identity still find within these groups sexism and racism that have to be dealt with – or if gathering on the basis of race, there is still sexism and homophobia to be confronted. Whole, not partial, people come to identity groups, carrying several identities. Some of liberation movements' major barriers to building a unified and cohesive strategy, I believe, come from our refusal to work directly on the oppressions – those fundamental issues of power – within our own groups. A successful liberation movement cannot be built on the effort to liberate only a few or only a piece of who we are.

Diversity and identity politics are responses to oppression. In confronting oppressions we must always remember that they mean more than people just not being nice to one another. They are systemic, based in institutions and in general society, where one group of people is allowed to exert power and control over members of another group, denying them fundamental rights. Also, we must remember that oppressions are interconnected, operating in similar ways, and that many people experience more than one oppression.

As I have stated, I believe that all oppressions in this country turn on an economic wheel; they all, in the long run, serve to consolidate and keep wealth in the hands of the few, with the many fighting over crumbs. Oppressions are built, in particular, on the dynamic intersection of race and gender and class. Without work against economic injustice, against the dehumanizing excesses of capitalism, there can be no deep and lasting work on oppression. Why? Because it is always in the best interest of the dominators, the greedy, to maintain and expand oppression – to feed economic and social injustice.

Unless we understand both the interconnections of oppressions and the economic exploitation of oppressed groups, we have little hope of succeeding in a liberation movement. The theocratic Right has been successful in driving wedges between oppressed groups because there is little common understanding of the linkages common to all oppressions. Progressives, including lesbians and gay men, have contributed to these divisions because, generally, we have dealt only with single pieces of the fabric of injustice. Often we have no knowledge of a shared history. We stand ready to be divided. If, for example, an organization has worked only on sexual identity issues and has not worked internally on issues of race and gender, then it is ripe for division on those issues.

As analyzed in an earlier chapter, the Right has had extraordinary success in using homosexuality as a wedge issue, dividing people on the issues clustered around the Right's two central organizing points, traditional family values and economics. It has been successful in using economics to divide "illegal" immigrants from legal immigrants; in using race, gender, and economics to divide people of color and women from low income white men on the issue of affirmative action.

The question, as ever, is what to do? I do not believe that either a diversity or identity politics approach will work unless they are changed to incorporate a multi-issue analysis and strategy that combine the politics of inclusion with shared power. But, one might say, it will spread us too thin if we try to work on everyone's issue, and ours will fall by the wayside. In our external work (doing women's anti-violence work, working against police brutality in people of color communities, seeking government funding for HIV/AIDS research), we do not have to work on "everybody's issue" – we can be focused. But how can we achieve true social change unless we look at all within our constituency who are affected by our particular issue? People who have HIV/AIDS are of every race, class, age, gender, geographic location, but when research and services are sought, it is women, people of color, poor people, who are most overlooked. The spread of HIV rages on because those in power think that the people who contract it are dispensable. Are we to be like them? To understand why police brutality is so much more extreme in people of color communities than in white, we have to understand also why, even within these communities, it is even greater against poor people of color, women who are prostitutes, and gay men and lesbians of color. To leave any group out leaves a hole for everyone's freedoms and rights to fall through. It becomes an issue of "acceptable" and "unacceptable" people, deserving and undeserving of rights, legitimate and illegitimate, deserving of recognition as fully human or dismissible as something less.

Identity politics offers a strong, vital place for bonding, for developing political analysis. With each other we struggle to understand our relationship to a world that says that we are no more than our identity, and simultaneously denies there is oppression based on race or gender or sexual identity. Our challenge is to learn how to use the experiences of our many identities to forge an inclusive social change politic. The question that faces us is how to do multi-issue coalition building from an identity base. The hope for a multi-racial, multi-issue movement rests in large part on the answer to this question.

Our linkages can create a movement, and our divisions can destroy us. Each point of linkage is our strongest defense and also holds the most possibility for long-lasting social change.

If our organizations are not committed internally to the inclusion and shared power of all those who share our issue, how can we with any integrity demand inclusion and shared power in society at large? If women, lesbians and gay men are treated as people undeserving of equality within civil rights organizations, how can those organizations demand equality? If women of color and poor women are marginalized in women's rights organizations, how can those organizations argue that women as a class should be moved into full participation in the mainstream? If lesbian and gay organizations are not feminist and anti-racist in all their practices, what hope is there for the elimination of homophobia and heterosexism in a racist, sexist society? It is an issue of integrity.

In the larger social change community our failure to connect issues prevents us from being able to do strong coalition and alliance work with one another. Most frequently, coalitions and alliances are created to meet crisis issues which threaten all of us. Made up of groups that experience injustice, they should have common ground. They most frequently fall apart, I believe, because of failure in relationships. As in all human relationships, it is difficult to solve the issue of the moment without a history of trust, common struggle, and reciprocity. Homophobia, for example, has kept us "quiet" and invisible in our anti-racist work; racism has kept us "quiet" in our lesbian and gay work. We needed to be visible in our work on all fronts. Working shoulder to shoulder on each other's issues enables us to get to know each other's humanity, to understand the broad sweep of issues, to build trust and solidarity.

Our separateness, by identity and by issue, prevents the building of a progressive movement. When we grasp the value and interconnectedness of our liberation issues, then we will at last be able to make true coalition and begin building a common agenda that eliminates oppression and brings forth a vision of diversity that shares both power and resources.

Trying to Walk the Talk: an Example

For the past fifteen years, we at the Women's Project in Arkansas have been trying to figure out how to develop political integrity and to follow a multi-issue agenda. Certainly it has not always been easy, but it has kept us relentlessly growing and learning, has built in each of us a powerful political conviction and determination, and has made all of us feel more whole. And while the organization is not always thought to be correct on all of its issues, it is respected for its efforts to maintain political integrity, internally and externally. We feel that we are participating every day in the creation of democracy and that we are as unfinished as it is, but the dream of justice and equality lifts us up and moves us forward.

The goal of the Women's Project is to eliminate racism and sexism. We believe these two are inextricably intertwined and must be dealt with equally, together, and head-on. We also think that all other oppressions are rooted in economics and connected to these two through similarity of method and intent. As a women's organizing and political education project, we have chosen to focus on economic injustice and violence against women and children as two major areas of discrimination against and control of both women of color and white women. Working on these issues includes working with men and boys and places us near the heart of community work.

In our community and nation our demand is for equality and justice, for shared power and resources, for opportunity and participation, for individual and group responsibility and freedom. In the search for political integrity, the challenge has been to create an internal philosophy and a structure and practice that reflect the vision of the world we seek for everyone.

Economics

Much of our political analysis is focused on economics as the root source of inequality, and we have seen economic injustice at work everywhere. Daily, we witness women unable to leave their batterers because they cannot afford to feed their children. We witness people condemned because of their poverty. We see the poverty of people of color viewed as an indication of their lack of value in society. Hence, we address the internal economic issue first.

We pay everyone at the Women's Project the same salary, no matter what job she does, and no matter how long she has worked there. At any time we have only four to five full-time employees, and pay such as a bookkeeper, child care providers, and layout designers for the newsletter on an hourly basis at the same rate the full-time staff is paid. Longevity is rewarded with other forms of compensation: a month yearly vacation after two years of employment; a retirement pension after five years; a five-month paid sabbatical after every five years worked.

We believe that an hour of one woman working as hard as she is able is equal to another woman's hard work, no matter what the task at hand, whether it is writing funding proposals, providing care for children, giving speeches, clipping newspaper articles and documenting violence, or cleaning the office. What is most important to us is commitment to the work and working hard. Consequently, we try to be very careful in our hiring. As a community-based, social change organization, our first concern is that a potential employee have a passion for social and economic justice and a desire to give her best self to the job. After that, we look at skills and the way needed skills can be learned during employment. Using these criteria, we are able to hire women whose life experiences are rich but who may not be formally educated or are inexperienced in a conventional workplace.

Our annual budget is almost $250,000, derived from foundation grants, churches, individual donors and pledges, compensation for services, and sales of books and products. Every member of the staff participates in fundraising. This way, we understand where our salaries and resources come from, participate in their creation, and are prepared to make decisions about their distribution.

When describing the organizational structure of the Women's Project, I am often told by people from larger organizations that such a pay structure could work only in a small place. Perhaps so, but a variation on it could also work. Larger organizations could create a policy to allow no more than a 20% differential between the highest paid employees and the lowest paid. If we do not do this, then the structure of our social change organizations reflects the economic pyramid of this country. Those at the apex (the fewest) make the most money and have the most power (control of decision-making and distribution of resources).

Accountability should be horizontal rather than vertical. Those at the bottom make the least and are not allowed to take part in the decisions that affect their lives and the life of the organization and its constituency. For instance, it is common in many social change and social service organizations for those who have the most contact with the constituency (battered women, for instance) to make the least money. Those who have the most contact with power (funders, com-munity leaders) make the most money.

Historic Inequality: Beyond Affirmative Action

As a women's organization working to eliminate racism, we try to do what we call "tilting the balance of historic inequality." We live in a country that has systematically withheld access to opportunity and participation from people of color, has practiced genocide, in particular against American Indians and African Americans and blamed them for causing it, has induced poverty, has dealt the blows of substandard education and health care, and has both appropriated the culture of people of color and condemned it as primitive and inferior – all leading to enforced inequality. We do not believe this history of injustice and inequality can be easily overcome, but we try to make major changes both organizationally and individually. We want to change ingrained thinking and assumptions.

We believe that when everything is placed in the balance, racial parity is more than simply creating an accurate reflection of the racial makeup of the population, or balancing 50% white women and 50% women of color. White women belong to only one of many racial groups in this country but that particular group has been the dominant power and has created the historic inequality. Quite simply, once domination has been ingrained for generations, for centuries, it is extremely difficult to throw off its assumptions and behaviors during efforts toward equality. Major structural and policy changes have to be made to ensure and support lasting results. And it is still difficult.

The way we try to tilt the balance is to make the majority of our organization women of color who earn equal salaries and have equal decision-making power. Our board is composed of twelve women, eight African American, one Asian, and three white, with the staff ratio 50/50. Out of sixteen women on the board and staff, five are lesbians, four are over 50, half are rural, and most are working-class. Where we are weak is in our development of participation by youth and of women of color other than African Americans.

Changing the Agenda

Increasing numbers of historically underrepresented groups gives an organization integration or diversity, but it does not necessarily bring about *a shift in power*. One of the ways we have tried to bring about this shift is to equalize access to decision-making. We believe that when there are predominantly women of color on the staff and board and everyone has equal say in the decision-making, then the agenda and how resources are used to support it will change.

Much responsibility is required: knowing about all aspects of the organization, attending weekly staff meetings and quarterly retreats, communicating well, and talking through issues until group agreement is reached. Each staff member is a lead organizer for a portion of the work. It is her job to oversee the vision and strategy, to recruit volunteers and other staff, to keep the rest of the staff abreast of what is happening, etc. However, each staff member does some work on each project, not just the one she is responsible for. In an annual board and staff retreat, we assess the year's work and lay out strategy for the next year. The staff meets quarterly to do the same, and then at the beginning of each month we provide each other with a work plan for what we hope to accomplish during the month. There are constant opportunities for analysis, criticism, disagreements, and revision. In addition to a strong framework of meetings and exchange, we have autonomy and independence; we are expected to dream big, to take on hard personal challenges, to think on our feet and be creative.

If we were a much larger organization, we would have to modify this structure, e.g., have people meet together in smaller work or issue groupings. The principle would be the same: all should take part in the decision-making that affects their work and lives at the organization.

Our ability to do good work and participate fully in decision-making is affected by the opportunities we have to gain new ideas both from the local community and nationally. We constantly work to try to equalize the privilege of access. For instance, I spend a lot of my time traveling, making speeches, attending conferences, and doing strategic work with groups. Each trip gives me great opportunities to learn new ideas, to make contacts with helpful people. If others on the staff do not have similar opportunities, then the way we work and interact together is affected. We look for opportunities for everyone to travel, to represent the organization in meetings and conferences, to be spokesperson with the press. All honoraria go to the Women's Project. Our policy is to provide financial support for each staff member to attend one conference a year just for her own education, not as a representative of the Project.

Relationships

All of what we do is built on a foundation of developing and maintaining strong relationships with one another. We not only work with each other, we know and care about each other's lives. In a world of entrenched racism, strong relationships between women of color and white women are not built overnight. There are many stops and starts and uneven, rough terrain to cross.

One very difficult issue in the work to create equality is that of white privilege. What is one to do with the privilege that society gives a person simply because of the color of one's skin – so that when a white woman and an African American woman are together in public they are always treated differently? One cannot change the color of one's skin or society's response, but one can change how that privilege is used. It can be used – or spent – for oneself or on behalf of those who do not receive it.

"Spending privilege" is not just a matter of becoming an advocate and a friend, though those are important roles. It also means using privilege to make gains for others rather than for oneself, using it to open doors to helpful people, to sources of money, to information, etc. It means moving out of the way for someone else to be in leadership, be the face of the organization, be the major contact. It does not mean paternalism or off-and-on involvement in issues that are more crucial to the lives of others than one's own.

For trust to be built, those with privilege have to take great risks, putting the loss of that privilege at risk on behalf of the liberation of others. Why, for example should a black woman ever trust a white woman unless she sees that white woman is willing to take risks in the effort to bring about racial justice? A common slang expression is "you get my back for me," meaning I trust you to cover my vulnerable side that I cannot see or protect. That trust is not to be placed in someone who, when the bottom line is reached, is going to escape into her privilege to save her own skin. The rhetoric of race relations has to be moved into action. As white people we have to be traitors to the domination politics of our race. The same is true for all areas of domination. Heterosexuals, to earn trust, have to be willing to put their privilege at risk on behalf of lesbians and gay men, that is, by never hiding behind their heterosexuality and by being willing to let the public think that they are homosexual. Men, in fighting sexism, have to be willing to be seen as foes of male supremacy, as gender traitors, as not "real men," for that is how they will be attacked. People who believe in equality have to be willing to be identified with the oppressed and willing to give up their unearned privilege in the process. We have to be willing to go to the line for each other. Otherwise, we are dealing only with rhetoric and good intentions.

All of us constantly have to check the assumptions that come from our privilege. It is no easy task, but the reward of struggling for shared power and the elimination of privilege is the expansion of possibility for genuine friendship and the bond of common humanity. At the Women's Project, we seek friendships in our work. African American and white women, lesbians and heterosexuals socialize with each other outside the office. Much of our best thinking and work occurs in raucous, no-holds-barred conversations in the office hallway, around the copier, at the local blue plate diner. We joke, tease, disagree, fuss with each other, and talk, talk, talk. Our work is often enough to break our hearts, but we also believe wholeheartedly in fun, in the outrageous, in high waves of satirical response to the morning newspaper or the telephone call that pushed us over the line. Mostly, we believe that we have to bring our whole selves to these many hours we work together each day, that we have to be living the vision of the world we want to create.

Results

Does it work? Not always. Sometimes we are overwhelmed by the murders of women we document, the entrenched poverty of so many of our constituency, the relentless racism, the reactionary legislature, the crack cocaine in our neighborhoods, the obscene greed of the billionaire Tysons and Waltons of our state. We do not always bring our best selves to the work. We have had our share of conflicts about race, class, and sexual identity. We have sometimes failed the community through lack of imagination or understanding of issues. We stumble. We sometimes move too fast without thinking through our strategy and possible outcomes.

Most of the time, however, it works. Our board meetings are day-long political conversations, with lots of food and laughter – we have to chase people out at the end. Even our most stressful days at the office are lightened by laughter and a sense of some accomplishment. Every staff member grows tremendously during her tenure with us and if she leaves, she goes as a strong social change worker.

But mostly we point to the work for our assessment. We think these policies account for our ability to get so much done with so few people and so little money. With our small budget and a current staff of four full-time and one part-time, we

- Conduct an African American Women's Institute that works with women in local communities to develop leadership, to organize to solve community problems, to conduct political education;

- Monitor racist, religious, sexist, anti-gay and lesbian violence, as well as the activities of the white supremacists and theocratic Right, document these activities and publish them in a yearly log, publish bimonthly reports, work with community groups to do hate violence education and to organize against biased violence, work with allies to make public policy change, do political education about the economic and racist underpinnings of incarceration;

- Produce written materials analyzing the Right, work with national groups to produce strategies to oppose them, provide political education nationally;

- Provide incarcerated women with weekly sessions for battered women, work with United Methodist women to transport children to visit their mothers in prison, work with allies to change prison policies;

- Publish an economic analysis of women's work and income in Arkansas; provide political education on economics; work with women in the Arkansas Delta on economic issues;

- provide HIV/AIDS education and training for women – especially lesbians, women of color, and incarcerated women;

- Operate a lending library and a feminist bookstore;

- Produce a bi-monthly newsletter of political analysis and opinion;

- Operate a monthly women's coffeehouse, conduct a lesbian support group, produce women's concerts, organize statewide conferences and national strategy meetings.

The work is slow but it sustains us. It is hard but we draw inspiration from it. We recognize that every day we are struggling uphill against centuries of prejudice and injustice. We are all too aware that we do not have all the answers, but we are deeply convinced that we have a significant beginning. This is the only way we know how to advance a progressive agenda: to practice our politics as close to home as possible.

Hope: Crossing Borders, Building Bridges

Sometimes the organization and expansion of the Right is almost overwhelming to me. It seems so all-encompassing that I waver momentarily in my faith that ordinary people with few resources can resist its destruction and build a just, liberating society. Then I recall those people who are pioneering new ways for people to work and live together. I am also sustained in my work by the examples of courageous people who are crossing borders into territory that traditionally has been inaccessible or forbidden, and of those people who are building bridges over divisions of fear, ignorance, and misunderstanding. They are pushing boundaries, seeking common ground, and opening new spaces for all of us to enjoy in our lives together. Their resistance to the limitations placed upon them and their willingness to enter uncharted territory often makes them endangered, but that resistance also offers us great hope for change.

Because the Right's strategy is to divide people and pit them against one another, we resist their organizing best by making real our vision of bringing people together to share common ground that is liberating for all of us. There are many examples of people traversing difficult territory to open a place for all of us to thrive. One of my favorites is Billings, Montana in 1993, when the community organized together to create safety for its Jewish, African American and Native American members. For some time there had been an increase in Klan activity in the area. During a Martin Luther King birthday rally, people found anti-King leaflets on their cars, and hateful flyers about lesbians and gay men had been posted around town. Though there were no direct linkages to the Klan, it was in this charged atmosphere that rocks were thrown through windows displaying Hanukkah decorations. A community coalition, made up of many different groups, individuals, and a large number of Christian churches, was created to respond. They persuaded *The Billings Gazette* to print a full-page picture of a menorah and encouraged people to put it in their windows. More rocks were thrown through windows that posted the picture, including one into the window of the Methodist church. In response, even more people put menorahs in their windows – an estimated 10,000. The vandalism stopped.

In another instance, when swastikas and the words "Die Indian" were spray-painted on a Native American woman's house, 30 members of the local Painters' Union and other volunteers painted her house. When skinheads began attending the African American Episcopal church, people of different races and religious backgrounds began attending services to block the skinheads' effort to intimidate. Working together in coalition, people sent the message that Billings was a town of open borders, a place of acceptance and inclusion.

Common ground and strong working relationships can develop when people who are very different from one another have time to explore both their differences and their commonalities in a setting that supports equality. In 1991, I was privileged to be an organizer of a dialogue on violence against women at the Blue Mountain Center in upstate New York. We focused on creating an analysis of violence which integrated race, class, gender, and sexuality. Of the 30 participants, 6 were African American, 6 Latina, 6 Native American, 6 Asian, and 6 white. For some of us white women, it was the first time we had been treated as part of a race numerically equal to other races and given no more than our proportionate time and space. The experience was profoundly moving. What was most exciting were the changes in the content of the discussion as everyone had an opportunity to speak the truth of her experience. Many of us had entered the conversation thinking we had a strong integrated analysis, but as we spoke of our commonalties and especially our differences a far broader and deeper analysis emerged. Of equal importance, however, were the relationships the thirty participants forged. I have fond memories of watching the Latina participants leading women in new dances late into the night, but my favorite memory of all is of twenty or so women sitting around the long dining table roaring with laughter as both heterosexuals and lesbians ranked themselves on the infamous "butch/femme" scale and gave hilarious reasons for their ranking. Bridges were built.

Some of the most important bridges are being constructed by people who possess more than one identity and lay claim to more than one world: multi-racial youth who refuse to be categorized into only one racial identity; transsexual, transgender and bi-sexual individuals who struggle with both heterosexuals and lesbians and gay men for recognition of their identities; lesbians and gay men of color who confront racism among white lesbians and gay men and homophobia among people of color. These people draw us into broader understanding of the complexity of who each individual is and the fact that identity cannot be harnessed, regulated or coerced into restrictive little packages. Many times they are pivotal in our resistance to the Right's organizing.

With admiration I have watched Mandy Carter lead the National Call to Resist, an effort to counter the Right's organizing within African American communities. Mandy works with other African American lesbians and gay men to create bridges of dialogue and understanding, especially within African American churches that have been a primary target of the Right. As the Right tries to stir up homophobia and division within these churches, African American lesbians and gay men speak from the congregation and the pulpit to expose the strategies of scapegoating and division.

One of the most successful and loathsome strategies of the Right is the exploitation of people's concern for children and the family. Yet it is in this realm that I feel some of my greatest hope. No matter how hard the Right works to return us to a nostalgic notion of families, there is an unorganized alternative movement that continues to redefine and broaden the idea of what a family is and how it functions. There is no longer a tight border around families. There are blended families in which couples bring together children and relatives from previous marriages, families with single parents or two parents that are not married, families of gay men or lesbians and their children from prior or present relationships, adult children caring for their parents, single or married parents with adopted children, families of grandmothers caring for their grandchildren, chosen families such as circles of beloved friends or of those who provide support for the ill or dying. These families are not defined by a formula that requires a married man and woman plus children, but instead by relationships that are marked by mutual responsibility, common concern, shared interests, and commitment to one another.

Some of my strongest hope comes from two experiences of family in my own life where demands for change have been made and borders have been crossed, opening up ways to live more fully as whole people. My relationship with my rural uncle and aunt, George and Mary Pharr, now 87 and 80 respectively, has been a beacon of hope for social change. During the several decades since I first told them I was a lesbian, their willingness to address homophobia has enabled me to draw them fully into my life, and this has brought significant gains for all of us. Because of this openness, they share a wide community of my friends and their experiences, and I have beloved family involved in every aspect of my life. We visit each other, travel together, share books and recipes – their family and mine. We talk philosophy and sex, tell stories and jokes. Rather than the narrow lives of secrets and the unspoken, we have rich fullness of experience with each other. It is family built upon authenticity.

That truthful, open relationship has prevented these two rural, working-class people from becoming susceptible to the Right's organizing in their community. When people in their small United Methodist church began repeating the divisive messages of the Right, my aunt stood up and confronted them from the pew. She told them in no uncertain terms that she knew many lesbians and gay men, her niece among them, and that she admired them and the lives they lived. At other times she has taken church members aside to talk with them about their comments and her own positive, direct experience with lesbians and gay men. The bridges we build one by one between individuals are the strongest, as we can see from the polls indicating that the people less likely to condemn homosexuals are those who know a lesbian or gay man.

The idea of family expanded greatly for me when my former lover, Ann Gallmeyer, diagnosed with an inherited terminal disease, Marie's ataxia, came to live her final years with me. Lovers for almost a decade and beloved friends for over two more, we had a lifelong commitment to each other. The demands of Ann's illness led us to remember our experiences with the women's health movement in the 1970s when we created care circles to surround those who were dying. We combined these memories with new information gained from gay men who cared for those living and dying with HIV/AIDS, and we created a care team for Ann. Though some came to the team because they knew one of us, all joined because they shared a common commitment to lesbians and an understanding of how difficult health care is for a lesbian dying in a homophobic world. Over several years, this team of 10 women became extended family to Ann.

We benefited greatly from our work with each other, but so did health care providers as we presented ourselves as open lesbians who made a family of support. When the time came for Ann to enter a nursing home in Portland, Oregon, we interviewed staff at almost a dozen homes, asking each about their social policies concerning lesbians. In almost every instance, there was a shocked response, with a quick answer that they had no problems with lesbians and that they had never had one in their facility – or that "what people do privately is their business." This provided us an opportunity for conversation about lesbian lives. At the home Ann chose, we led many of the staff away from the irrational fear that they would contract HIV/AIDS from touching Ann to an appreciation of the large gay freedom flag flying proudly on her door and of us as family that came visiting every day.

When Ann entered hospice care, one of our most emotional moments was when we realized we were honored as a legitimate family for Ann and that our relationship was respected for the depth of love and commitment that we brought to our care for her and each other. We took a moment to acknowledge that those bridges had been built by gay men and their lovers and friends who had gone before us in this beautiful place of comfort for the dying and their families.

Mrs. Daisy Bates has long been a source of hope for me. I lived for ten years in a house across the street from Central High School in Little Rock, Arkansas, where Mrs. Bates led the drive for integration in 1957. Every day I could sit on my screened porch and look across the garden at a rainbow of kids entering a fully integrated high school that is one of the best in the U.S. Looking at that school made me think about how for 15 years my life has been privileged by Mrs. Daisy Bates, a friend, a mentor, and a member of the Women's Project.

Then, in 1992, while I was away working against the theocratic Right in Oregon, I called my office one day and heard this story of hope and vision: There had been a small gathering of friends at my house overlooking Central High School where three of us then lived, white and middle-aged, African American and young, white and living in a wheelchair. At this dinner of friends, there were five lesbians, three white and two African American, and Mrs. Daisy Bates in her wheelchair, all eating Chinese food together and watching a slide show about Mrs. Bates' life. Of these lesbians, one created the Women's Project's lending library of women's and African American literature, another was an activist for disability rights, one was writing a book about Mrs. Bates' life, another wrote poetry and incisive political articles about lesbian battering, and one spent her days working to end biased violence against people of color, women, Jews and Catholics, lesbians and gay men. All sat there together, eating and laughing and talking, sharing friendship and politics and common cause. Hearing about it I thought, this is a glimpse of what the world can and should be.

I also thought, this is a truly moral vision. The theocratic Right frames our political efforts in terms of immorality and offers in the place of politics a narrow moral prescription. Yielding this terrain to the Right, progressive people do not talk often enough about the morality of our own vision. Could there be anything more moral than the idea that all people are of equal worth and deserve justice and full participation in their society? Is there anything more moral than the idea that people are connected to and responsible for one another? I don't think so.

My life is sustained by visions of the inclusive, liberating actions I see around me: people who with great courage and imagination cross borders and build bridges into new territory where generosity, tolerance, empathy and understanding reign.

Pieces of a Progressive Agenda

What we have learned from the failures of our past and what the present anti-democratic organizing teaches us is that we cannot separate the work against economic exploitation and oppression. If we do, we fail. A united agenda that intertwines economic justice and human rights offers the best possibility of building a strong political base for creating change. It is what we are lacking now, and all of the media political ads and sound bites in the world will not take the place of a politically educated and motivated grassroots base committed to a pro-democracy agenda.

To do this work we have to create local organizations who work in combination with national resource centers and are committed to the cause of participatory democracy. We can forge a vision and strategy from our core beliefs to create a movement for economic justice and human rights. It is not coincidental that these two areas are the Right's weakest. As noted earlier, when we talk about the redistribution of wealth upward over the past two decades, we are accused by the Right of fostering class warfare – when, instead, the war against working people has been launched from the corporation board rooms for years. This response is a sure indication of the Right's Achilles' heel. There is no honest way to defend robbing working people for the benefit of the rich, for the destruction of human lives in the name of well-documented greed.

For change to come about, we must continue to point out contradictions, let conflicts arise, and then organize around them. There are enormous numbers of disaffected people who are hurt deeply by the economic practices of corporations and of the Right which serves them. Almost everyone knows that the social contract between employers and employees has broken down; that no matter how much one gives to the company in time, labor and loyalty, the company will not be loyal in return. Jobs will be eliminated, companies will move to cheaper labor markets, work will be doubled for less pay, workers will be made part-time. Everyone from the unemployed factory worker to the fast food minimum wage worker to the middle manager is feeling this crunch and beginning to understand it. We must speak to the sense of injury and injustice that workers experience, name the cause of their mistreatment, and present a strategy for change.

"Owner/manager/worker" class analysis does not fit easily; our organizing also must be around the broader issues of economic justice and economic democracy. Working people, the unemployed, and the poor are poised to enter a movement that fights for them. Unfortunately, at the moment, it is the Right that is most successfully organizing many of them using the issue of scapegoating and anti-government sentiment (the latter being another form of scapegoating since the government is negatively identified as promoting the rights of women, people of color, poor people and the environment over "true Americans").

We must give people a vision of hope and possibility, renewing their belief in participatory democracy as an alternative to the Right's agenda of exclusion. In our organizing for social change, we have to be intentional in our work to prevent the development of a new fascism.

Here are some strategies. End the social chaos in our communities which makes people willing to accept authoritarianism and the loss of their democratic rights as an answer to their desperate problems. Create a strong economy that offers secure, decent employment for all workers, with livable wages and full benefits. Intensify our efforts to defend and protect those who are the targets of scapegoating. Expose and oppose the leaders of the repressive movement and their policies.

The following strategies can be incorporated into an overall agenda that works against fascism and promotes democracy:

Human Rights

Place what is happening to people in this country in a human rights framework and link it to human rights struggles in other countries. Organize to hold the U.S. government accountable for its human rights abuses both in this country and internationally. Demand that the government sign and comply with international human rights agreements and treaties. Expand our understanding of human rights to include food, clothing, shelter, livable income, education, and safety. Work for these by creating, for example, publicly funded childcare, affordable housing, a guaranteed income. Direct public attention to the human rights abuses found in the U.S. – for example, in violence against women and in the U.S. system of incarceration. Work on the barriers and oppressions that prevent access to human rights

Economic Democracy

Organize to hold corporations and the government accountable for economic decisions that hurt the poor and help the rich. Demand that corporations put money back into salaries, production, development, and job creation. Point to the contradictions between salaries of CEOs, corporate profits, and salaries of workers. Push for equal distribution of wealth as opposed to the redistribution of the past twenty years that has sent wealth upward into the higher income brackets; support progressive taxation. Be prepared for red-baiting or accusations of fostering a class war when we talk about economic injustice; remember that the rich have declared war on the poor and we must call it what it is and defend ourselves. Accept no diversionary tactics, especially scapegoating, that keep us from looking at and changing the source of the problem. Broaden organized labor's constituency to include people in jobs and workplaces that do not lend themselves to traditional union organizing. Renew, overhaul, and rebuild the union movement, and work to change laws that restrict the rights of workers to organize.

Taxation for Human Needs

Organize to demand a national budget based on fair, graduated taxation that will address human needs first. Through political education, help people understand that economics first represents a value system, and that the way a country (or person) spends its money is a reflection of its deepest values. Mount opposition to enormous expenditures on the military/industrial establishment and the use of the military as the primary job training program in the U.S. Insist upon a budget that reflects a desire to provide people decent jobs, benefits, and working conditions; healthy food and adequate shelter; publicly funded child care, universal health care, and education; and a safe environment. Demand, for example, a budget that spends more on education than on prisons. On the individual level, make equally difficult changes: end consumerism by practicing thrift and buying only what we need. Share our commitment to others by tithing a portion of our income to social change organizations to help solve the problems and meet the human needs of our communities.

Campaign Reform

Work for elimination of the current form of "bought and sold" campaign financing, which depends on the contributions of corporations and the rich. Work for publicly funded campaigns which provide each candidate with the same amount of money and resources. Until this change is made, all of the other changes in our governing process will mean little. Campaigns will continue to be high-priced media shows lacking substance. Those who govern will still dance to the tune of those who paid their way.

Racial Justice

Organize across racial lines to change the racist policies and practices of institutions. Develop political education that keeps alive an understanding of racial discrimination and injustice. Help our constituencies recognize that people of color are the focal point in the Right's development of the scapegoating necessary for the groundwork of fascism. For instance, confront and expose coded language such as the use of the words "crime," "welfare," "affirmative action," "under-class," "immigrants," "inner city," "gangs," "drug dealers" to mean people of color. This current attack is the continuation of a very old war against people of color, and once again it carries the potential for mass genocide. Link issues of discrimination and injustice.

Community-building

Organize efforts on the local level to build and strengthen communities, emphasizing responsibility both to the community and individuals' rights. Develop ways to place multi-culturalism at the heart of community life as the centerpiece of democracy. Strengthen the capacity of community organizations by developing *political integrity* which draws people toward hope and a desire for action, and which begins to develop a moral framework for our lives. Strengthen the capacity of individuals within the community by providing support for wholeness, for fairness, for generosity, for responsibility for oneself and for others.

Political Education and Grassroots Organizing

All politics is local – work on the local level to provide accurate, truthful information and skills to develop a political base for change. Examine issues and policies in light of their impact on historically marginalized groups: women, people of color, old people, children, people with disabilities, lesbians and gay men, religious minorities. Work for the inclusion and leadership of these people in every aspect of local organizing. Make national organizations accountable to local organizations and activists. Develop individuals and organizations that exhibit political and personal integrity and provide hope. Create access for new activists and support their leadership development. Include young people in all of the work.

Longevity

Create a pace that can be maintained for the long haul. This is ongoing work, not a short campaign that can be won or lost in one encounter. Be thoughtful about organizational and individual health. Create principled internal politics and healthy standards for work and working conditions. Be respectful of everyone. Do not act martyred. Build relationships that include more than work:

celebration, ritual, play. Use positive humor whenever possible and often. Get a life, have a life, live a life – as fully and as joyously as imaginable.

The strategies and tactics learned from decades of movement building for social change still serve us well: direct action, media messages, political education, progressive candidacies, electoral campaigns, civil disobedience, study circles, voter registration and education, linkages through cultural/political events, the arts and the internet, creation of alternative institutions, advocacy, legal challenges, and creation of activities and events that invite people to bring their passion for justice and put it to use. Organizing, organizing, organizing. However, as we know, tactics are neutral and can be used equally well to repress rather liberate a society. The central issue is developing a pro-democratic consciousness in those who participate in these tactics and strategies. We now seek ways to bring them into a vision of solidarity in the creation of a multi-issue, multi-racial, multi-cultural progressive movement that creates a democracy that works for all of us.

And finally...

We are living in a time of social, cultural, economic and political conflict in which many values are shifting and being redefined. It is a time of upheaval, change and fear of loss. Much of the conflict centers around what we believe the U.S. should be – a pluralistic (many ethnicities, religions, cultures), democratic society that finds a place and resources for everyone – or what the Right envisions – a mono-cultural, authoritarian society that puts tight limits on people's participation. Should we have a society that uses its resources for the common good or a two-tiered society with increased economic stratification and poverty? It is a conflict between the politics of inclusion and sharing and the politics of exclusion and selfishness.

At stake is the historical dream of this country and the values we seek in the ongoing struggle to make that dream real: that this country is open, providing a place where people can come in search of freedom; where people can find a place to be who they are and to live peacefully; where people can be equal partners with each other in the creation of family, community and government; where people have hope and resources to meet their basic needs.

We are living in a time of danger. Because of decisions made by corporate leaders in response to increased global economic competition, our standard of living has been in decline for twenty years. Concerted corporate efforts to escape rightful tax responsibility and structural changes in the economy, such as automation, "downsizing," and sending our plants and production overseas where "underdeveloped" countries provide cheap labor, have accelerated the economic crisis in the U.S. during the past decade. Economic and social problems, coupled with a sense that a flawed government is failing the average citizen, make people seek answers in easy but aggressive rightwing populist solutions. People's fears make them susceptible to rightwing propaganda that tells them there are not enough civil rights and resources to go around. It could become the majority "will of the people," unchecked by democratic processes, that literally kills minority voices and rights. Economic hard times make people particularly susceptible to authoritarian leadership that scapegoats "minority groups" as the cause of social and economic problems. Worldwide, due to similar economic stresses bringing cultural disruption, there is a danger that regressive populism could slip into fascism.

It is a time when we must all be particularly vigilant that justice is even-handed, that all rights are equally protected, that there is equal access to educational and employment opportunity for everyone, and that we are careful to recognize and work on the complex causes of our social and economic unrest. Avoiding emotional, unexamined nationalism, we need to see ourselves as world citizens, and act as responsible stewards of the honored trust to develop and protect democracy and civil liberties. We must caretake and expand the moral ground of justice and equal participation in democracy.

As world citizens, we must find ways to end corporate imperialism and our government's support of human rights abuses when economic gain is at stake. We must hold our government accountable as a participant in the stewardship of the world's peoples, resources, and environment. A new definition of human rights (which goes beyond that of political torture or abuse to recognize food, shelter, employment, safety, education, health) must be held up as standard for people both of this country and of the world.

The work before us can be done one step at a time, beginning at the local community level and moving out to the international. Acknowledging the worth and dignity of every individual and developing an understanding of our vital connection to one another and to the natural world, we can create a society where children can be safe, healthy and educated; where people can have decent jobs that enable us to afford housing in clean, safe neighborhoods; where the rights and responsibilities of the individual and the community are balanced; where, worldwide, the health and well-being of people and the environment are considered the highest goals humans can pursue. Working together, crossing barriers and borders together, we will build a movement that makes real our dream of justice, equality, and freedom.

About the Author

Suzanne Pharr is a southern queer feminist and anti-racist organizer. She founded the Women's Project in Arkansas in 1981, was a co-founder of Southerners on New Ground in 1984, and was director of the Highlander Center from 1999 to 2004. Pharr is an organizer and political strategist who has spent her adult life working to build a broad-based, multi-racial, multi-issued movement for social and economic justice in the United States. Major themes in her movement work include intersectional issues and strategies, anti-violence, racial and gender equality, cross-generational collaboration, democratic participation, economic justice, and human rights based on equality and justice. At the center of Pharr's every effort is the question, "How can we make it possible for everyone to live as a whole person, to have self-determination, to be treated with dignity and respect, and to have access to material necessities as well as joy?" Based on six decades of work across movements, she now thinks of herself as a political handywoman, working across issues with activists of diverse races, genders, sexual identities, classes, ages, abilities, and cultures to develop strategies for justice and equality.

At http://www.suzannepharr.com there are also various video recordings that expand on the different themes in this book.

About the Editor

Christian Matheis is faculty in Community and Justice Studies in the Department of Justice and Policy Studies at Guilford College in Greensboro, NC. Matheis specializes in scholarship and practice that bridge social and political philosophy, ethics, public policy, and direct-action organizing.